By Brant Pitre

Introduction to the Spiritual Life
The Case for Jesus
Jesus and the Jewish Roots of the Eucharist
Jesus and the Jewish Roots of Mary
Jesus the Bridegroom

INTRODUCTION *to the* SPIRITUAL LIFE

INTRODUCTION
to the
SPIRITUAL LIFE

Walking the Path of Prayer

with Jesus

BRANT PITRE

Image | New York

Imprimatur: +Most Reverend Shelton J. Fabre
Bishop of Houma-Thibodaux

Nihil Obstat: Rev. Joshua Rodrigue, STL
Censor Librorum

The *Nihil Obstat* and *Imprimatur* are official declarations that a book or pamphlet is free of doctrinal or moral error. No implication is contained therein that those who have granted the *Nihil Obstat* or *Imprimatur* agree with the content, opinions, or statements expressed.

LIBRARY OF CONGRESS CATALOGING-IN-PUBLICATION DATA

Names: Pitre, Brant James, author.
Title: Introduction to the spiritual life / Brant Pitre.
Description: First edition. | New York: Image, 2021.
Identifiers: LCCN 2021012930 (print) | LCCN 2021012931 (ebook)
ISBN 9780525572763 (hardcover) | ISBN 9780525572770 (ebook)
Subjects: LCSH: Spiritual life—Catholic Church. | Spiritual formation—Catholic Church.
Classification: LCC BX2350.3.P564 2021 (print) | LCC BX2350.3 (ebook) | DDC 248.4/82—dc23
LC record available at https://lccn.loc.gov/2021012930
LC ebook record available at https://lccn.loc.gov/2021012931

Printed in Canada on acid-free paper

crownpublishing.com

2 4 6 8 9 7 5 3

First Edition

Book design by Virginia Norey

For Hannah Rose

Hannah also prayed and said,
"My heart exults in the LORD."
—1 Samuel 2:1

CONTENTS

Introduction

∽

If any one thirst, let him come to me and drink.
—Jesus of Nazareth (John 7:37)

MANY YEARS AGO, A FRIEND OFFERED TO GIVE ME SOME FREE BOOKS from his personal theological library. At the time, I was a young professor with a new PhD and a mountain of student debt. Needless to say, I accepted. Little did I know that by "some," he meant well over a thousand. In the end, he sent me over fifty large boxes, filled with books on the Old Testament, ancient Judaism, the New Testament, and early Christianity—all topics I had studied during my doctoral program at the University of Notre Dame.

Several boxes, however, contained books on *spiritual theology*—a subject about which I knew next to nothing. These included works by ancient Christian writers like John Cassian and John Climacus; medieval mystics like Catherine of Siena and Thomas à Kempis; and modern spiritual masters like Ignatius of Loyola, Teresa of Avila, and John of the Cross.

Once I started reading the spiritual classics, I couldn't stop. It was like drinking water from a well after spending years in the desert. I began to learn for the first time about meditation, contemplation, the seven capital sins, their opposing virtues, and other topics. That year, when asked to teach an elective, I knew immediately it would be on spiritual theology. However, because my doctoral research was in biblical studies, I chose to focus on the scriptural roots of Christian spirituality.

To this day, that course remains the most powerful experience I have ever had in the classroom.[1] Studying the scriptural foundations of the spiritual life was not just informative; it was *transformative*. It changed me. It also seemed to have a similar impact on my students. More than once they asked, "Why have we never heard this before?" Together, we realized we were tasting something precious, which Jesus himself calls the "one thing" that is "necessary" (Luke 10:42).[2] During that time, I made several discoveries that ultimately laid the foundations for this book.

THREE KINDS OF PRAYER

The first thing I learned was that there are different kinds of prayer. Growing up as a Catholic, I had always assumed that prayer simply involved saying the words of certain memorized prayers, like the Our Father. However, once I started reading the spiritual classics, I quickly discovered that the spiritual life involves much more. Although vocal prayer is essential, there are at least three major forms of prayer:

1. *Vocal Prayer:* praying with words, whether memorized or spontaneous.
2. *Meditation:* praying with the mind, especially by reading and reflecting on Scripture and entering into dialogue with God.
3. *Contemplation:* praying with the "eyes" of the heart, with a loving desire to "see" the face of God.

Each of these is deeply biblical. Jesus himself teaches his disciples a vocal prayer when he gives them the Lord's Prayer (see Matthew

6:9-13). Likewise, the book of Psalms begins by blessing anyone who "meditates" on Scripture "day and night" (Psalm 1:1-2). Finally, the book of Exodus gives a classic description of contemplation when it describes Moses' practice of praying in the Tabernacle. There "the LORD used to speak to Moses *face to face*" (Exodus 33:11). According to the spiritual classics, the life of every disciple of Jesus should involve all three kinds of prayer.

THE STAGES OF SPIRITUAL GROWTH

The second thing I discovered was that the spiritual life consists of certain *stages* of growth. When I was younger, I tended to think of my spiritual life as a kind of "revolving door." On one side was deadly sin, or "mortal sin." On the other side was repentance and forgiveness, or a "state of grace." My primary aim was to die on the right side of the door! For many years, I felt like I was spiritually going in circles. I never had any sense of making progress. If anything, I felt like I was constantly backsliding.

To my surprise, this was *not* how the great spiritual writers describe the Christian life. Instead, just as a person's biological life ordinarily goes through certain stages—childhood, adolescence, and adulthood—so, too, a person's spiritual life normally goes through stages of growth. Over the centuries, these stages have been described by some spiritual writers as three "ways" or paths:

1. *The Purgative Way:* the path of spiritual childhood, focused on keeping the commandments, rooting out the capital sins (hence "purgative"), and learning to pray to the Father and practice meditation.
2. *The Illuminative Way:* the path of spiritual adolescence, focused on a deeper understanding of the mysteries of the

life of Christ (hence "illuminative"), growing in virtues, and contemplation.

3.   *The Unitive Way:* the path of spiritual adulthood, focused on union with God (hence "unitive") through the power of the Holy Spirit and the perfection of faith, hope, and love.

Although this exact terminology took time to develop, the basic idea of three stages of spiritual growth is rooted in the Bible. For example, the apostle Paul contrasts spiritual "children" in Christ with those who have attained "mature manhood" (Ephesians 4:13–14). Likewise, the apostle John distinguishes three spiritual "ages" in the Church: "little children" are the beginners, "young men" are those who have made spiritual progress, and "fathers" are the spiritual adults (1 John 2:12–13).[3]

Over the centuries, different spiritual writers have given a variety of names to these stages of the interior life. Nevertheless, the identification of three stages—the beginning, the middle, and the end—can be found in ancient, medieval, and modern spiritual writers, in both Eastern and Western Christianity.[4] Together they testify that the spiritual life is not a revolving door, but a *process of growth*. With that said, it's important to keep in mind that each person's *experience* of this process is going to be unique. For in the end, the spiritual life of each human soul is a mystery.[5]

At the same time, in the Sermon on the Mount, Jesus himself describes a *single* "way" or "path" (Greek *hodos*) upon which *all* of his disciples must walk (Matthew 7:14). This image of a path presupposes a starting point and progress toward a final destination. It also reflects the fact that Jesus describes his followers as "disciples" or, more literally, "students" (Greek *mathētai*).[6] This means he expects them to learn his teachings and to *walk together* down the path of their spiritual master and rabbi (see Matthew 10:24–25; 23:8–10).[7] For according to Jesus, his path is the "way" that "leads to eternal life" (Matthew 7:14; 19:16–17).

THE UNIVERSAL CALL TO HOLINESS

Third, and perhaps most important, I discovered to my surprise that all Christians—myself included—are called to be saints. Now, I don't recall anyone ever actually saying that holiness was unattainable for a layperson like me. Yet, somewhere along the way, I had picked up the idea that while monks, nuns, priests, bishops, and popes might be called to contemplation and union with God, the best I could shoot for was spiritual mediocrity and (hopefully) not going to hell. However, the more I studied the spiritual classics, the more I realized that *every person*—old or young, man or woman, unmarried or married alike—is called to real holiness.[8]

Now, this shouldn't have come as a surprise. After all, in the Sermon on the Mount, Jesus says, "You, therefore, must *be perfect, as your heavenly Father is perfect*" (Matthew 5:48). With these words, Jesus is alluding to God's call to the people of Israel: "You shall *be holy;* for I the LORD your God am holy" (Leviticus 19:2). Likewise, the apostle Paul says that the Corinthians—who were all former pagans and laypeople—are all "called to be *saints*" (1 Corinthians 1:2). Finally, the letter to the Hebrews calls its readers to "the *holiness* without which no one will see the Lord" (Hebrews 12:14). Perhaps the most beautiful example of the universal invitation to holiness comes from Jesus' encounter with the Samaritan woman at the well:

> There came a woman of Samaria to draw water. Jesus said to her, "Give me a drink." . . . The Samaritan woman said to him, "How is it that you, a Jew, ask a drink of me, a woman of Samaria?" For Jews have no dealings with Samaritans. Jesus answered her, *"If you knew the gift of God, and who it is that is saying to you, 'Give me a drink,' you would have asked him, and he would have given you living water."* The woman said to him, "Sir, you have nothing to draw with, and the well is

deep; where do you get that living water?" . . . Jesus said to her, "Every one who drinks of this water will thirst again, but whoever drinks of the water that I shall give him will never thirst; the water that I shall give him will become in him a spring of water welling up to eternal life." The woman said to him, "Sir, give me this water, that I may not thirst, nor come here to draw."

(John 4:7, 9–11, 13–15)

We will have more to say about the image of "living water" later.[9] For now, the main point is that Jesus is not referring to ordinary water. He is talking about quenching the woman's *spiritual* thirst by giving her the gift of the Holy Spirit. As Jesus says elsewhere in the Gospel of John,

> *If any one thirst, let him come to me and drink.* He who believes in me, as the scripture has said, *"Out of his heart shall flow rivers of living water."* Now this he said about *the Spirit,* which those who believed in him were to receive.
>
> (John 7:37–39)

At first glance, the Samaritan woman may seem an unlikely candidate for the gift of the Holy Spirit. For one thing, she is not a Jew. The Samaritans descended from pagans who had invaded the Holy Land centuries earlier (see 2 Kings 17:24–41). Although they accepted the God of Israel, the Samaritans rejected the Jerusalem Temple (see John 4:19–24). For another thing, the Samaritan woman is in a state of grave sin. Not only has she been married five times, but she is currently living with a man who is not her husband (see John 4:17–18). In an ancient Jewish context, this would put her in a public and permanent state of fornication.

Yet none of this stops Jesus from offering her the gift of the Holy Spirit. Apparently, *her sin is not a barrier to Jesus' calling her.* To be sure, as soon as she asks him to give her this water, the first thing she will need to do is address the sin in her life. That is why Jesus says, "Go, call your husband, and come here" (John 4:16). Nevertheless, it is Jesus who waits beside the well for her. It is *he* who first asks her for a drink. The reason for this is simple: Jesus' invitation to holiness—his offering of the gift of the Holy Spirt—is universal. It is not just for some, but for all. In other words, no matter who you are or what you've done, if you are spiritually thirsty, then Jesus is inviting *you* to come to him and drink.

JESUS AND THE JEWISH ROOTS OF SPIRITUALITY

This brings me to the fourth and final thing I discovered. The more I read, the more I realized the greatest spiritual writers were not making up their teachings out of thin air. They were getting them from the Bible—especially the Gospels. Consider the opening lines of Thomas à Kempis' classic work *The Imitation of Christ*:

> If we truly want to be enlightened . . . , then let our principal study be meditation on the life of Jesus Christ. The doctrine of Christ surpasses all the doctrines of the saints.[10]

In other words, in the end, *Jesus himself is the supreme teacher of the spiritual life.* He is the master and model of all Christian spirituality. As Jesus says, "You have one teacher, the Christ" (Matthew 23:10).[11]

But there are a couple of problems. For one thing, the spiritual teachings of Jesus are not always easy to understand. To take just one example: What does Jesus mean when he says, "Be perfect, as your heavenly Father is perfect" (Matthew 5:48)? Is this even possible? For another thing, when Jesus first gave his teachings, he spoke to a Jewish audience, using words and images deeply rooted in Jewish Scripture. However, many Christians today just don't know the Old Testament as well as they would like to. In order to really understand the words and actions of Jesus, we need to situate them in their ancient Jewish context. That is what we are going to do in this book. We are going to explore *Jesus and the Jewish roots of the spiritual life.*

Before we begin, I want to stress that everything I'm going to say in the following pages draws directly on ancient, medieval, and modern Christian spiritual classics. Readers interested in digging deeper into these works are encouraged to study the endnotes. The main text, however, will focus on the biblical foundations of key topics in Christian spirituality, including

- Vocal Prayer, Meditation, and Contemplation
- Three Major Temptations and Three Remedies
- Spiritual Exercises: The Lord's Prayer, Fasting, and Almsgiving
- The Seven Capital Sins and the Seven Opposing Virtues
- *Lectio Divina:* How to Meditate on Scripture
- The Dark Night of the Soul[12]

I should also emphasize that this is not a comprehensive study of the entire spiritual path. It is an *introduction* to the first stage of spiritual growth—commonly known as the purgative way. Each chapter will begin with a brief glimpse into what the spiritual classics say about each topic before exploring what Jesus himself has to say about it. Then we'll conclude with some practical implications, drawing on the wisdom of the spiritual classics. You can think of this book as a kind of "biblical road map of the spiritual life," with Jesus as the primary guide. The ultimate goal is to shed light on the first steps of the spiritual "path" taught by Jesus himself (see Matthew 7:14).

In conclusion: if you, like me, grew up thinking the spiritual life was mainly about saying your prayers and hoping not to go to hell; or if you've ever started to pray but given up after experiencing dryness or distraction; or if you've ever tried to read the writings of the mystics but felt lost or confused by what they were saying; or even if you know the spiritual classics well but are curious about the biblical roots of their teachings—whoever you are, wherever you are on the journey—if you're thirsting for the "living water" that only Jesus can give, then this book is for you. Just as Jesus spoke directly to the woman at the well in the Gospels, he is still speaking to us today.

But *how* exactly do we talk to God? In order to answer this question, we need to begin our journey down the spiritual path of Jesus by turning to the topic of prayer.

PRAYER

1

VOCAL PRAYER

When you pray, say: "Father, hallowed be thy name."
—Jesus of Nazareth (Luke 11:2)

THE BEATING HEART OF THE SPIRITUAL LIFE IS PRAYER. OVER THE centuries, Christian spiritual writers have often singled out three major forms: vocal prayer, meditation, and contemplation.[1] Before we start walking down the spiritual path Jesus taught his disciples, it is necessary to first define our terms and clarify what the Bible teaches about each of these. We begin with vocal prayer.

On its most basic level, vocal prayer can be defined as *using words to communicate with God*. Over the centuries, Christian spiritual writers have often emphasized the use of spoken words in prayer. Consider, for example, the following statements from ancient, medieval, and modern times:

Prayer is by nature a dialogue . . . with God.
—John Climacus (7th century)[2]

Prayer is . . . the requesting of good things from God.
—John Damascene (8th century)[3]

In vocal prayer the mind and heart must be attentive
to what you say.
—Teresa of Avila (16th century)[4]

Since human beings have souls and bodies, the translation of interior thoughts and feelings into exterior words is a natural form of communication. For this reason, vocal prayer has always been regarded as an essential part of the spiritual life. In the sixteenth century, the great Spanish mystic Teresa of Avila once described vocal prayer—when spoken from the heart—as "the door of entry" to the interior life of the soul.[5]

Why is praying with words so important? Why not just skip over vocal prayer and go straight to silent meditation or contemplation? The answer: Jesus himself, following the Jewish Scriptures, used words when he prayed. Moreover, when asked by his disciples to teach them how to pray, Jesus gave them specific words to say, in the Lord's Prayer (see Luke 11:1–4). In this chapter, we'll take a few moments to look at Jesus and the Jewish roots of vocal prayer.

The Jewish Roots of Vocal Prayer

In order to understand the teaching of Jesus on vocal prayer, we have to begin by looking at vocal prayer in the Jewish Scriptures.

Vocal Prayer in Jewish Scripture

In the Old Testament, using words to communicate with the God of the universe goes all the way back to the beginning of human history. In the Garden of Eden, Adam uses words to speak to God when he hears him coming near: "I heard the sound of you in the garden, and I was afraid, because I was naked; and I hid myself" (Genesis 3:10). Likewise, Abraham uses words to intercede for Lot and the people of Sodom: "Behold, I have taken upon myself to speak to the Lord, I who am but dust and ashes" (Genesis 18:27). When God appears to Moses in the burning bush, Moses uses words to say to God, "Here am I" (Exodus 3:4).

Sometimes, vocal prayer can be spoken so quietly that it is virtually silent, as when Hannah, the mother of Samuel, begs God to give her the gift of a son: "Hannah was speaking in her heart; only her lips moved, and her voice was not heard" (1 Samuel 1:13). When her request is granted by God, Hannah responds with one of the most famous vocal prayers in all of Jewish Scripture, known as the "Song of Hannah":

> My *heart* exults in the LORD;
>> my strength is exalted in the LORD.
> My *mouth* derides my enemies,
>> because I rejoice in your salvation.
> (1 Samuel 2:1)

Notice that in both cases, Hannah speaks to God from her "heart." In context, this does not refer to an organ in her body. In Jewish Scripture, the "heart" (Hebrew *leb*) refers to the deepest part of a human being, the hidden center, the *inner person*.[6] In the Hebrew conception of a human being, the "heart" is not only the seat of emotions; it is also the seat of memories, thoughts, and decisions. Above all, it is the heart that chooses to *love*. Thus, speaking from the heart is the essence of true vocal prayer.

The Book of Psalms: Masterpiece of Vocal Prayer

The book of Psalms is the indisputable masterpiece of vocal prayer in the Jewish Scriptures. Indeed, it is nothing other than a collection of 150 vocal prayers. In the original Hebrew, these "psalms" are called "praises" (Hebrew *tehillim*) because many of them are prayers of thanksgiving, adoration, and praise.[7] The psalms explain not only what vocal prayer is but how it is to be practiced.

For example, the book of Psalms makes clear that the most basic definition of "prayer" (Hebrew *tephillah*) is speaking "words" to God:

> Hear my *prayer*, O God;
>> give ear to *the words of my mouth*.
>> (Psalm 54:2)

At the same time, the Psalter emphasizes that true vocal prayer involves not just the lips but also the heart:

> Let *the words of my mouth* and *the meditation of my heart*
>> be acceptable in your sight,
> O Lord, my rock and my redeemer.
>> (Psalm 19:14)

Finally, the book of Psalms even goes so far as to describe vocal prayer as a kind of sacrifice offered to God every morning and every evening:

> O Lord, in the morning *you hear my voice;*
>> *in the morning I prepare a sacrifice for you,* and watch.
>> (Psalm 5:3)

> Let *my prayer* be counted as *incense* before you,
>> and the lifting up of my hands as an *evening sacrifice*!
>> (Psalm 141:1–2)

According to the Jewish Bible, vocal prayer is something that should be done every day. Each day should begin and end by offering one's "soul" back to the God who gave it in the first place (Psalm 86:3–4).

Jesus and Vocal Prayer

When we turn from vocal prayer in the Jewish Scriptures to the life of Jesus, we quickly discover that Jesus practiced vocal prayer himself and instructed his disciples to follow his example.

Jesus Prayed the Psalms

At the time of Jesus, the book of Psalms was the fundamental "prayer book" of the Jewish people.[8] As a first-century Jew, Jesus would have known the Psalms by heart from singing them during festivals such as Passover. He also would have used the words of the Psalms in his own vocal prayer. To take just one example: at the very end of his life, as he is dying on the cross, Jesus cries out to God,

> *"Father, into your hands I commit my spirit!"* And having said this he breathed his last.
>
> (Luke 23:46)

With these words, Jesus is offering his life to the Father. This is the supreme example of vocal prayer as a *sacrifice*. However, that is not all Jesus is doing. He is also quoting the book of Psalms:

> *Into your hand I commit my spirit;*
> you have redeemed me, O LORD, faithful God.
> (Psalm 31:5)

Jesus not only knows the words of Psalm 31 by heart but also makes these words his own in the last prayer he ever utters. However, whereas the psalm itself is addressed to "the LORD" (Hebrew *YHWH*), Jesus addresses his prayer to the "Father" (Greek *patēr*). One of the most distinctive aspects of the prayer of Jesus is his repeated insistence that his disciples address God as their Father.

Jesus Prayed in His Own Words

In addition to memorized vocal prayers, Jesus also prays using his own words. On more than one occasion, Jesus prays to the Father in public, where everyone can hear him (see Luke 10:21–22; John 11:41–42). During the Last Supper, Jesus speaks the longest vocal prayer recorded in the Gospels—his so-called "high priestly prayer"—in the presence of his chosen disciples when he prays for unity (see John 17:1–26). Perhaps most moving of all is the prayer during his agony in Gethsemane:

> Jesus went with them to a place called Gethsemane, and he said to his disciples, "Sit here, while I go there and pray." . . . And going a little farther he fell on his face and prayed, *"My Father, if it be possible, let this cup pass from me; nevertheless, not as I will, but as you will."* And he came to the disciples and found them sleeping. . . . Again, for the second time, he went away and prayed, *"My Father, if this cannot pass unless I drink it, your will be done."* And again he came and found them sleeping, for their eyes were heavy. So, leaving them again, *he went away and prayed for the third time, saying the same words.*
>   (Matthew 26:36, 39–40, 42–44)

Note well that Jesus uses words to pray, even when he is alone. Obviously, he does not need to do this, but he chooses to. Notice also that Jesus even *repeats himself* when he prays, "saying the same words" (Matthew 26:44). His prayer is fully human. In the agony in Gethsemane, Jesus models for his disciples the importance of spontaneous and persistent vocal prayer to the Father, spoken from the heart.

Jesus Taught His Disciples a Vocal Prayer

Finally, when Jesus is asked by his disciples to teach them how to pray, he gives them certain words to say, in the form of the Lord's Prayer:

> *He was praying in a certain place,* and when he ceased, *one of his disciples said to him, "Lord, teach us to pray,* as John taught his disciples." And he said to them, *"When you pray, say: 'Father,* hallowed be your name. Your kingdom come. Give us each day our daily bread; and forgive us our sins, for we ourselves forgive every one who is indebted to us; and lead us not into temptation.' "
>
> (Luke 11:1–4)

We will look more closely at the longer version of the Lord's Prayer later (see Matthew 6:9–13). For now, the main point is that when Jesus' disciples ask him to teach them how to pray, he gives them certain words to say—the first of which is "Father." In doing so, he is beginning to teach them to pray like he prays. In giving the Lord's Prayer, Jesus shows that he is both the master and the model of vocal prayer.

VOCAL PRAYER IN CHRISTIAN TRADITION

It should be clear by now that Jesus, following the Jewish Scriptures, considers vocal prayer *an essential part* of the spiritual life of his disciples. Several practical implications flow from this fact.

Memorized and Spontaneous Vocal Prayer

If Jesus himself prayed both memorized vocal prayers (like the Psalms) and spontaneous vocal prayers (like his prayer in Gethsemane), then disciples of Jesus should practice *both*. As Jesus himself says:

> *A disciple is not above his teacher*, nor a servant above his master; *it is enough for the disciple to be like his teacher,* and the servant like his master.
>
> (Matthew 10:24–25)

In other words, followers of Jesus should begin by imitating the prayer of their spiritual master. Some people are very comfortable reciting memorized prayers but virtually never speak to God in their own words. Others are very comfortable praying spontaneous prayers but look down on memorized prayers as empty words. Neither extreme is biblical. On the one hand, if we are going to talk to God the Father in the same way that Jesus did, we need to pray using our own words. On the other hand, if we never pray the words of the Psalms or the Lord's Prayer, then we are choosing not to pray like Jesus himself prayed. If Jesus is truly the model and master of Christian prayer, then we should follow his example by writing the words of the Psalms and the Lord's Prayer into our hearts so that they can teach us how to pray and what to say.

Speaking from the Heart

Whatever words we use, we should always strive to speak to God *from the heart*. In other words, we need to say what we mean, and mean what we say.

But what about the problem of distraction during vocal prayer? How do we avoid saying the words of prayer while thinking about something else altogether? As the great medieval theologian Thomas Aquinas pointed out centuries ago, "Even holy men sometimes suffer from a wandering of the mind when they pray."[9]

For this reason, the first practical step is to always begin our prayers by taking a moment to place ourselves in the presence of

God. In the words of the seventeenth-century Christian writer Francis de Sales:

> *Begin all your prayers, whether mental or vocal, in the presence of God.* Keep this rule without any exception and you will quickly see how helpful it will be.[10]

The second step is this: when you begin to speak, remember that you are not just saying words, but speaking *to someone*—God. As Teresa of Avila writes:

> When you approach God, then, *try to think and realize Whom you are about to address* and continue to do so while you are addressing him. . . . Do not, I beg you, address God while you are thinking of other things.[11]

By developing the habit of placing ourselves in God's presence before we begin to pray, and remembering whom we are praying to, our vocal prayer can be transformed from a distracted monologue with ourselves into a heartfelt dialogue with the living God.

The Path to Meditation and Contemplation

Finally, when Jesus teaches his disciples how to pray, he *begins* by giving them *words* to say. While some people may be tempted to skip over vocal prayer in the desire to begin practicing "higher" forms of prayer, such as meditation or contemplation, this would be a mistake. In fact, according to Teresa of Avila, vocal prayer said well can lead directly to contemplation:

> It may seem to anyone who doesn't know about the matter that vocal prayer doesn't go with contemplation; but I know that it does. Pardon me, but I want to say this: *I know there are many persons who while praying vocally . . . are raised by God*

to sublime contemplation without their striving for anything or understanding how. It's because of this that I insist so much . . . upon your reciting your vocal prayer well.[12]

In sum, if Jesus himself talked to God the Father using words, and if he taught his disciples to do the same, then vocal prayer is an essential part of the spiritual life of a Christian. It is also the beginning of the path to meditation and contemplation.

Of course, vocal prayer is just one form of prayer. According to the Bible, we also need to learn to pray with our minds. We need to learn to meditate.

2

MEDITATION

You shall love the Lord your God . . . with all your mind.
—Jesus of Nazareth (Mark 12:30)

THE SECOND MAJOR FORM OF PRAYER—MEDITATION—CAN BE DE-fined as *praying with the mind,* especially by prayerfully reading and pondering the word of God. Just as vocal prayer uses words to communicate with God, so meditation uses thoughts to reflect on God. And just as vocal prayer involves the body, so meditation involves the mind. (For this reason, some spiritual writers refer to meditation as "mental prayer.") And just as true vocal prayer is spoken from the heart, so, too, the goal of meditation is not just growth in knowledge but the transformation of the heart.

In the history of Christian spirituality, the importance of meditation—especially meditation on Scripture—has repeatedly been emphasized. Consider the following quotations from ancient, medieval, and modern Christian writers:

> Meditating on [Scripture] should consume
> all the days and nights of our life.
> —John Cassian (5th century)[1]

> Let our principal study be meditation on
> the life of Jesus Christ.
> —Thomas à Kempis (15th century)[2]

Meditation is the basis for acquiring all the virtues, and to
undertake it is a matter of life and death for all Christians.
—Teresa of Avila (16th century)[3]

Isn't this putting it a bit too strongly? Is meditation really a matter of life and death for *all* Christians? After all, the word "meditation" never occurs in the New Testament. Why do the spiritual
classics insist on it?

The answer lies in the Bible itself. On more than one occasion,
the Jewish Scriptures are absolutely unequivocal that the person
who loves God should also love God's word and should meditate
on it day and night. Likewise, although Jesus himself never uses
the word "meditation," when we interpret his words about the
greatest commandment and the Parable of the Sower in their ancient Jewish context, we discover that Jesus is equally emphatic
about the necessity of meditating on the word of God. In this
chapter, let's take a few moments to explore Jesus and the Jewish
roots of meditation.

THE JEWISH ROOTS OF MEDITATION

In order to understand the teaching of Jesus on meditation, we
have to begin by looking at what the Jewish Scriptures teach us
about the practice of meditation. In this regard, two passages
stand out as of supreme importance: the command to love God
with all one's heart, soul, and strength, commonly known as the
Shema (see Deuteronomy 6:4–6), and the book of Psalms, which
begins by declaring "blessed" anyone who "meditates" on the
word of God "day and night" (Psalm 1:1–2).

Moses and the Shema

The first major example of meditation in Jewish Scripture is perhaps the most well-known passage in the entire Old Testament. I am speaking here of the words of Moses given to the people of Israel at the end of the exodus from Egypt:

> Hear, O Israel: The LORD our God is one LORD; and you shall love the LORD your God with all your heart, and with all your soul, and with all your might. *And these words which I command you this day shall be upon your heart; and you shall teach them diligently to your children, and shall talk of them when you sit in your house, and when you walk by the way, and when you lie down, and when you rise.*
> (Deuteronomy 6:4–7)

In later Jewish tradition, the first part of this passage came to be known as the *Shema,* from the first word: "Hear (Hebrew *shema'*), O Israel" (Deuteronomy 6:4). At the time of Jesus, the *Shema* was recited by devout Jews several times a day as *the* fundamental daily prayer.[4] As we will see in a moment, Jesus himself identifies the *Shema* as the greatest commandment (see Mark 12:28–30).

For our purposes here, however, it is the second half of the passage that stands out. How exactly does one love God with all one's "heart," "soul," and "might"? According to Moses, *by writing his "words" upon one's heart,* by teaching them diligently to one's children, by speaking about them everywhere (whether at home or traveling), and by thinking about them every day (morning and night). In other words, according to the Bible, one of the primary ways to love God is by meditating on his word. And notice here that Moses is speaking to all the people of Israel—parents and families included. According to Jewish Scripture, remembering, discussing, and pondering the word of God is supposed to be a daily part of *ordinary* family life.

The Book of Psalms and Daily Meditation

The second major example of meditation in Jewish Scripture comes from the opening lines of one of the most popular and well-known books of the Bible:

> *Blessed is the man*
> who walks not in the counsel of the wicked,
> nor stands in the way of sinners,
>   nor sits in the seat of scoffers;
> but *his delight is in the law of the* LORD,
>   and *on his law he meditates day and night.*
> (Psalm 1:1–2)

According to the book of Psalms, what is the key to being "blessed"—or, more literally, "happy" (Hebrew *'asher*)? Not just reading the "law" but taking "delight" in it and meditating on it. Significantly, the word "meditate" (Hebrew *hagah*) comes from a Hebrew word that also means to "sigh" or "moan" in longing.[5] In the ancient Greek version of the Bible, it was translated as "think about" or "meditate" (Greek *meletaō*) (Psalm 1:2 LXX).[6] Either way, meditation involves the mind. And note well how often the Bible says meditation should be practiced: "day and night" (Psalm 1:2). Finally, notice its positive effects. A person who meditates regularly is like a "tree" that not only bears fruit but whose leaves never dry up because its roots are constantly drinking (Psalm 1:3). According to the Jewish Scripture, meditation is the antidote for spiritual dryness.

JESUS AND MEDITATION

When we turn from the Old Testament to the teaching of Jesus, we quickly discover that Jesus nowhere uses the word "meditate."

However, on two key occasions, Jesus uses the exact same passages from Jewish Scripture that we just studied to teach his disciples the importance of loving God with their minds by keeping his word in their hearts.

The Greatest Commandment

The first teaching of Jesus that stresses the importance of meditation on Scripture comes to us in his famous answer to a Jewish scribe's question about which of the biblical commandments is greatest:

> One of the scribes came up and heard them disputing with one another, and seeing that he answered them well, asked him, "Which commandment is the first of all?" Jesus answered, "The first is, 'Hear, O Israel: The Lord our God, the Lord is one; and *you shall love the Lord your God* with all your heart, and with all your soul, and *with all your mind,* and with all your strength.' "
>
> (Mark 12:28–30)

Notice here that Jesus answers the question by quoting the *Shema:* "Hear, O Israel . . ." (Deuteronomy 6:4). At first glance, his answer looks like standard Jewish teaching. However, as any first-century Jew would have noticed, Jesus also does something remarkable. He *adds* a new command: "You shall love the Lord your God . . . *with all your mind*" (Mark 12:30). This line is not present in the Hebrew Scriptures.[7] The word Jesus uses for "mind" (Greek *dianoia*) refers to a person's "intelligence" or "understanding."[8]

In other words, Jesus expects his disciples to love God not only with their heart, soul, and strength but also with their intellect. He expects his disciples to love God *by thinking about him.* Moreover, since the *Shema* itself is specifically focused on loving God by writing his "words" on the "heart" (Deuteronomy 6:6), Jesus implies that his followers are likewise to love the one God of the universe by remembering and pondering his word—every day and every night.

The Parable of the Sower

Another major teaching of Jesus that emphasizes meditation comes from his famous Parable of the Sower. Although the parable is well-known, it is important to read it carefully, focusing on the four different kinds of soil:

> When a great crowd came together and people from town after town came to him, he said in a parable: "A sower went out to sow his seed; and as he sowed, *some fell along the path,* and was trodden under foot, and the birds of the air devoured it. And *some fell on the rock;* and as it grew up, it withered away, because it had no moisture. And *some fell among thorns;* and the thorns grew with it and choked it. And *some fell into good soil* and grew, and yielded a hundredfold." As he said this, he called out, "He who has ears to hear, let him hear."
>
> (Luke 8:4–8)

What is the meaning of this parable? And what does it have to do with meditation?

If all we had was the parable itself, we might not be able to see any connection. Thankfully, Jesus also gives his disciples an explanation of the parable. For the sake of clarity, I've organized Jesus' explanation according to each of the four different kinds of soil:

> Now the parable is this: The seed is *the word of God.*
>
> [1] The ones along *the path* are those who have heard; then the devil comes and takes away the word from their hearts, that they may not believe and be saved.

[2] And the ones *on the rock* are those who, when they hear the word, receive it with joy; but these have no root, they believe for a while and in time of temptation fall away.

[3] And as for what fell *among the thorns,* they are those who hear, but as they go on their way they are choked by the cares and riches and pleasures of life, and their fruit does not mature.

[4] And as for that in *the good soil,* they are those who, hearing the word, hold it fast in an honest and good heart, and bring forth fruit with patience.

(Luke 8:11–15)

According to Jesus, the entire Parable of the Sower is really about four different responses to "the word of God" (Luke 8:11).[9]

Four Responses to the Word

The first group of people hear the word of God, but the devil comes and takes it "from their hearts" (Luke 8:12), so they *stop believing.*

The second group of people hear the word of God and are happy at first, but because their faith is so shallow—it has "no root" (Luke 8:13)—they believe only for a while. As soon as temptation comes, they end up *falling away.*

The third group of people hear the word of God and even begin to bear some spiritual "fruit." However, as time goes by, God's word is choked to death by "cares" and the pursuit of earthly "riches" and "pleasures" (Luke 8:14). Notice Jesus says nothing about sins like adultery or murder. Anxiety about worldly cares and *the pursuit of wealth and pleasure* are more than enough to choke the life out of the soul.

The fourth and final group of people also hear the word of God, but they do something different. They "hold it fast" in their hearts (Luke 8:15). Significantly, the word for "hold fast" (Greek *katechō*) also means to "keep in one's memory."[10] (We get the English word "catechesis" from this term.) In other words, these people respond to the word of God by *memorizing* it and writing it *in their hearts*—the deepest part of themselves, where they encounter God.[11] This is exactly what meditation is: pondering the word of God with the mind and storing it up in the heart in order to grow in love of God.

The Fruits of Meditation

Notice how this affects a person's soul. Not only does his heart become "honest and good" (Luke 8:15), but he also begins to bear superabundant "fruit"—up to one hundredfold (see Luke 8:8, 15)! In using this imagery of bearing fruit, Jesus is alluding to what the book of Psalms teaches about meditation:

> Blessed is the man . . .
> [whose] delight is in the law of the LORD,
>   and *on his law he meditates day and night.*
> He is like a tree
>   planted by streams of water,
> *that yields its fruit in its season.*
>   (Psalm 1:1–3)

According to Jewish Scripture, the key to being "blessed"—or, more literally, "happy" (Hebrew *'asher*)—is daily meditation on the word of God. A person who meditates on Scripture regularly is like a "tree" that bears much spiritual "fruit" because its roots are constantly drinking from the living water of God's word.

In short, although Jesus never uses the word "meditation," he clearly expects his disciples to love God with their minds and store up the word of God in their hearts. In other words, Jesus insists that his disciples meditate, lest they risk becoming like the first three kinds of fruitless soil in the Parable of the Sower.

MEDITATION IN CHRISTIAN TRADITION

By now it should be clear that we don't have to go to the classic works of Christian spirituality in order to discover the importance of meditation on God's word. The Law of Moses teaches it. The book of Psalms teaches it. Jesus himself teaches it. At the same time, later Christian spiritual writers have given us some helpful practical advice about daily meditation from the heart, including how to do it.

Set Aside Time Every Day for Meditation
The first thing that needs to be said is that prayerful meditation on the Bible takes time. It cannot be rushed. Exactly how much time will differ from person to person, depending on one's state in life, age, health, occupation, and familial or professional duties. However, the common teaching of the spiritual classics is about an hour of prayer and meditation each day.

For example, in his adaptation of the *Spiritual Exercises* for ordinary working people, the sixteenth-century Spanish writer Ignatius of Loyola recommends that "a person who is involved in public affairs or pressing occupations" should devote "an hour and a half each day" to prayer and meditation on Scripture.[12] Along similar lines, consider the advice of Francis de Sales' classic *Introduction to the Devout Life,* which was explicitly written for "ordinary" Christians living in the world:

> I especially counsel you to practice mental prayer, the prayer of the heart. . . . Set aside *an hour every day* before the midday

meal, if possible, early in the morning, when your mind is less distracted and fresher after the night's rest.[13]

Clearly, both Ignatius and Francis expect ordinary Christians who are serious about making spiritual progress to do more than just "say their prayers" before meals or before they go to bed at night. Just as a person who wants to grow in bodily strength will need to devote at least an hour a day to regular physical exercise, so, too, anyone who really wants to grow spiritually. This is why Ignatius himself begins his famous book *Spiritual Exercises* by stating that "just as taking a walk, journeying on foot, and running are bodily exercises, so we call Spiritual Exercises every way of preparing and disposing the soul to rid itself of all inordinate attachments and, after their removal, of seeking and finding the will of God in the disposition of our life for the salvation of our soul."[14]

And, just as with physical exercise, if we need to start with just thirty minutes of prayer per day and then gradually work our way up to an hour, that's okay. The important thing is to *read the Bible and meditate on it every single day*, without fail. Of course, this will entail using our time well by avoiding useless distractions. In the words of Thomas à Kempis:

> If you avoid unnecessary conversation and idle visits, as well as a preoccupation with news and various reports, you will find sufficient and appropriate time for good meditations.[15]

Oftentimes, many of us who think it impossible to carve out an hour alone with God each day will easily spend one or two hours (or more!) on the internet, social media, or personal entertainment. It's simply a question of prioritizing our time of prayer: for where our *time* is, there will our *hearts* be also.

Be Faithful to Meditation, and Resolve to Continue

But what do we do if we should happen to miss our morning meditation for some reason? Francis de Sales continues:

> If it happens that the whole morning passes without your having spent time in mental prayer, either because you have been busy or for any other reason—*you should not allow this to happen, as far as you possibly can*—try to make up this omission after the midday meal. . . . *With all this, make a firm determination to take up the practice of daily mental prayer the following day.*[16]

In other words, commit yourself to meditating on the word of God every single day. And if you should happen to miss your morning meditation, do it that evening or start up again the next day. Whatever happens, *don't stop meditating*. As Jesus himself says to his disciples, if you "hold fast" to the "word" in your heart, you will "bring forth fruit with patience" (Luke 8:15).

Begin with the Lord's Prayer and the Gospels

Finally, some readers may be wondering, Where do I begin? What parts of the Bible should I read and meditate on first? According to the spiritual classics, two excellent places to begin are with (1) the words of the Our Father (Matthew 6:9–13) and (2) the life of Jesus in the four Gospels.

For example, in the sixteenth century, the founder of the Jesuits, Ignatius of Loyola, recommended slowly meditating on each of the words of the Lord's Prayer in the following manner:

> One may kneel or sit, as may be better suited to his disposition and more conducive to devotion. He should keep his eyes closed, or fixed in one position without permitting them

to roam. Then let him say, "Father," and continue meditating upon this word as long as he finds various meanings,
comparisons, relish, and consolation in the consideration of
it. *The same method should be followed with each word of the Our
Father.* . . . He should continue for an hour in the way described, going through the whole Our Father.[17]

One reason this way of meditating on the Our Father is a good
place to begin is because so many people already know the words
of the prayer by heart. (It may even be the most well-known passage of Scripture in the entire Bible.) Moreover, as we will see in
chapter 9, although the Lord's Prayer is short, when explained in
the light of Jewish Scripture, every line of the prayer is filled with
meaning and mystery.

   Regarding meditation on the Gospels, as we saw earlier,
Thomas à Kempis begins his classic work *The Imitation of Christ* by
stating in no uncertain terms that "if we truly want to be enlight-
ened," our "principal study" should be "meditation on the life of
Jesus Christ."[18] Along similar lines, in the late nineteenth century,
Thérèse of Lisieux—perhaps the most popular spiritual writer of
modern times—singled out the four Gospels as having pride of
place in her spiritual life:

> But it is especially the Gospels that sustain me during my hours
> of prayer, for in them I find what is necessary for my poor
> little soul. I am constantly discovering in them new lights,
> hidden and mysterious meanings.[19]

Why is it so important to focus on the Gospels? Because if we
want to follow the spiritual path of Jesus, we need to ponder his
teachings, which are found above all in the Gospels. Moreover,
the practice of meditating on his life not only forms our minds
but also transforms our hearts. After all, when we love someone,

we spend time *thinking* about that person.[20] As Ignatius of Loyola says, when meditating on the Gospels, we should ask God for "an intimate knowledge" of Jesus so that we can *"love Him more* and follow Him more closely."[21]

We will have more to say about meditation on Scripture later in the book when we look at the ancient Christian practice known as *lectio divina.* For now, we need to turn to the third major form of prayer, which is especially focused on the heart: contemplation.

3

CONTEMPLATION

One thing is necessary. Mary has chosen the good portion.
—Jesus of Nazareth (Luke 10:42)

THE THIRD MAJOR FORM OF PRAYER—CONTEMPLATION—DERIVES
its name from the Latin verb *contemplor,* which means to "look
at," "behold" or "gaze attentively."[1] While vocal prayer uses exterior words to talk to God, and meditation uses interior thoughts
to think about God, contemplation, in its most basic form, is *a
"gaze of love"* between the soul and God. In contemplative prayer,
a person takes time to be alone with God out of a simple desire to
be in his presence, to listen to his voice, and to seek his "face."

Over the centuries, Christian spiritual writers have provided a
variety of descriptions of contemplative prayer.[2] Consider, for example, the following descriptions from ancient, medieval, and
modern spiritual classics:

> The Lord . . . placed the highest good not in carrying out
> some work, however praiseworthy, but in the truly simple
> and unified contemplation of him.
> —John Cassian (5th century)[3]

> Contemplation regards the simple act
> of gazing on the truth.
> —Thomas Aquinas (13th century)[4]

What is more tranquil than a simple gaze directed at God alone? . . . Lost in contemplation, [we] see that you, the Creator of all, have no equal among creatures.

—Thomas à Kempis (15th century)[5]

The simple gaze of contemplation . . . differs from meditation, which almost always is made with difficulty, labor, and reasoning.

—Francis de Sales (17th century)[6]

Notice the emphasis in these definitions on the loving desire to "see" the face of God. Taken together, they lead to the conclusion that contemplative prayer is perhaps best described as "a *gaze of faith fixed on Jesus*, an attentiveness to the Word of God, a silent love."[7]

Where do the spiritual writers get the idea of contemplation? Although the word itself never occurs in the Bible, the mystery of contemplation is a central feature of the spiritual life in both the Old and New Testaments. In this chapter, we will take a few moments to look at Jesus and the Jewish roots of contemplative prayer.

THE JEWISH ROOTS OF CONTEMPLATION

When we open the pages of the Jewish Scriptures, three classic examples of contemplative prayer stand out: Moses' practice of being alone with God in "face to face" prayer (Exodus 33–34); David's "one" desire to see the "face" of the Lord and be with him forever in the Temple (Psalm 27); and Elijah's famous encounter with God's "still small voice" (1 Kings 19). Let's look now at each in turn.

Moses' "Face to Face" Prayer with God

The first example of contemplation from Jewish Scripture comes from the life of Moses.[8] Although many readers of the Bible nowadays tend to think of Moses primarily as a lawgiver, he is also a man of contemplative prayer. Consider, for example, Moses' practice of regularly entering alone into the mysterious "tent of meeting" to speak with God face to face:

> *Moses used to take the tent and pitch it outside the camp, far off from the camp; and he called it the tent of meeting.* And every one who sought the LORD would go out to the tent of meeting, which was outside the camp. . . . When Moses entered the tent, the pillar of cloud would descend and stand at the door of the tent, and the LORD would speak with Moses. . . . *Thus the LORD used to speak to Moses face to face, as a man speaks to his friend.*
>
> (Exodus 33:7, 9, 11)

Notice here that Moses pitches the tent of meeting—a kind of portable sanctuary—outside the camp so that he can be alone with God. Notice also that whenever Moses enters into the tent of meeting, the "pillar of cloud" overshadows it as a visible sign of God's presence. Most important of all, when Moses enters the tent, God speaks with him in a unique way: "face to face" (Exodus 33:11). In context, this does not mean that Moses sees the invisible face of God with his human eyes. Just a few verses later, God himself tells Moses, "You cannot see my face; for man shall not see me and live" (Exodus 33:20). What it does mean is that when Moses prays, he enters into God's *presence*. In Hebrew, the word for "face" (Hebrew *panim*) and "presence" (Hebrew *panim*) are the same. "Face to face" thus can also mean "presence to presence."[9] In other words, Moses' communication with God is intimate and personal, like that of a friend rather than a subject or servant. In fact, Moses' prayer is so powerful that it actually changes his appearance: "The skin of his face shone because he had been talking with God" (Exodus 34:29). According to the Bible, Moses does not just talk *to* God; he talks *with* God in a way that transforms him.

King David's One Desire

The second classic example of contemplative prayer in Jewish Scripture comes from the book of Psalms.[10] In Psalm 27, King David declares that his one longing—his deepest desire—is to be with God in the Temple, to see his face, to listen to his voice:

> *One thing have I asked of the* LORD,
> *that will I seek after;*
> that I may dwell in the house of the LORD
> all the days of my life,
> *to gaze upon the beauty of the* LORD,
> *and to inquire in his temple. . . .*
> Hear, O LORD, when I cry aloud,
> be gracious to me and answer me!
> You have said, *"Seek my face."*
> *My heart says to you,*
> *"Your face,* LORD, *do I seek."*
> Hide not your face from me.
> (Psalm 27:4, 7–9)[11]

At the heart of this psalm is David's loving desire for "one thing": to be in God's presence in the Temple forever. There David longs both to "behold," or "gaze upon," God and to "inquire" of him (Psalm 27:4).[12] The first expression refers to David's desire to contemplate the beauty of God, while the second refers to his desire to hear God's voice. Just as Moses would enter regularly into the tent of meeting to be alone with God "face to face," so, too, David wants to dwell in "the house of the LORD"—forever. Notice here that David does not want to just ask God for things using words (as in vocal prayer) or to just think about God using his mind (as in meditation). His deepest desire is to *see* the "face" of God—that is, God's holy and mysterious "presence" (Hebrew *panim*) (Psalm 27:8). This is the heart of contemplative prayer: the loving desire to be with God forever, face to face.

Elijah and God's Still Small Voice

A third major example of contemplation comes from the figure of Elijah. Again, while many contemporary Bible readers think of Elijah primarily as a miracle worker or prophet, in the history of Christian spirituality, he was widely regarded first and foremost as a man of prayer.[13] Nowhere is this clearer than in the famous account of God speaking to Elijah in silence on Mount Sinai:

> There he came to a cave, and lodged there; and behold, the word of the LORD came to him. . . . *"Go forth, and stand upon the mount before the LORD."* And behold, *the* LORD *passed by,* and a great and strong wind rent the mountains, and broke in pieces the rocks before the LORD, but the LORD was not in the wind; and after the wind an earthquake, but the LORD was not in the earthquake; and after the earthquake a fire, but the LORD was not in the fire; and after the fire *a still small voice. And when Elijah heard it, he wrapped his face in his mantle and went out and stood at the entrance of the cave.*
>
> (1 Kings 19:9, 11–13)

Two aspects of this encounter are important for understanding contemplative prayer. First, notice that Elijah, like Moses and David, goes up Mount Horeb to be alone with God. This is different from the kinds of prayers offered by the people of Israel to

God as a community when they gather in worship. Second, when God speaks to Elijah, he does not do so in a visible, tangible way through the wind, the earthquake, or the fire, but in "a still small voice" (1 Kings 19:12). In Hebrew, this expression can be translated as "a *silent* small voice."[14] In other words, *God "speaks" to Elijah in sheer silence.* The exchange between them transcends human words.

JESUS AND CONTEMPLATION

With this biblical background in mind, we can now turn to the life of Jesus. Although Jesus himself never uses the word "contemplation," since ancient times, one episode in particular has been singled out over and over again throughout the centuries as *the* classic example of contemplative prayer.[15] I am speaking here of the famous account of Martha, Mary, and the "one thing . . . necessary" (Luke 10:38–42).[16]

Martha, Mary, and the One Thing Necessary
Although the story of Jesus, Martha, and Mary is very well known, we need to look at it carefully in order to understand why it is so frequently interpreted as a prime example of the life of contemplation:

> As they went on their way, he entered a village; and a woman named Martha received him into her house. *And she had a sister called Mary, who sat at the Lord's feet and listened to his teaching.* But Martha was *distracted* with much serving; and she went to him and said, "Lord, do you not care that my sister has left me to serve alone? Tell her then to help me." But the Lord answered her, "*Martha, Martha, you are anxious*

and troubled about many things; one thing is necessary. Mary has chosen *the good portion,* which shall not be taken away from her."

(Luke 10:38–42)[17]

In order to see the relationship between Mary and contemplative prayer, several points are necessary.

When Mary sits at the feet of Jesus, she is *taking the posture of a Jewish disciple* listening attentively to the teaching of a rabbi.[18] Consider, for example, the words of one ancient Jewish tradition outside the Bible:

> Let your house be a meeting-house for the Sages and *sit amid the dust of their feet* and drink in their words with thirst.
>
> (Mishnah, *Aboth* 1:4)[19]

In a first-century Jewish context, Mary's act of sitting at Jesus' feet is not negligent relaxation. Instead, Mary is focused on looking at Jesus and listening to his words, attentively drinking them in. By the very act of sitting still, Mary is doing the "work" of a student and walking the "path" of a disciple.

When Martha devotes herself to "serving" Jesus, she is taking the role of hostess, most likely by preparing the food for a meal. In an ancient Jewish context, Martha's "serving" (Greek *diakonia*) was an act of hospitality that would have been regarded as both necessary and important.[20]

Contrary to what many readers assume—Jesus does *not* rebuke Martha for serving him.[21] If you go back and read the Gospel carefully, you will see that he reproves her for being *distracted* and *anxious.* The Greek word for "distracted" literally means "to be pulled/dragged away from."[22] In other words, *Martha's anxiety about serving Jesus is literally pulling her away from him.* It is making her unable to focus her attention on Jesus himself and listen quietly to his words, like her sister Mary did. Her problem is not that she is serving him but that she is "anxious and troubled about many things" (Luke 10:41).

The Good Portion = God Himself

Finally, when Jesus tells Martha that there is only "one thing" necessary, he is referring to Mary's act of choosing to sit still and listen to him. Just as King David's "one" desire was to enter into God's presence in the Temple, behold his beauty, and inquire about God's word (Psalm 27:4), so, too, the one thing necessary for a disciple of Jesus is to sit at his feet, gaze at his face, and listen to his words. That is why he says that Mary has chosen the "good portion" (Luke 10:42). For in the book of Psalms, the good portion chosen by David is God himself:

> I say to the LORD, "You are my Lord;
> *I have no good apart from you."* . . .
> The LORD *is my chosen portion.*
> (Psalm 16:2, 5)[23]

In other words, Jesus is teaching Martha to put *looking at him* and *listening to him* above *doing things for him.* Although serving Jesus through works is good, the loving contemplation of Jesus and his words is better.

CONTEMPLATION IN CHRISTIAN TRADITION

In this chapter, we have only scratched the surface of the mystery of contemplative prayer. We will have more to say over the course of our study. For now, I want to conclude with a few practical points.

The One Thing Necessary

Although vocal prayer and meditation are essential, throughout the centuries, spiritual writers have identified contemplative prayer as "the one thing . . . necessary" spoken of by Jesus (Luke 10:42). Consider, for example, the words of the late-sixth-century writer Gregory the Great:

> Mary was actually listening to our Redeemer's word as she sat at his feet, while Martha was busy with her service. . . . What is meant by Mary, who sits and listens to the Lord's words, but the contemplative life? What does Martha, who is occupied with external service, signify but the active life? Martha's solicitude is not censured, but Mary's role is praiseworthy. Great indeed is the value of active life, but contemplation is better, so Mary's role is said never to be taken away. Whereas the works of the active life disappear with the body, the joys of contemplation wax greater with the end of this life.[24]

With these words, Gregory warns followers of Jesus against the perennial temptation to abandon silent, contemplative prayer for the sake of good works or activity that—although virtuous in themselves—can easily become an excuse for not spending time alone with Jesus.

The Silent Gaze of Love

Along similar lines, if contemplation in its simplest form is a gaze of love between the soul and God, then it's important to emphasize that we don't have to say anything, do anything, or think about anything in particular during contemplative prayer. There is no need to be anxious about doing many things for Jesus during prayer (like Martha was). All that is necessary is to silently gaze at him with love and listen (like Mary did). In the words of Teresa of Avila:

> I am not asking you now to think of Him, or to form numerous conceptions of Him, or to make long and subtle meditations with your understanding. *I am asking you only to look at Him.* For who can prevent you from turning the eyes of your soul (just for a moment, if you can do no more) upon this Lord? You are capable of looking at very ugly and loathsome things: can you not, then, look at the most beautiful thing imaginable? Your Spouse [Jesus] never takes His eyes off you.[25]

Notice here that contemplative prayer involves *two* people: you look at Jesus *and he looks back at you.* After all, Jesus is God. Not only can he see you, but he is looking *at* you—right now. All that is necessary is to look back at him. As the book of Psalms says, "*Be still,* and know that I am God" (Psalm 46:10).

The Transforming Power of Contemplation

Last, but certainly not least, the final reason contemplative prayer is so important is because it has the power to actually *change* us— and for the better. When Moses comes down the mountain after being with God for forty days, his very face is altered; it is radiant with the light of God (see Exodus 34:29). In the same way, if we regularly focus our prayer upon the face of Christ, we, too, will be transformed. As the apostle Paul himself says:

> We all, with unveiled face, *beholding the glory of the Lord, are being changed into his likeness* from one degree of glory to another.
>
> (2 Corinthians 3:18)

When we love someone and spend time with him or her, we tend to become more and more like that person. In the words of John of the Cross:

> Contemplation . . . is an infused and loving knowledge of God, which enlightens the soul and at the same time enkindles it with love, until it is raised up step by step, even unto God its Creator.[26]

Indeed, to the extent that contemplation is rooted in the heart's desire to "see" the face of God, contemplative prayer is a kind of foretaste or *"glimpse" of eternal life*. As Jesus himself says in the Sermon on the Mount, "Blessed are the pure in heart, for they shall see God" (Matthew 5:8).

Of course, before we can ever see the face of God, our hearts will need to be purified from sin. In order for that to take place, we need to actually start walking down the spiritual path given by Jesus himself. The first step on that path is repentance.

THE SPIRITUAL PATH

4

THE FIRST STEP

There is joy before the angels of God over
one sinner who repents.
—Jesus of Nazareth (Luke 15:10)

IF THERE IS ONE THING THE SPIRITUAL CLASSICS AGREE UPON, IT IS
that a person will not make it very far down the spiritual path of
Jesus without making a conscious decision to *repent*—that is, to
turn away from sin and turn toward God. Consider, for example,
the following words of ancient, medieval, and modern spiritual
writings:

The beginning of repentance is the beginning of salvation.
—John Climacus (7th century)[1]

If you wish to make spiritual progress . . . Apply yourself to
repentance of heart, and you will find devotion.
—Thomas à Kempis (15th century)[2]

Interior penance consists in sorrow for one's sins and a firm
purpose not to commit them or any others. Exterior penance
is the fruit of the first kind.
—Ignatius of Loyola (16th century)[3]

But why is repentance so necessary? And does anyone who has
lived a life of sin really have the power to change so radically?

In order to answer these questions, we need to look carefully at what the Bible itself says about repentance. As we will see, the concept of repentance in Jewish Scripture is much richer than the English word suggests, and Jesus himself *begins* his proclamation of the gospel by inviting people to turn away from sin and return to God.

THE JEWISH ROOTS OF REPENTANCE

In order to properly understand Jesus' message of repentance, we first need to take a brief look at repentance in Jewish Scripture and the teaching of the most famous Jewish preacher of repentance in history: John the Baptist.

Turning from Sin and Returning to God

In English, the word "repent" is commonly defined as "to feel regret" or "remorse" over having done something wrong.[4] From a biblical point of view, this definition is partially correct, but it does not capture the fullness of what authentic repentance means in the Jewish Scriptures.[5]

In Hebrew, the word commonly translated as "repent" literally means to "turn" (Hebrew *shūb*).[6] It can be used in two ways. On the one hand, to repent means to "turn away" from sin. As God says to the people of Israel:

> *Repent and turn* [Hebrew *shūb*] *from all your transgressions.* . . .
> Cast away from you all the transgressions which you have committed against me, and get yourselves *a new heart* and *a new spirit*!
>
> (Ezekiel 18:30–31)

On the other hand, to repent means to "return" to God. Consider, for example, the words of King David in the book of Psalms, in which he repents for having committed adultery:

> *Create in me a clean heart, O God,*
>> *and put a new and right spirit within me.* . . .
> Then I will teach transgressors your ways,
>> *and sinners will return* [Hebrew *shūb*] *to you.*
> (Psalm 51:10, 13)

Notice that both passages associate repentance with a "new heart" and a "new spirit." From a biblical point of view, repentance is not just a human choice; it is a gift of God's spirit that actually *changes* the human heart. It is God who gives human beings the power to turn away from sin and return to him. It is not something they can accomplish apart from the transforming power of his grace.

John's Baptism of Repentance

With this Jewish concept of repentance in mind, we can better understand the message of Jesus' forerunner, John the Baptist:

> John the baptizer appeared in the wilderness, preaching *a baptism of repentance for the forgiveness of sins*. And there went out to him all the country of Judea, and all the people of Jerusalem; and they were baptized by him in the river Jordan, *confessing their sins*. . . . And he preached, saying, "After me comes he who is mightier than I, the thong of whose sandals I am not worthy to stoop down and untie. *I have baptized you with water; but he will baptize you with the Holy Spirit*."
> (Mark 1:4–5, 7–8)

Three aspects of John the Baptist's ministry need to be highlighted here.[7]

First, John's baptism is explicitly called one of "repentance." As we've already seen, in Jewish Scripture, repentance involves turning away from sin and returning to God. However, the Greek word for "repent" (Greek *metanoeō*) has an added layer of meaning: it literally means to "change one's mind."[8] Thus, John's baptism is being offered to those who have changed their minds about sin and want to be forgiven.

Second, John's baptism involves both *washing* with water and the verbal *confession* of sins.[9] In an ancient Jewish context, the washing emphasizes that it is God who forgives sin and has the power to "cleanse" a person's heart. As King David says to God after having committed adultery, "Wash me thoroughly from my iniquity, and cleanse me from my sin!" (Psalm 51:2). On the other hand, the confession emphasizes that the person also takes responsibility for his own sin. As the Jewish Torah says, "When a man or woman commits any of the sins that men commit . . . , he shall confess his sin" (Numbers 5:6–7).

Finally, as we learn elsewhere, the people coming to John are not pagans; they are fellow Jews who have broken one or more of the commandments. They include people such as "tax collectors" and "harlots" (Matthew 21:32). In a first-century Jewish setting, both groups would have been viewed as sinners—that is, people who had publicly and repeatedly broken two of the Ten Commandments: "You shall not commit adultery" and "You shall not steal" (Exodus 20:14–15). They are men and women who want to change their lives and return to God.

JESUS AND THE GOOD NEWS OF REPENTANCE

When we turn from John the Baptist to Jesus, we discover something extremely significant: as soon as he begins to preach, *the very first thing Jesus does* is invite people to turn away from sin and return to God:

> After John was arrested, Jesus came into Galilee, preaching the gospel of God, and saying, "The time is fulfilled, and the kingdom of God is at hand; *repent* [Greek *metanoeō*], *and believe in the gospel* [Greek *euangelion*]."
>
> (Mark 1:14–15)

In light of these words, one can truly say that, for Jesus, *there is no true evangelization*—no sharing of the "gospel" (Greek *euangelion*)—*without the call to repentance*. In order to illustrate this, we will take a few moments to look at three of Jesus' most famous parables, all of which are focused on repentance: the Lost Sheep, the Lost Coin, and the Prodigal Son (Luke 15:4–32).

The Parable of the Lost Sheep

Jesus' first parable of repentance is the famous story of the lost sheep:

> What man of you, having a hundred sheep, if he has *lost* one of them, does not leave the ninety-nine in the wilderness, and go after the one which is *lost,* until he *finds* it? And when he has *found* it, he lays it on his shoulders, *rejoicing.* And when he comes home, he calls together his friends and his neighbors, saying to them, "*Rejoice* with me, for I have found my sheep which was *lost.*" *Just so, I tell you, there will be more joy in heaven over one sinner who repents* than over ninety-nine righteous persons who need no repentance.
>
> (Luke 15:4–7)

The key to understanding this parable is in the last line, when Jesus reveals that the shepherd represents God and the lost sheep represents a sinner who "repents." Both of these are standard images in Jewish Scripture.[10] Once this is clear, the parable reveals several key truths: just as the lost sheep gets separated from the flock and the shepherd, so, too, sin separates a person from others and from God. And just as the shepherd goes after the lost sheep and does not rest until he finds it, so, too, it is *God* who initiates the search for those who are lost; he will not stop until he finds them.[11] Notice here that the shepherd carries the lost sheep home on his shoulders; so, too, it is *God's grace* that carries a sinner back home. He or she cannot do it alone. Finally, just as the shepherd rejoices with his friends when he finds the lost sheep, so, too, there is "joy in heaven" when even "one sinner" repents and returns to God.

The Parable of the Lost Coin

Jesus' second parable of repentance is the story of the lost coin:

> What woman, having ten silver coins, if she loses *one coin,* does not light a lamp and sweep the house and *seek diligently until she finds it*? And when she has found it, she calls together her friends and neighbors, saying, "Rejoice with me, for I have found the coin which I had lost." *Just so, I tell you, there is joy before the angels of God over one sinner who repents.*
>
> (Luke 15:8–10)

Once again, the key to understanding this parable is the last line, where Jesus reveals that the woman represents God, her friends are the angels, and the coin is "one sinner who repents." Once this is clear, several truths emerge: just as the "one coin" is valuable to the woman, even though she has nine others, so, too, the "one sinner" is *precious* to God.[12] And just as the woman seeks diligently until she finds the lost coin, so, too, it is God who seeks after the lost sinner and *will not stop* until he finds him or her. Finally, just as the woman rejoices with her friends and neighbors, so, too, God *himself* rejoices when even "one sinner . . . repents."[13]

The Parable of the Prodigal Son

Jesus' third parable of repentance is the most famous of them all: the story of the prodigal son. For the sake of space, I will focus here only on the first half of the parable:

> There was a man who had two sons; and the younger of them said to his father, "Father, give me the share of property that falls to me." And he divided his living between them. Not many days later, the younger son gathered all he had and took his journey into *a far country,* and *there he squandered his property in loose living.* And when he had spent everything, a great famine arose in that country, and he began to be in want. So he went and joined himself to one of the citizens of that country, *who sent him into his fields to feed swine.* And he would gladly have fed on the pods that the swine ate; and no one gave him anything. *But when he came to himself* he said, "How many of my father's hired servants have bread enough and to spare, but I perish here with hunger! *I will arise and go to my father, and I will say to him, 'Father, I have sinned against heaven and before you; I am no longer worthy to be called your son;* treat me as one of your hired servants.' " And he arose and came to his father. *But while he was yet at a distance, his father saw him and had compassion, and ran and embraced him and kissed him.* And the son said to him, "Father, I have sinned against heaven and before you; I am no longer worthy to be called your son." But the father said to his servants, "Bring quickly the best robe, and put it on him; and put a ring on his hand, and shoes on his feet; and bring the fatted calf and kill

it, and let us eat and make merry; *for this my son was dead, and is alive again; he was lost, and is found.*"

(Luke 15:11–24)

Although Jesus does not use the word "repentance," when we look at the Prodigal Son in light of the Lost Sheep and the Lost Coin, the reality of repentance and forgiveness is at its very heart.

Far from making him happy, the sin of the prodigal son isolates him, defiles him, and fills him with shame. It isolates him by taking him to "a far country"—that is, pagan territory. It defiles him by leading him to live among "swine," which Jewish Scripture identifies as an "unclean" animal (Leviticus 11:7–8).[14] And it so fills him with shame that he does not even feel "worthy" to be called his father's son.

The repentance of the prodigal son involves changing his mind, returning to his father, and confessing what he has done. Notice that the moment of his repentance takes place when "he came to himself" and remembered *who* he really was (Luke 15:17). This realization is the beginning of his repentance.[15] Of course, it's not enough to just change his mind. He has to get up and start walking home. When he arrives, he makes his confession simply, without excuses or explanations: "Father, I have sinned against heaven and before you" (Luke 15:21).

Most important of all, the father responds to his son's repentance with compassion and joy. Not only is his father watching for him while he is still at a distance, but as soon as he sees the son returning, the father does not wait but runs, embraces him, and kisses him. Why so much joy? Because in the father's eyes, the prodigal son has done much more than just repent. He has come *back to life*. He has *come home*. "This my son was dead, and is alive again; he was lost, and is found" (Luke 15:24).

In the end, that is why Jesus puts the preaching of repentance at the very center of his gospel. Because if sin really does kill, if it really leads to being lost, then sinners don't just need a good teacher. They need a *savior*. And that is the whole point of Jesus' mission. As he says elsewhere, "The Son of man came to seek and to save the lost" (Luke 19:10). True repentance doesn't just bring us back to ourselves; it brings us home to God.

Repentance in Christian Tradition

Given how important repentance is in Jewish Scripture and for John the Baptist and Jesus himself, it is not surprising that it is also central in later Christianity. Just as Jesus begins by preaching the gospel of repentance, so, too, the apostle Peter ends his first sermon on Pentecost with the call to "repent" (Greek *metanoeō*) (Acts 2:38). Likewise, the apostle Paul describes his preaching as calling people to "repent and turn to God" (Acts 26:20). Finally, the letter to the Hebrews describes "repentance" (Greek *metanoia*) as the "foundation" of the spiritual life (Hebrews 6:1–2).

The Foundation of the Spiritual Life
Of course, repentance can look different for different people. For those who have not yet been baptized, turning away from a life of sin ordinarily leads to receiving forgiveness in baptism. As Peter goes on to say, "Repent, and be *baptized* every one of you in the name of Jesus Christ for the *forgiveness* of your sins" (Acts 2:38).

For those who have broken the commandments after baptism, repentance ordinarily requires the confession of sins. As the apostle John says, "If we *confess* our sins, he is faithful and just, and will *forgive* our sins and cleanse us from all unrighteousness" (1 John 1:9). Likewise, the letter of James teaches: "*Confess your sins to one another*, and pray for one another, that you may be healed" (James 5:16).

Either way, true repentance consists of both remorse and the resolution to avoid sin in the future. In the words of Francis de Sales:

> What is your state of soul with respect to mortal sin? Are you firmly resolved never to commit it for any reason whatsoever? . . . In this resolution consists the foundation of the spiritual life.[16]

Is Francis right about this? How can he say the resolution never to commit a "mortal sin" really is the "foundation of the spiritual life"?

The answer is simple: If you have broken any of the Ten Commandments and have not yet repented, then you've not even really begun the journey home to the Father's house. You are either stuck on the path or (more likely) going backward. To be sure, no matter what you've done, you're still his child and he's still your Father. But like the prodigal son, you have to "come to yourself" and change your mind about who you are and who God is. You have to get up and start walking home to the Father. He is already watching and waiting for you. And when you do, as Jesus said, *there will be "joy in heaven"* (Luke 15:7).

Of course, that leaves us with the question of exactly what a mortal sin is and where it comes from in the Bible. To answer this question, we have to turn to our next topic: the Ten Commandments.

5

THE TEN COMMANDMENTS

If you would enter life, keep the commandments.
—Jesus of Nazareth (Matthew 19:17)

AFTER THE NECESSITY OF TURNING AWAY FROM SIN, PERHAPS THE second most widely agreed upon point is that the person who wishes to follow the spiritual path of Jesus cannot do so without keeping the Ten Commandments. If repentance is the *foundation* of the spiritual life, the commandments are the *entryway*. Consider the following words of ancient, medieval, and modern spiritual writers:

> The first step of humility is taken when a man obeys all of God's commandments.
> —Benedict of Nursia (6th century)[1]

> Blessed the simplicity that . . . walks on in the plain and sure path of God's commandments.
> —Thomas à Kempis (15th century)[2]

> It is the function of charity to enable us to observe all God's commandments in general and without exception.
> —Francis de Sales (17th century)[3]

Why are the Ten Commandments so important? Aren't they just a set of rules? And furthermore, don't they belong to the Old Testament? Why should followers of Jesus and the new covenant have to keep them?

In this chapter, we will focus on the role of the Ten Commandments in the spiritual life. Although many people are likely to be familiar with memorized lists of the commandments, if we want to really understand the teaching of Jesus, we need to look carefully at the biblical form of the Ten Commandments in Jewish Scripture. As we will discover, far from being just a set of rules, the Ten Commandments are *a spiritual path* that leads to love rather than hatred, life rather than death.

THE JEWISH ROOTS OF THE TEN COMMANDMENTS

When we open the pages of Jewish Scripture, several aspects of the Ten Commandments stand out as crucial for understanding their role in the spiritual teaching of Jesus.[4]

The Ten Words

The first thing to notice is that the Bible itself never actually uses the phrase "the Ten Commandments." In Jewish Scripture, they are called the "ten words" (Hebrew *'asereth ha-debarim*) (Exodus 34:28).[5] Consider, for example, what Moses says to the people of Israel:

> *The* LORD *spoke to you out of the midst of the fire; you heard the sound of words,* but saw no form; there was only a voice. *And he declared to you his covenant,* which he commanded you to perform, that is, *the ten words;* and he wrote them upon two tables of stone.
>
> (Deuteronomy 4:12–13)

In this passage, the "ten words" are not some arbitrary set of rules. They are spoken directly, by God himself, in the midst of a theophany (an appearance of God) on Mount Sinai. The context of God's appearance is the exodus from Egypt, shortly after God leads Israel through the Red Sea (see Exodus 1–15). Thus, when God speaks the "ten words" to Israel, he has already shown his love for them by saving them from slavery to Pharaoh. Now, at Mount Sinai, God is inviting them into a special relationship with him, known as a "covenant."[6] Like all relationships, this relationship has certain rules. In context, the purpose of the "ten words" is to show them how to remain in covenant with God.

The Call to Holiness

Equally important, God gives the Ten Commandments to Israel in the context of calling them to be "holy":

> *If you will obey my voice* and keep my covenant, you shall be my own possession among all peoples; . . . and you shall be to me a kingdom of priests and *a holy nation*.
> (Exodus 19:5–6)

In ancient Hebrew, the word "holy" (Hebrew *qadosh*) literally means "set apart."[7] It has two distinct connotations.

On the one hand, "holiness" means being "set apart" *from evil*. As God says elsewhere, "You shall be holy; for I the Lord your God am holy" (Leviticus 19:2). Just as God is totally separated from evil, so Israel is called to avoid sin by keeping God's commandments. At the same time, "holiness" also means being "set apart" *for God*. As God says elsewhere, "You shall be holy to me; for I . . . have separated you from the peoples, that you should be mine" (Leviticus 20:26). In other words, God gives the Ten Commandments to Israel so that they can be set apart from sin and set apart for a covenant relationship with him.

The Two Tablets: Love of God and Neighbor

Notice also there are two tablets of commandments. Although there are different traditions of exactly how to count each of the Ten Commandments, since ancient times, interpreters have agreed that the first tablet is focused on love of God, while the second tablet is focused on love of neighbor.[8] In order to see this twofold love clearly, we have to look closely at the original biblical form of the commandments. On the first tablet, God says that those who practice idolatry "hate" him, while those who keep his

Tablet 1: Love of God	Tablet 2: Love of Neighbor
1. Idolatry: "You shall have no other gods."	4. Honoring Parents: "Honor your father and your mother."
2. Blasphemy: "You shall not take the name of the LORD . . . in vain."	5. Murder: "You shall not kill."
3. Sabbath Rest: "Remember the sabbath day, to keep it holy."	6. Adultery: "You shall not commit adultery."
	7. Theft: "You shall not steal."
	8. False Witness: "You shall not bear false witness against your neighbor."
	9–10. Coveting: "You shall not covet . . . anything that is your neighbor's."
(Exodus 20:1–11)	(Exodus 20:12–17)

commandments "love" him (Exodus 20:5-6). Likewise, on the second tablet, the focus shifts to the expression "your neighbor," which occurs four times in a couple of short verses (Exodus 20:16-17).

Taken together, the upshot of these two tablets is clear: those who love God will worship him alone, avoid taking his name in vain, and keep the Sabbath day "holy"—or "set apart" for God—by resting from work. Likewise, those who love their neighbor will honor their parents and avoid murder, adultery, theft, bearing false witness, and coveting their neighbor's spouse or possessions. Far from being randomly arranged, the Ten Commandments give the basic rules for living life in a loving relationship with God and other human beings. At their very heart, the "ten words" of God are about love.

The Ten Commandments: A Path to Life

Finally, the Ten Commandments are not just rules. They are a spiritual path that leads to life. Consider once again the words of Moses, after he gives the commandments to Israel for the second time:

> You shall walk in all the way which the LORD your God has commanded you, that you may live, and that it may go well with you, and that you may live long in the land which you shall possess.
>
> (Deuteronomy 5:33)

When Moses speaks of walking in "the way" of God's commandments, the Hebrew word literally means a "path" or "road" (Hebrew *derek*).[9] Thus, God gives the commandments so that Israel can know "*the way* in which they must walk" (Exodus 18:20). From this point of view, the commandments are a kind of spiritual road map that teaches Israel not only how to love but also how to have spiritual life, and have it abundantly. As the book of Psalms says, "The path" of God's "commandments" fills the soul with "delight," and God's "words" are "sweeter than honey" (Psalm 119:35, 103).

One reason this idea of the Ten Commandments as a spiritual path to life is important is because it helps us better understand the biblical concept of *sin*. According to the Bible, one of the primary reasons God gives the Ten Commandments is so that Israel can avoid "sin" (Exodus 20:20). Although many people nowadays think of sin primarily as breaking a rule or violating a law, in Jewish Scripture, the word "sin" (Hebrew *chata'*) literally means to "miss the mark" or to *"miss the path."*[10] Consider the following examples, in which the same word for "sin" is used to describe someone getting lost:

> Do not fear, for God has come to prove you . . . that you may not *sin* [Hebrew *chata'*].
>
> (Exodus 20:20)

> He who makes haste with his feet *misses* [Hebrew *chata'*] *his way.*
>
> (Proverbs 19:2)

In other words, in the Hebrew Bible, to sin by breaking one of the commandments is to "miss the path"—to stray from God's path that leads to life.

In Jewish Scripture, this connection between keeping the Ten Commandments and having life was quite literal. To break one of the Ten Commandments was, literally speaking, a "mortal" sin: it was punishable by death. Although modern-day readers sometimes assume that in Old Testament times a person could be put to death for virtually anything, that is not true. According to the Bible, only grave violations of the Ten Commandments—such as kidnapping, murder, or adultery—were capital offenses.[11] In short, those who break the commandments "sin" because they literally "miss the path" that leads to life. Instead of acting in ways that are loving and life-giving, they act in ways that are selfish and bring death.

JESUS AND THE TEN COMMANDMENTS

When we turn from the Jewish Scriptures to the life of Jesus, we see two key places in which he emphasizes the absolute necessity of keeping the Ten Commandments.[12]

The Doorway to Eternal Life

First, when Jesus is asked by a rich young man what good deed to do in order to have eternal life, Jesus tells him to keep the commandments:

> [Jesus] said to him, ". . . *If you would enter life, keep the commandments.*" He said to him, "Which?" And Jesus said, "You shall not kill, You shall not commit adultery, You shall not steal, You shall not bear false witness, Honor your father and mother, and, You shall love your neighbor as yourself."
>
> (Matthew 19:17–19)

Notice here that when Jesus speaks about "life," he is not talking about ordinary earthly life. He is responding to the young man's question about "eternal life" (Matthew 19:16). Notice also that when Jesus speaks of "the commandments," he lists those from the second tablet, which is focused on love of neighbor. Most important of all, Jesus describes keeping the commandments as a kind of doorway or entry to eternal life. In other words, *the Ten Commandments are the starting point, not the goal.* Indeed, in the Sermon on the Mount, Jesus calls his disciples to do much more than just avoid breaking the commandments. He calls them to be "perfect" as God is "perfect" (Matthew 5:48)—more on this momentarily. Nevertheless, Jesus states in no uncertain terms that keeping the commandments is a necessary *first step* on his spiritual path.

The Two Greatest Commandments

Second, the reason Jesus says that keeping the Ten Commandments is necessary for salvation is because he knows that, at their heart, the commandments are about love. Consider his famous exchange with a Jewish scribe:

> One of the scribes came up and heard them disputing with one another, and seeing that he answered them well, asked him, *"Which commandment is the first of all?"* Jesus answered, *"The first is,* 'Hear, O Israel: The Lord our God, the Lord is one; and *you shall love the Lord your God* with all your heart, and with all your soul, and with all your mind, and with all your strength.' *The second is this,* 'You shall love your neighbor as yourself.' *There is no other commandment greater than these."*
> (Mark 12:28–31)

Given the importance of the Ten Commandments, one might expect Jesus to identify God's prohibition of idolatry as the "first" commandment (Exodus 20:2–3). However, Jesus instead quotes two other passages from Jewish Scripture: the command to love God with all one's heart, soul, and strength (Deuteronomy 6:4–5) and the command to love one's neighbor as oneself (Leviticus 19:18). In doing this, Jesus is not rejecting the Ten Commandments. Instead, he is summing up the essence of the commandments: the love of God and the love of neighbor.[13]

In support of this, recall Jesus' famous exhortation to his followers to be "perfect" (Greek *teleios*) as God is "perfect" (Matthew 5:48). Admittedly, the Greek word used here is difficult to translate: it can mean "perfect," as well as "blameless," "whole," or "complete."[14] In the Sermon on the Mount, however, Jesus is clearly calling his disciples to the spiritual "perfection" that requires us to *love those who do not love us,* in the same way that God does.[15] Look at his words in context:

> You have heard that it was said, "You shall love your neighbor and hate your enemy." *But I say to you, Love your enemies and pray for those who persecute you, so that you may be sons of your Father who is in heaven; for he makes his sun rise on the evil and on the good, and sends rain on the just and on the unjust.* For if you love those who love you, what reward have you? Do not even the tax collectors do the same? And if you salute only your brethren, what more are you doing than others? Do not even the Gentiles do the same? *You, therefore, must be perfect, as your heavenly Father is perfect.*
> (Matthew 5:43–48)

In other words, the essence of keeping the commandments—and the heart of the spiritual path taught by Jesus—is learning to *love* our enemies like the heavenly Father loves.

THE TEN COMMANDMENTS IN CHRISTIAN TRADITION

With all this in mind, we can bring our discussion to a close with a couple of brief points about the role of the Ten Commandments in Christian spirituality.

The Necessity of Keeping the Commandments

Like Jesus before them, later Christians consistently teach that fidelity to the Ten Commandments is not optional. It is an essential element of the spiritual life. Consider, for example, the words of the apostles Paul and John:

> Neither circumcision counts for anything nor uncircumcision, but *keeping the commandments of God.*
>   (1 Corinthians 7:19)

> This is the love of God, that we *keep his commandments.*
>   (1 John 5:3)

Because the commandments were an indispensable part of life with God, any violation of them was seen as a "mortal sin"—that is, one that leads to spiritual death. As the apostle John states, *"There is sin which is mortal"* (1 John 5:16). In other words, if the Ten Commandments are truly the path that leads to eternal life, then the deliberate and grave violation of them has no place in the life of a follower of Jesus.

The Commandments and the Examination of Conscience

For this reason, over time, it became customary for Christians to regularly examine their lives to see whether they strayed from the path of life by breaking any of the commandments. This practice, known as the "examination of conscience," is famously and beautifully described by the sixteenth-century Spanish writer Ignatius of Loyola:

> I ask God our Lord for grace to know how I have failed in the observance of the Ten Commandments, and also for grace and help to amend for the future. I will beg for a perfect understanding of them in order to observe them better and glo-

rify and praise the Divine Majesty more. In this first method of prayer I should consider and think over the First Commandment, asking myself, how I have observed it, and in what I have failed. . . . This same method will be followed with each of the Ten Commandments.[16]

Examining oneself according to the Ten Commandments is especially important in the beginning stages of the spiritual life. As we saw earlier, after baptism, any grave violation of the commandments will require both repentance and confession in order to stay on the path that leads to life (see 1 John 1:9).

Of course, all this raises another question: Why do human beings sin at all? In order to answer this question, we have to look closely at the reasons for the very first sin ever committed in the Bible. We have to go back to the fall of Adam and Eve.

6

THE THREE TEMPTATIONS

When the devil had ended every temptation,
he departed from him.
—The Gospel of Luke (4:13)

IN THE LAST TWO CHAPTERS, WE LOOKED AT REPENTANCE AS THE foundation of the spiritual life and the commandments as the doorway. But as soon as we start to walk down the path, a problem arises: even after we repent and resolve to keep the commandments, the temptation to sin remains. Why is this so? Why is it so easy to sin, even after choosing to turn away from it? In order to answer this question, we need to look at the origin of human sinfulness and understand exactly how Jesus himself conquers temptation and gives the power to conquer it to his disciples. As we will see, it is impossible to fully understand the good news of salvation without first grasping the bad news of temptation to sin.

When it comes to the root causes of human sin, spiritual writers across the centuries have pointed to *three particular temptations.* Since ancient times, Christians have noted that Adam and Jesus are both tempted by three temptations that seem to correspond to one another. Consider the following examples:

> [Jesus] had to be tempted himself by the same passions by which Adam also was tempted. . . . By these three vices, then, we read that the Lord, the Savior, was also tempted.
> —John Cassian (5th century)[1]

Our ancient enemy rose up against the first human being [Adam], our ancestor, in three temptations. . . . But the means by which he overcame the first man [Adam] were the same ones which caused him to yield when he tempted the second [Jesus].

—Gregory the Great (6th century)[2]

In this chapter, we will look more closely at exactly what the Bible says these three temptations are and how they correlate with the three principal temptations faced by every fallen human being.

This will mean studying what eventually came to be known as "the triple concupiscence"—the disordered human desire for *pleasure, possessions, and pride*.[3] The New Testament refers to these three temptations as "the lust of the flesh and the lust of the eyes and the pride of life" (1 John 2:16). As we will see, these three disordered desires are the key to understanding all human sin as well as the salvation Jesus brings by conquering them.

THE THREE TEMPTATIONS IN JEWISH SCRIPTURE

In order to understand how Jesus overcomes the triple temptation, we need to go back to Jewish Scripture and look carefully at the role of these temptations in the fall of Adam and Eve. We begin with one common question: If the first man and woman are created "very good" (Genesis 1:31), then why do they sin? What is the reason for the Fall?

The Three Reasons for the Fall of Adam and Eve
According to Genesis, after God places Adam in the Garden of Eden, he explicitly commands him not to eat the fruit of the "tree of the knowledge of good and evil," under penalty of death (Gen-

esis 2:8, 15–17). So why does Adam disobey? One key factor is because Eve listens to the words of the "serpent," who assures her that she and her husband will not "die" but will "be like God" or—more literally, "like gods" (Hebrew *'elohim*) (Genesis 3:1–5). However, what is sometimes overlooked are the *three reasons* Eve gives in to the serpent's suggestion:

> When the woman saw that the tree was *good for food,* and that it was *a delight to the eyes,* and that the tree was *to be desired to make one wise,* she took of its fruit and ate; and she also gave some to her husband, who was with her, and he ate.
>
> (Genesis 3:6)[4]

According to Jewish Scripture, there is a triple motivation for the first sin. The reason Adam and Eve disobey God is because of the *pleasure* of tasting the fruit ("good for food"), the longing to *possess* it once they see it ("a delight to the eyes"), and the *prideful* desire to be "wise" like God, but by disobeying him ("desired to make one wise").

It is important to emphasize that, in themselves, these three desires are *good.*[5] The desire for the pleasure of food is good. After all, God himself gives Adam and Eve "every plant" and "every tree with . . . its fruit . . . for food" (Genesis 1:29). Likewise, the desire to possess created things is good. God himself gives Adam and Eve "dominion" over everything in the world: the fish, the birds, the cattle, and all the earth (Genesis 1:26, 28). Finally, even the desire to be like God is good. God himself makes man and woman in his own "image" and "likeness" (Genesis 1:26–27). In other words, the whole reason God creates man and woman is so that they can share in what is good ("good for food"), and beautiful ("a delight to the eyes"), and true (to be "like God"). The problem is that Adam and Eve try to acquire these three things by *abusing their freedom* and disobeying God. They want to be like God, but apart from his will.

By freely choosing to disobey God, Adam and Eve transform these three good desires into three *disordered* desires—for pleasure, possessions, and pride. These are the three reasons for the first human sin.

JESUS AND THE THREE TEMPTATIONS

When we turn from the fall of Adam and Eve to the life of Jesus, we discover a striking parallel between the three reasons for the first sin and the mysterious account of Jesus' three temptations in the desert.

The Temptations of Jesus in the Desert

Immediately after being baptized by John in the river Jordan, Jesus goes into the desert and fasts for forty days, during which time he experiences three temptations. For the sake of clarity, I have enumerated them:

[1] The devil said to him, "If you are the Son of God, *command this stone to become bread.*" And Jesus answered him, "It is written, 'Man shall not live by bread alone.'" [2] And the devil took him up, and *showed him all the kingdoms of the world in a moment of time,* and said to him, "*To you I will give all this authority and their glory; for it has been delivered to me,* and I give it to whom I will. If you, then, will worship me, it shall all be yours." And Jesus answered him, "It is written,

'You shall worship the Lord your God, and him only shall you serve.'"

[3] And he took him to Jerusalem, and set him on the pinnacle of the temple, and said to him, "*If you are the Son of God, throw yourself down from here;* for it is written,

'He will give his angels charge of you, to guard you,'

and

'On their hands they will bear you up,
lest you strike your foot against a stone.' "

And Jesus answered him, "It is said, 'You shall not tempt the Lord your God.' " And when the devil had ended *every temptation,* he departed from him until an opportune time.

(Luke 4:3–13)

Just as the book of Genesis says the forbidden fruit was pleasurable to the taste, a delight to the eyes, and desirable to make Adam and Eve "like gods" (Genesis 3:5), so now the devil tempts Jesus with the *pleasure* of eating, the desire to *possess* the "glory" of all the wealth and power of this world, and the *pride* of exalting himself by performing a miracle where everyone could see. Consider the chart on the opposite page.

Since ancient times, Christian writers have recognized that the parallels between the fall of Adam and the temptations of Jesus in the desert show that he is not just the Messiah. He is also the new Adam.[6] Whereas Adam gave in to the temptations to pleasure, possessions, and pride, and brought sin and death into the world, Jesus triumphs over all three. In other words, the temptations of Jesus in the desert show that his mission is not just to save humanity from sin but also to conquer the power of the very temptations that plunged humanity into sin to begin with.

Fall of Adam	Jesus in the Desert	Three Temptations
1. Good for food	Stone into bread	Pleasure
2. Delight to eyes	All kingdoms of the world	Possessions
3. To make wise	If you are the Son of God	Pride
(Genesis 3:6)	(Luke 4:3, 5–7, 9)	

THE THREE TEMPTATIONS IN CHRISTIAN TRADITION

Should there be any doubt about the importance of understanding that Jesus conquers sin by conquering the three temptations of Adam, we need only turn to the writings of the apostles and later Christian tradition.

Jesus, the New Adam
For example, in his letter to the Romans, the apostle Paul has this to say about the parallel between Adam and Jesus:

> As by one man's disobedience many were made sinners, so by one man's obedience many will be made righteous.
> (Romans 5:19)

According to Paul, Jesus saves humanity not only through his death on the cross; he saves humanity through his *obedience,* by which he undoes the disobedience of Adam in the face of the first temptation.

The Apostle John and the Triple Lust

Consider also the words of the apostle John, who specifically describes human sin as a triple "lust":

> All that is in the world, *the lust of the flesh* and *the lust of the eyes* and *the pride of life,* is not of the Father but is of the world. And the world passes away, and *the lust of it;* but he who does the will of God abides for ever.
>
> (1 John 2:16–17)

In order to understand this passage, it's important to emphasize that though the word "lust" in English normally refers to a disordered desire for sexual pleasure, in Greek, it can refer to *any* disordered "craving" (Greek *epithymia*).[7] Similarly, the word translated here as "pride" literally means "arrogance" (Greek *alazoneia*).[8]

Fall of Adam	Jesus in the Desert	Triple Lust	Three Temptations
1. Good for food	Stone into bread	Lust of the flesh	Pleasure
2. Delight to eyes	All kingdoms of the world	Lust of the eyes	Possessions
3. To make wise	If you are the Son of God	Pride of life	Pride
(Genesis 3:6)	(Luke 4:3, 5–7, 9)	(1 John 2:16–17)	

Thus, according to John, the triple "lust" consists of a sinful desire for the pleasures of the flesh (e.g., food, drink, physical pleasure), the longings of the eyes (e.g., possessions, wealth), and the "arrogance" of exalting oneself over others. These three desires correspond precisely to the three temptations of Adam and Jesus.

The Triple Root of All Human Sinfulness

In light of such striking parallels, later Christian spiritual writers would repeatedly emphasize that these three temptations are at the root of all sin and the evil that results from it. Consider, for example, the words of the great North African bishop Augustine of Hippo and the Spanish mystic John of the Cross:

> *These are the three,* and apart from either the desire of the flesh or the desire of the eyes or the ambition of the world you [will] find nothing to tempt human selfishness.
>
> —Augustine of Hippo (5th century)[9]

> Concupiscence of the flesh, concupiscence of the eyes, and pride of life . . . give rise to all the other appetites.
>
> —John of the Cross (16th century)[10]

If we step back for a moment and reflect, it doesn't take long to realize that this is all too true. *Every conceivable sin* that is part of this fallen world flows in some way from these three temptations.

Think, for example, of the incalculable suffering, brokenness, and pain experienced by individuals, families, and communities because of drunkenness, drug abuse, pornography, human trafficking, and rape. What is at the root of it all? The "lust of the flesh"—the selfish desire for physical pleasure. Think also of the inestimable violence and damage done to human life because of slavery, robbery, fraud, corruption, pollution, and the exploitation of the poor, the elderly, the sick, and the powerless. What is the cause of all this? The "lust of the eyes"—the selfish craving for acquiring wealth at any cost. Finally, imagine the ocean of evil that has swept over human history because of the arrogance of kings, queens, princes, presidents, and politicians who exalt themselves at the expense of those around them. How many wars have been fought, how much blood spilled, because of "the pride of life"?

And we don't even have to look at the tragedy of human history. We need only look into our own hearts. There we will quickly discover our own disordered cravings for pleasure, possessions, and selfish pride.

Jesus Gives His Disciples Three Remedies

So how do followers of Jesus fight against the triple lust? Who among us has power to overcome it?

As we will see over the course of the next three chapters, in the Sermon on the Mount, Jesus gives his disciples *three spiritual exercises* that are remedies for the triple lust that dwells in every human heart. Consider the following:

Fall of Adam	Jesus in the Desert	Triple Lust	Sermon on the Mount
1. Good for food	Stone into bread	Lust of the flesh	Fasting
2. Delight to eyes	All kingdoms of the world	Lust of the eyes	Almsgiving
3. To make wise	If you are the Son of God	Pride of life	Prayer
(Genesis 3:6)	(Luke 4:3, 5–7, 9)	(1 John 2:16–17)	(Matthew 6:2, 5, 16)

As these parallels make clear, Jesus did not overcome temptation so that his followers don't have to. He overcame temptation *so that we can overcome it too.*

In order to see this clearly, however, we will have to look more carefully in the next three chapters at each of these spiritual remedies. We will begin with the antidote to the lust of the flesh—fasting.

7

FASTING

> When you fast . . . wash your face, that your fasting may
> not be seen by men but by your Father who is in secret.
> —Jesus of Nazareth (Matthew 6:17–18)

IN THE SERMON ON THE MOUNT, JESUS GIVES HIS DISCIPLES THREE
spiritual exercises—prayer, fasting, and almsgiving—as antidotes
to "the lust of the flesh and the lust of the eyes and the pride of
life" (1 John 2:16). In this chapter, we will focus on fasting as the
remedy for "the lust of the flesh"—the disordered desire for physical pleasure. As we will see, Jesus teaches his disciples to develop
the habit of *secret fasting*—privately abstaining from food in order
to draw closer to the Father.

In contemporary times, the practice of fasting is not something many people would identify as essential to Christianity. Yet
over the centuries, many spiritual writers have described it as a
central part of the Christian life:

> You will find that fasting guided all the saints to
> a godly way of life.
> —Basil the Great (4th century)[1]

> The author of our death [Adam] broke the commandments by
> eating the fruit of the forbidden tree. . . . Let us who have

fallen away from the joys of paradise through food, rise up to
them again . . . through fasting.

—Gregory the Great (6th century)[2]

The enemy has greater fear of us when he sees
that we can fast.

—Francis de Sales (17th century)[3]

This emphasis on the importance of fasting should not come as a
surprise. After all, in the Sermon on the Mount, Jesus assumes
that fasting will be a regular part of the spiritual life of his followers: "When you fast, anoint your head and wash your face" (Matthew 6:17). It is significant that Jesus says, "*When* you fast . . . ," not
"*If* you fast . . ." Jesus does not consider fasting to be optional.

But what is the reason for fasting? After all, food is necessary
for human life. So why does Jesus expect his followers to sometimes secretly abstain from eating? In this chapter, we will examine where fasting is found in the Bible, why Jesus requires his
disciples to practice it, and how fasting is an antidote to the lust
of the flesh.

THE JEWISH ROOTS OF FASTING

When we open the pages of Jewish Scripture, we discover several
important features of the biblical practice of fasting.[4]

Fasting and the Fall of Adam and Eve

First, a case can be made that the practice of fasting goes all the
way back to the Garden of Eden. Although God's first commandment is "be fruitful and multiply" (Genesis 1:28), the second
commandment explicitly involves abstaining from food:

> The LORD God commanded the man, saying, "You may freely
> eat of every tree of the garden; but of the tree of the knowl-
> edge of good and evil *you shall not eat,* for in the day that you
> eat of it you shall die."
>
> (Genesis 2:16–17)

Long before God ever says, "You shall not kill" (Exodus 20:13), he
says, "You shall not eat" (Genesis 2:17).[5] In other words, Adam
commits the very first sin by *failing to control his desire to eat.* If he
had "fasted" from the tree of knowledge, he would not have been
cast out of Eden. However, because the tree is "good for food," he
gives in to his desire and eats (Genesis 3:6). As a result, not only
are Adam and Eve banished from Eden (Genesis 3:22–23), but all
human beings are born into this fallen world with a disordered
craving for the pleasure of food, which the apostle John calls "the
lust of the flesh" (1 John 2:16). Seen in this light, the biblical
practice of fasting is firstly about *reversing the effects of the Fall* by
training the desires of the body to obey the will of the soul. If a
person can learn to control cravings for good things, like food, he
or she will more likely be able to control cravings for evil things,
like sin.

Preparation for Entering God's Presence

In Jewish Scripture, fasting is also done in order to prepare to
enter the presence of God. Consider the examples of Moses on
Mount Sinai:

> *[Moses] was there with the* LORD *forty days and forty nights; he
> neither ate bread nor drank water.* . . . When Moses came down
> from Mount Sinai, . . . Moses did not know that the skin of
> his face shone because *he had been talking with God.*
>
> (Exodus 34:28–29)

Along similar lines, the prophet Elijah fasts for "forty days and forty nights" (1 Kings 19:8) before climbing Mount Horeb and meeting God:

> There [Elijah] came to a cave, and lodged there. . . . And behold, *the* LORD *passed by,* and a great and strong wind rent the mountains . . . but the LORD was not in the wind; and after the wind an earthquake, but the LORD was not in the earthquake; and after the earthquake a fire, but the LORD was not in the fire; and after the fire *a still small voice.*
>
> (1 Kings 19:9, 11–12)

In both cases, fasting from food and drink prepares Moses and Elijah to encounter God and to hear his voice.

A Sign of Interior Repentance

Finally, in the Jewish Scriptures, fasting is also practiced as an outward sign of inward repentance. Consider the words of the prophet Joel:

> "Yet even now," says the LORD,
>   "*return to me with all your heart,*
> *with fasting,* with weeping, and with mourning;
>   and *rend your hearts* and not your garments."
> *Return to the* LORD, *your God,*
>   for he is gracious and merciful. . . .
> Blow the trumpet in Zion;
>   *sanctify a fast;*
> call a solemn assembly;
>   gather the people.
> Sanctify the congregation;
>   assemble the elders;

> gather the children,
> > even nursing infants.
> Let the bridegroom leave his room,
> > and the bride her chamber.
> > (Joel 2:12–13, 15–16)

Notice here that all Israelites—men, women, and children—are called to participate in the fast as a way of turning away from sin and returning to God with all their hearts (Joel 2:12). This link between outward fasting and interior repentance was often signified by outward actions such as wearing "sackcloth" and "ashes" (Isaiah 58:3–5). Indeed, once a year, on the Day of Atonement, the entire people of Israel would "afflict" themselves, a Hebrew expression for abstaining from food and drink (Leviticus 16:29).[6] In sum, the biblical practice of fasting is all about turning *away* from sin and turning *to* God.[7]

JESUS AND SECRET FASTING

When we turn from the Jewish Scriptures to the life of Jesus, we discover three more important features of fasting.

Jesus Is the Model for Fasting
First, after he is baptized and led out into the desert by the Holy Spirit, Jesus himself fasts:

> Then Jesus was led up by the Spirit into the wilderness to be tempted by the devil. And *he fasted forty days and forty nights,* and afterward he was hungry.
> > (Matthew 4:1–2)

During his public ministry, Jesus was of course known for "eating and drinking" with sinners as part of his effort "to seek and to save the lost" (Matthew 11:19; Luke 15:1–2; 19:10). Nevertheless, when it came time to do battle with temptation, Jesus fasted. In this way, Jesus himself becomes the "principal example" of fasting for his disciples.[8]

The Power of Prayer and Fasting

According to Jesus, when prayer is combined with fasting, it is especially powerful. Consider the words of Jesus to his disciples after he heals a boy with a mute spirit that they were unable to cast out (see Mark 9:14–27). Later, they ask him privately,

> "Why could we not cast it out?" And he said to them, "This kind cannot be driven out by anything but *prayer and fasting.*"
> (Mark 9:28–29)[9]

Significantly, Jesus does not say that it was the disciples' sin that made them spiritually weak. It was just that they were *not fasting*. By itself, prayer is powerful. But in especially difficult situations, it needs to be combined with fasting.[10]

Jesus Teaches His Disciples to Fast in Secret

Finally, in the Sermon on the Mount, Jesus teaches his disciples to practice secret fasting:

> When you fast, do not look dismal, like the hypocrites, for they disfigure their faces that their fasting may be seen by men. Truly, I say to you, they have received their reward. *But when you fast, anoint your head and wash your face, that your fasting may not be seen by men but by your Father who is in secret;* and your Father who sees in secret will reward you.
> (Matthew 6:16–18)

Notice here that Jesus is addressing the *private* fasting of his disciples, not the *public* fasting of the Jewish people as a whole. As we saw above, the Bible itself teaches the people of Israel to wear ashes on solemn days of community-wide fasting and repentance (see Isaiah 58:3–9). Here, Jesus is teaching his disciples to do more than keep the annual days of public fasting, like the Day of Atonement. He is teaching them to develop the habit of *secret fasting*. This emphasis on secrecy is meant to safeguard the disciples against doing the right thing (fasting) for the wrong reason (seeking human praise).[11] Moreover, because only God can see it, secret fasting helps draw them closer to the "Father who is in secret." In short, Jesus calls his disciples to make privately abstaining from food a regular part of their spiritual lives.

FASTING IN CHRISTIAN TRADITION

When we turn from the teaching of Jesus to later Christian tradition, we discover that—no matter how far back one goes—fasting was treated as a central feature of Christian life.

Community Fasting and Christian Worship

For example, from the earliest days of the Church, fasting by the whole community was practiced in conjunction with worship. As the Acts of the Apostles tells us,

> In the church at Antioch . . . they were *worshiping* the Lord
> and *fasting*.
>
> (Acts 13:1–2)

This combination of liturgy and fasting is extremely important since worship in the apostolic Church revolved around the "breaking of bread" (Acts 2:42). Apparently, just as Moses and Elijah fasted to prepare to enter into God's presence, and just as ancient Jews fasted in preparation for Passover (Mishnah, *Pesahim*

10:1), so, too, ancient Christian fasting was linked with partaking of the "body of Christ" and the "blood of Christ" in the Lord's Supper (cf. 1 Corinthians 10:16; 11:20).[12]

Private Fasting and the Passion of Jesus

In addition, early Christians also engaged in private fasting on special days of the week. For example, several ancient Christian writings instruct believers to fast on Wednesdays and Fridays (*Didache* 8:1; *Lives of the Desert Fathers* 8.58; *Apostolic Constitutions* 5.15).[13] In particular, the Friday fast was linked with Jesus' words to the disciples:

> Can the wedding guests fast while the bridegroom is with them? . . . The days will come, when the bridegroom is taken away from them, and *then they will fast in that day*.
> (Mark 2:19–20)

From this point of view, fasting on Friday is a way of *remembering the Crucifixion*—the day on which Jesus was taken away. Just as anyone who has ever lost a spouse or loved one not only remembers the day the loved one died but also keeps that day solemn and sacred, so, too, Christians fast on Fridays as a way of remembering his passion and sharing in the sufferings of Jesus.

By the Middle Ages, this connection between fasting and the sufferings of Jesus made its way into Thomas à Kempis' spiritual classic, *The Imitation of Christ*:

> *[Jesus] finds many companions at table, but few in fasting.* All desire to rejoice with him, but few are willing to suffer something for him and with him.[14]

Seen in this light, fasting is not just something to do in imitation of Jesus. It is about *union with Jesus*. Christian fasting is a way of being with Jesus while he is alone in the desert and suffering on the cross. Since ancient times, Christians have fasted during the forty days of Lent as a way of uniting themselves to "the mystery of Jesus in the desert."[15]

A Remedy for the Lust of the Flesh

Last, but certainly not least, if we have a problem with giving in to the cravings of our flesh, then we need to start fasting. For fasting is a remedy for "the lust of the flesh" (1 John 2:16). Consider the words of the ancient Christian writer Basil the Great:

> If fasting were to preside over our life . . . it would have taught all people not only to control themselves with regard to food, but also to completely avoid and be utterly estranged from avarice, greed, and every kind of vice.[16]

Nowadays, people sometimes suggest that instead of fasting from food, Christians should just "fast" from sins and bad habits. This sounds good in principle, but if we can't control our tongue's cravings for food and drink, what makes us think we will be able to control our cravings for gossip, obscenity, rudeness, and insults? If, on the other hand, we are able to voluntarily give up good things like food, then we will more likely be able to voluntarily resist bad things, like sin. The ability to control the body and the soul go hand in hand. With that said, it is crucial to remember that when it comes to the practice of fasting, we need to ask God for the *grace* to grow in self-control. As Jesus himself says to his disciples at the Last Supper, "Apart from me you can do nothing" (John 15:5).

With this in mind, we can now turn our attention to the remedy for the lust of the eyes that Jesus gives in the Sermon on the Mount—almsgiving.

8

ALMSGIVING

When you give alms, do not let your left hand
know what your right hand is doing,
so that your alms may be in secret.

—Jesus of Nazareth (Matthew 6:3–4)

THE SECOND SPIRITUAL EXERCISE JESUS GIVES TO HIS DISCIPLES IN
the Sermon on the Mount is almsgiving—the practice of giving
money or possessions to the poor and those in need. Just as fasting
is a spiritual remedy for the disordered desire for pleasure ("the lust
of the flesh"), so almsgiving is a spiritual remedy for the disordered
desire for possessions ("the lust of the eyes"). And just as Jesus
teaches his followers to practice secret fasting that only God can
see, so also he exhorts them to practice *secret almsgiving*—discreetly
and voluntarily giving money or other possessions to those in need.

For two thousand years, there have been countless Christian
examples of almsgiving and love for the poor (think here of
Mother Teresa of Calcutta). One reason for this is that ancient,
medieval, and modern spiritual writers regarded the practice of
regularly giving to the poor as not just advisable for Christians,
but as necessary for salvation. Consider the following statements:

It is impossible, though we perform ten thousand other good
deeds, to enter the portals of the kingdom without almsgiving.
—John Chrysostom (4th century)[1]

Some are punished eternally for omitting to give alms.
                —Thomas Aquinas (13th century)[2]

Frequently give up some of your property by giving it with a
generous heart to the poor.
                —Francis de Sales (17th century)[3]

Is this true? Is it really impossible to enter the kingdom of God
apart from almsgiving? Is giving to the poor actually *necessary* for
salvation? Should Christians really give alms frequently, or just
occasionally?

    In this chapter, we will look at the biblical roots of almsgiving,
with a particular focus on how it is a remedy for the lust of the
eyes—the disordered human desire to possess what we see. Moreover, as we will discover, it is Jesus himself who states in no uncertain terms that almsgiving is necessary for salvation.

THE JEWISH ROOTS OF ALMSGIVING

In Jewish Scripture, there are two classic passages devoted to the
practice of almsgiving: Moses' commandment to give generously
to the poor (Deuteronomy 15), and the book of Proverbs' teaching on almsgiving as a "loan" to God (Proverbs 19:17). Let's take
a few moments to look at each of them.[4]

The Commandment to Give to the Poor

When we open the pages of Jewish Scripture, the first thing we
discover is that, according to the Torah of Moses, giving to the
poor and needy is not a suggestion but a commandment:

> The poor will never cease out of the land; *therefore I command*
> *you, You shall open wide your hand to your brother, to the needy*
> *and to the poor.*
>
> (Deuteronomy 15:11)

Notice here that Moses *commands* the Israelites to give to those in
need. This is extremely significant. According to the Torah, almsgiving is not optional. The duty to give to the poor is a "commandment" (Hebrew *mitzvah*) (Deuteronomy 15:5)—the exact
same Hebrew word used for the Ten "Commandments" (Hebrew
mitzvoth) (Exodus 20:6). Notice also that the Israelites are commanded to give generously: they shall "open wide" their hands to
anyone in need.

Whoever Gives to the Poor Lends to God

The second key passage is from the book of Proverbs, which goes
even further than the Law of Moses.[5] According to Proverbs, whoever gives alms to the poor actually "lends" money to God:

> *Whoever is kind to the poor lends to the* LORD,
>   and will be repaid in full.
>   (Proverbs 19:17)[6]

It's worth pointing out here that the word for being "kind" (Hebrew *chanan*) to the poor will later be translated as "mercy" (Greek
eleōn) (Proverbs 19:17 LXX). As we will see in a moment, in Greek,
the word for "almsgiving" (Greek *eleēmosynē*) comes from the
word "mercy" (Greek *eleos*). It's also important to emphasize that
when Proverbs says whoever gives to the poor "lends" (Hebrew
lawah) to the Lord (19:17), this is the technical term for giving a
"loan" that will be repaid.[7] In other words, according to the Jewish Bible, when you give alms to the poor, *you actually "loan" them*

to God, who will eventually "repay" you for the kindness shown to those in need.[8]

JESUS AND SECRET ALMSGIVING

When we turn from the Old Testament to the teaching of Jesus, we discover just how deeply rooted his words are in Jewish beliefs about almsgiving.

The Sermon on the Mount and Secret Almsgiving

Just as Moses commands the Israelites to give to the poor, so, too, in the Sermon on the Mount, Jesus *commands* his disciples to give to whoever begs from them.

> *Give to him who begs from you,* and *do not refuse* him who would borrow from you.
>
> (Matthew 5:42)

Moreover, as with prayer and fasting, Jesus teaches them to give alms secretly, and not for the sake of praise:

> Thus, when you give alms, sound no trumpet before you, as the hypocrites do in the synagogues and in the streets, that they may be praised by men. Truly, I say to you, they have their reward. *But when you give alms, do not let your left hand know what your right hand is doing, so that your alms may be in secret;* and your Father who sees in secret will reward you.
>
> (Matthew 6:2–4)

Once again, note well that Jesus does not say, "*If* you give alms . . ." but "*When* you give alms . . ." Jesus assumes that "almsgiving" or "acts of mercy" (Greek *eleēmosynē*) will be a regular part of the spiritual life of his followers. Notice also that, just like the book of Proverbs, Jesus promises that God will "reward"—or, more literally, "repay" (Greek *apodidōmi*)—anyone who practices almsgiving, as long as it is done in secret. Why is giving secretly so important? The answer is simple but significant: if the disciples give alms for the sake of being praised rather than for the sake of showing mercy, they make pride rather than love the primary motive for doing spiritual exercises that are supposed to be remedies (not causes) for sin.

Almsgiving and "Treasure" in Heaven

In addition, just as the book of Proverbs describes almsgiving as making a "loan" to God, so Jesus describes almsgiving as storing up "treasure" in a heavenly bank:

> *Sell your possessions, and give alms; provide yourselves* with purses that do not grow old, *with a treasure in the heavens that does not fail,* where no thief approaches and no moth destroys. For where your treasure is, there will your heart be also.
> (Luke 12:33–34)

According to Jesus, the way a person lays up "treasure in the heavens" is precisely by giving away treasure on earth. To this end, Jesus describes the practice of almsgiving by using the striking image of filling up a heavenly "treasure box" or "treasure chest" (Greek *thēsauros*) (Luke 12:33).[9] Why does he do this? In order to show that almsgiving has the power to change the human heart. After all, people put only things that are precious to them in treasure chests. By commanding his disciples to give to the poor, he is teaching them to love their neighbor more than they love their possessions.

The Parable of the Sheep and the Goats

Finally, and most important of all, Jesus himself clearly teaches that giving to the poor is *necessary for salvation*. Nowhere is this clearer than in his famous Parable of the Sheep and the Goats (see Matthew 25:31–46). This parable is a detailed description of Jesus' Second Coming and the Final Judgment of humanity.

Although the Parable of the Sheep and the Goats is too long to quote in full here, the main point for us is that the primary difference between the sheep and the goats is whether they gave to the poor. Consider the following words of Jesus:

The Sheep (= Those Who Give Alms)	The Goats (= Those Who Don't)
I was hungry and *you gave me food*	I was hungry and *you gave me no food*
I was thirsty and *you gave me drink*	I was thirsty and *you gave me no drink*
I was naked and *you clothed me*	I was . . . naked and *you did not clothe me*
As you did it to one of the least . . .	As you did it not to one of the least . . .
you did it to me.	*you did it not to me.*
[Go] into eternal life.	Go away into eternal punishment.
(Matthew 25:34–36, 40, 46)	(Matthew 25:41–43, 45–46)

Strikingly, Jesus never says the goats committed idolatry, adultery, or murder. He gives no hint that they broke one of the Ten

Commandments. They simply failed to care for the poor. They sinned by omission.

Equally startling is the fact that while Proverbs says that anyone who gives to the poor lends to *God* (Proverbs 19:17), Jesus says that anyone who cares for the poor cares for *him* (Matthew 25:40). With these words, Jesus is putting himself in the place of God. Ultimately, this is why almsgiving is necessary for salvation. Because to fail to love the poor is *to fail to love Jesus*. And if Jesus *is* God, then to refuse to love the poor is *to refuse to love God*.

ALMSGIVING IN THE CHRISTIAN TRADITION

Should there be any doubt about the necessity of Christian almsgiving, we need only turn to the writings of the apostles, the practice of the early Church, and later Christian tradition.

Weekly Almsgiving in the Early Church

For example, in his first letter to the Corinthians, Paul instructs believers to set aside money for the poor every Sunday:

> Concerning the contribution for the saints: . . . *On the first day of every week, each of you is to put something aside and store it up.*
>
> (1 Corinthians 16:1–2)

Notice here that Paul expects everyone—not just the wealthy—to put "something aside" for "the saints"—which is Paul's term for "the poor" living in Jerusalem (Romans 15:26; Galatians 2:10).

Faith Without Almsgiving Is Dead

Perhaps even more striking is the teaching of the letter of James. Although many people are familiar with the famous passage in which James declares that "faith" without "works" is "dead" (James 2:17), what often gets overlooked is that when James speaks about "works," he is talking primarily about almsgiving:

> *If a brother or sister is ill-clad and in lack of daily food,* and one of you says to them, "Go in peace, be warmed and filled," without giving them the things needed for the body, what does it profit? *So faith by itself, if it has no works, is dead.*
>
> (James 2:15–17)

In context, James is clearly teaching that faith without "works" *of charity* is dead (James 2:17). The kind of "faith" that turns a blind eye to the poor—especially to Christian brothers and sisters—does not have the power to "save" (James 2:14). In other words, if we say we have faith but we do not give to the poor, then our faith is dead.

Almsgiving and the Christian Home

Also important: if almsgiving really is necessary for salvation, then it should not be something occasional but rather a regular part of the spiritual lives of followers of Jesus. Consider, for example, the words of the fourth-century writer John Chrysostom:

> Therefore . . . let us collect money in the home for the explicit purpose of almsgiving. . . . *In this manner, therefore, let everyone's house become a church that will have sacred money stored up within it.* Wherever money is stored up for the poor, that place is inaccessible to demons; and the money that is collected together for almsgiving fortifies Christian homes more than a shield, spear, weapons, physical power, and multitudes of soldiers.[10]

By cultivating the habit of setting aside money for the poor, our homes will truly be transformed into what Chrysostom elsewhere calls a "little church" (Greek *mikra ekklēsia*) and what Augustine referred to as the "domestic church" (Latin *Ecclesia domestica*).[11]

A Remedy for the Lust of the Eyes

Last, but certainly not least, just as secret fasting is a spiritual remedy for "the lust of the flesh"—the disordered desire for pleasure—so, too, secret almsgiving is a spiritual remedy for "the lust of the eyes"—the desire to possess what we *see* (even if we don't need it). In the words of Francis de Sales:

> *Frequently give up some of your property by giving it with a generous heart to the poor.* . . . Oh, how holy and how rich is the poverty brought on by giving alms! Love the poor and love poverty, for it is by such love that you become truly poor.[12]

In other words, if we struggle with disordered desires for money, possessions, luxuries, and other "stuff," the best way to weaken that craving is by *regularly giving them away*. Not only is such almsgiving an act of mercy, but it also helps our hearts grow in love for the poor and, through them, in love for God.

Of course, neither fasting nor almsgiving will be of any spiritual value if it is not united to prayer. Thus, we turn now to the remedy that Jesus gives for the pride of life—prayer.

9

THE LORD'S PRAYER

When you pray, go into your room and . . .
pray then like this: Our Father . . .
—Jesus of Nazareth (Matthew 6:6, 9)

THE THIRD AND FINAL SPIRITUAL EXERCISE JESUS GIVES HIS DISCIples in the Sermon on the Mount is prayer. Of the three, Jesus devotes the most attention to prayer. Just as Jesus teaches his followers to fast and give alms secretly, so, too, he commands them to practice *secret prayer*—by going into their "room" and speaking to their "Father who is in secret" (Matthew 6:6). Moreover, Jesus not only teaches his disciples how to pray but also tells them what to say, by giving them the words of the Lord's Prayer, commonly known as the Our Father (Latin *Pater Noster*) (Matthew 6:9–13).

For over a thousand years, Christian spiritual writers have labored to unpack the meaning of the Lord's Prayer. Consider the following words of commentators across the centuries:

> A summary of the whole Gospel is to be found
> in the [Lord's] prayer.
> —Tertullian of Carthage (3rd century)[1]

> The Lord's Prayer is the most perfect of prayers. . . . In it we
> ask, not only for all the things we can rightly desire, but also
> in the sequence that they should be desired.
> —Thomas Aquinas (13th century)[2]

In the Our Father the Lord has taught us the whole method of prayer. . . . In its few words are enshrined all contemplation and perfection, so that if we study it no other book seems necessary.

—Teresa of Avila (16th century)[3]

These are striking claims. According to these writers, the Lord's Prayer is nothing less than *the summary of the Gospel* and *the greatest of all prayers.*

But what do the words of the Lord's Prayer actually mean? Also, why does Jesus insist that his disciples go into their "room" to pray to God the Father "in secret"? In order to answer these questions, we will need to take a closer look at the one prayer given to his disciples by Jesus himself.

THE JEWISH ROOTS OF THE LORD'S PRAYER

Virtually every word of the Lord's Prayer is deeply rooted in Jewish Scripture.[4] For our purposes here, however, we want to begin by simply focusing on Jesus' instruction to his disciples to call God "Father" (Matthew 6:9).

Prayer to the Father in Jewish Scripture

In Jewish Scripture, by far the most common name for God is "LORD" (Hebrew *YHWH*). For example, the book of Psalms refers to God as "LORD" almost seven hundred times.[5] In Hebrew, the name "LORD"—which means "He Who Is"—is revealed by God to Moses on Mount Sinai, along with the divine name "I AM" (Exodus 3:13–15). In context, both names emphasize the transcendent and eternal nature of God. He has no beginning and no end. He simply is.

On the other hand, Jewish Scripture does sometimes refer to

God as "Father." For example, in the book of Psalms, God is addressed as "Father" (Hebrew *'ab*) about three times.[6] This name emphasizes God's relationship to his people as their creator and savior. Consider the following:

> Is not he *your father, who created you,*
>   *who made you* and established you?
> (Deuteronomy 32:6)

> You, O LORD, are *our Father,*
>   *our Redeemer* from of old is your name.
> (Isaiah 63:16)

By calling God "Father," Jewish Scripture emphasizes that he is not only the transcendent God of the universe but also the one who saves his children from slavery in Egypt because he loves them and sees them as "the apple of his eye" (Deuteronomy 32:10).

Jesus and the Fatherhood of God

Thus, before we even get to the Lord's Prayer itself, the first thing that leaps out at us in Jesus' teaching on prayer is his repeated insistence on *addressing God as "Father"* (Matthew 6:9; Luke 11:2). Although prayer to God as "Father" is not unprecedented in Jewish Scripture, it is definitely not the norm. Yet in the Sermon on the Mount alone, Jesus refers to God as "Father" seventeen times.[7] And in the four Gospels as a whole, Jesus refers to God as "Father" over *170 times*! Clearly, one of the first things Jesus wants his disciples to learn is to speak to God not just as the "Lord" of the universe but as their "Father" (Matthew 6:9; Luke 11:2). In this way, Jesus emphasizes the intimacy with which they should speak to God in prayer.

JESUS AND THE LORD'S PRAYER

With this background in mind, we can now take a closer look at what Jesus teaches his disciples about prayer in the Sermon on the Mount.

Jesus Teaches His Disciples to Pray in Secret

Before telling them what to say, Jesus begins by teaching his disciples how to pray—in secret:

> When you pray, you must not be like the hypocrites; for they love to stand and pray in the synagogues and at the street corners, that they may be seen by men. Truly, I say to you, they have received their reward. *But when you pray, go into your room and shut the door and pray to your Father who is in secret;* and your Father who sees in secret will reward you.
>
> (Matthew 6:5-6)

With these words, Jesus is *not* prohibiting all public prayer. After all, he himself prays out loud in public (see Luke 10:21-22; John 11:41-42). Instead, Jesus is prohibiting prayer that is driven by pride—the desire to be exalted in the eyes of others. As an antidote to prideful prayer, Jesus teaches his disciples to practice secret prayer. This kind of prayer protects them from the temptation to pray simply for the sake of being seen by others. They are to go into their "inner room" or "bedchamber" and talk to God in private.[8] This is also how Jesus himself frequently chooses to pray—"alone" with God (Luke 9:18).[9]

Jesus Teaches His Disciples to Pray Simply

Next, Jesus teaches his disciples to speak simply and concisely when praying:

In praying *do not heap up empty phrases as the Gentiles do; for they think that they will be heard for their many words.* Do not be like them, for your Father knows what you need before you ask him.

(Matthew 6:7–8)

Once again, Jesus is *not* prohibiting all repetition in prayer. He himself repeats "the same words" when he prays during his agony in Gethsemane (Matthew 26:44). Instead, Jesus is rejecting the kind of "empty phrases" or "babbling" (Greek *battalogeō*) found in pagan incantations, which were often designed to force a god or goddess to act through mechanistic repetition.[10] As an antidote to such empty words, Jesus teaches his disciples to practice *simple prayer.* Jesus wants his disciples to speak to the Father from their hearts. True prayer is not manipulation but communication.

The First Three Petitions: Focused on God

The supreme example of simplicity in prayer is the Lord's Prayer itself, which consists of seven remarkably brief petitions. The first three begin by focusing on God:

> *Our Father who art in heaven,*
> Hallowed be *thy name.*
> *Thy kingdom* come,
> *Thy will* be done,
>> On earth as it is in heaven.
>> (Matthew 6:9–10)

In the first petition—more literally translated as "Let thy name be hallowed"—Jesus teaches his disciples to pray *that the Father's name be treated as holy.* That is what the word "hallow" (Greek *hagiazō*) means. It is a prayer for the whole world to stop taking God's name in vain and begin treating it as sacred.

In the second petition—"thy kingdom come"—Jesus teaches his disciples to pray for *God's eternal kingdom to come down to earth.* Although Jesus certainly inaugurates the kingdom of God through his miracles and mission, he also says that the final coming of the kingdom will take place only at the Last Judgment. On that day, as he says later, "the Son of man" will "sit on his glorious throne" and say, "Come, O blessed of my Father, inherit the kingdom prepared for you from the foundation of the world" (Matthew 25:31, 34). It is a prayer for the final advent of "eternal life" (Matthew 25:46).

In the third petition—"thy will be done, on earth as it is in heaven"—Jesus teaches his disciples to pray for *the salvation of the world.* As Jesus makes clear elsewhere, "It is not the will of my Father who is in heaven" that even "one" soul "should perish" (Matthew 18:14). At the same time, doing the Father's will is essential for salvation: "Not every one who says to me, 'Lord, Lord,' shall enter the kingdom of heaven, but he who does the will of my Father who is in heaven" (Matthew 7:21).

The Last Four Petitions: Focused on Human Beings

The second half of the Lord's Prayer consists of four more petitions, in which the focus shifts to the disciples' needs. Notice that every petition uses the plural "us." In this way, Jesus transforms each petition into a simultaneous act of intercession for all of humanity:

> *Give us* this day our daily bread;
> And *forgive us* our debts,
>> As we also have forgiven our debtors;
> And *lead us* not into temptation,
>> But *deliver us* from evil.
>> (Matthew 6:11–13)

In the fourth petition, Jesus teaches his disciples to *ask the Father for "daily bread."* The Greek word translated as "daily" (Greek *epiousious*) is ambiguous.[11] On the one hand, it can mean just "bread for the day"—though Jesus elsewhere tells his followers *not* to be anxious about earthly food and drink (Matthew 6:25–33). On the other hand, it can be translated as "bread for the coming day" or "supernatural bread." In an ancient Jewish context, either of these would call to mind the *miraculous manna from heaven,* which God gave Israel during their wandering in the wilderness (see Exodus 16:1–31).[12] If this is correct, the implications are enormous, since Jesus will later identify himself—in particular, his "flesh"—as the true "bread which came down from heaven" (John 6:48–51). Seen in this light, the first thing Jesus teaches the disciples to ask for in the Lord's Prayer is the gift of "the bread" that he will "give for the life of the world" (John 6:51).

In the fifth petition, Jesus teaches his disciples to ask the Father *to forgive their "debts"*—an ancient Jewish way of referring to "sins" (Matthew 6:13; compare Luke 11:4).[13] Interestingly, this is the only petition in the Lord's Prayer that is conditional. This point is so important that Jesus repeats it immediately:

> For *if* you forgive men their trespasses, your heavenly Father also will forgive you; but *if* you do not forgive men their trespasses, *neither will your Father forgive your trespasses.*
> (Matthew 6:14–15)

These may well be the most terrifying words in the Gospel. For Jesus states here in no uncertain terms that forgiveness by God depends *entirely* on whether his disciples forgive others.[14]

In the sixth petition—"lead us not into temptation"—Jesus teaches his disciples to ask the Father *not to allow them to be tested beyond their strength.* Contrary to what many people assume, this line does *not* mean that God tempts people to sin. For one thing, in ancient Hebrew, a causal verb can be used with a permissive meaning: thus, "Do not lead us into temptation" means "Do not *allow* us to fall into temptation."[15] Moreover, the New Testament clearly states that "God cannot be tempted with evil and he himself tempts no one" (James 1:13). However, in Greek, the word for "temptation" and "testing" are the same (Greek *peirasmos*). Here, Jesus is instructing his disciples to ask the Father to be merciful in the face of their own weakness by not allowing them to fall into temptation.

In the seventh petition—"deliver us from evil"—Jesus teaches his disciples to ask God to *deliver them from the power of Satan*. In the original Greek, the word "evil" literally means "the evil one" (Greek *ho poněros*). Seen in this light, the final line is not a prayer for protection from suffering and death but from the power of evil. For Jesus, prayer is not just a spiritual exercise; it is part of a great spiritual battle between good and evil.

Jesus, the Master and Model of Prayer

Finally, by the words of the Lord's Prayer, Jesus is teaching his disciples to pray to the Father *with the same words he himself uses*. In order to see this clearly, compare the words of the Lord's Prayer with the prayers of Jesus:

The Lord's Prayer	The Prayers of Jesus
Our Father	My Father
Hallowed be thy name	Keep them in thy name
Thy will be done	Not my will, but thine, be done
Forgive us our debts	Father, forgive them

The Lord's Prayer	The Prayers of Jesus
Lead us not into temptation	Pray that you may not enter into temptation
Deliver us from evil	Keep them from the evil one
(Matthew 6:9–10, 12–13)	(Matthew 26:39, 41; Luke 22:42; 23:34; John 17:11, 15)

What striking parallels! As they make crystal clear, the Our Father is no ordinary prayer. With its words, Jesus truly becomes "the master and the model of our prayer."[16]

THE LORD'S PRAYER IN CHRISTIAN TRADITION

Given the fact that Jesus himself gives his disciples the Lord's Prayer, it is not surprising that it quickly became central in early Christianity. By the first century, it was customary for Christians to pray the Our Father "three times a day" (*Didache* 8:3), as well as at baptisms and the Eucharist.[17] We'll close with a few points of practical advice about prayer in general and the Lord's Prayer in particular.

Secret Prayer and Intimacy with God

In its original context, Jesus taught his disciples to pray the Lord's Prayer in secret.[18] This is absolutely crucial. It is not enough to pray in public. Jesus wanted his disciples to pray alone precisely so that they could cultivate a relationship with God as their Father. As one ancient Christian writer put it, "Prayer is intimacy with God."[19] Likewise, Teresa of Avila pointed out long ago:

When you never communicate with a person he soon becomes a stranger to you, and you forget how to talk to him; and before long, even if he is a kinsman, you feel as if you do not know him, for both kinship and friendship lose their influence when communication ceases.[20]

In other words, *if the only time we ever speak to God is in public, then we probably don't have a real relationship with him.* By contrast, when we talk frequently with him in private, we will actually get to know him. This intimacy with God that naturally develops during secret prayer is essential to the spiritual life.

How to Avoid Distraction

At the same time, it is easy to slip into saying the words of the Lord's Prayer in a mechanical way. We all get distracted. So what can we do? For one thing, we must resist the temptation to rush. As Francis de Sales writes:

Do not hurry along . . . try to speak from your heart. *A single Our Father said with feeling has greater value than many said quickly or hurriedly.*[21]

Next, we also need to remember who we are talking to. As Teresa of Avila says:

If you are to recite the Our Father well, one thing is needful: *you must not leave the side of the Master Who has taught it you.* . . . *The best remedy I have found for [distraction] is to try to fix my mind on the Person by Whom the words were first spoken.* Have patience, then, and try to make this necessary practice into a habit.[22]

By developing this habit of fixing our minds on Jesus before beginning to say the Our Father, we take the place of the disciple who first humbly requested of him, "Lord, teach us to pray" (Luke 11:1).

A Remedy for the Pride of Life

Finally, just as fasting is a remedy for the "lust of the flesh" and almsgiving is a remedy for the "lust of the eyes," so, too, secret prayer is a remedy for the "pride of life" (1 John 2:16). For it takes humility for a human being to get down on his knees when alone and beg God for help:

> *Humility is the foundation of prayer.* Only when we humbly acknowledge that "we do not know how to pray as we ought," are we ready to receive freely the gift of prayer. "Man is a beggar before God."[23]

In other words, if we struggle with a disordered love of ourselves, the best antidote is humble prayer. By writing the words of the Lord's Prayer in our hearts, we will learn to pray like Jesus himself prayed, from the infinite depths of his own divine humility. In the words of one ancient Christian writer, "When we make our prayer, let the Father recognize the words of his own Son. May he who lives inside our heart be also in our voice."[24]

Now that we've looked closely at the three temptations every fallen human being experiences and at the three spiritual remedies given by Jesus in the Sermon on the Mount, it's time to take a closer look at some ways this "triple concupiscence" manifests itself in human life. In the next section, we will begin to look closely at how to identify and root out the seven capital sins and how to grow in their opposing virtues.

VICES AND VIRTUES

10

⁓

THE SEVEN SINS

Then he goes and brings with him seven other spirits
more evil than himself.

—Jesus of Nazareth (Matthew 12:45)

AS WE SAW IN THE LAST FOUR CHAPTERS, ACCORDING TO THE BIBLE,
the fall of mankind was brought about by three temptations that
later came to be known as the "triple lust": the disordered human
desire for pleasure, possessions, and pride (cf. Genesis 3:6; 1 John
2:16). Now that we've clarified the origins of human sinfulness,
we need to turn to specific examples of sins that need to be rem-
edied by those beginning to walk the spiritual path of Jesus.

Since ancient times, Christian writers have singled out seven
particular sins that need to be rooted out, especially in the beginning stages of the spiritual life.[1] For example, in the sixth century,
Pope Gregory the Great famously wrote about the "seven principal vices."[2] In medieval times, Thomas Aquinas standardized the
list of "seven capital vices."[3] By the modern period, the sixteenth-
century Spanish writer Ignatius of Loyola considered avoidance
of "the Seven Capital Sins" to be an essential component of the
first stage of spiritual growth.[4]

The reason these seven vices or sins are called "capital" is because they stand at the "head" (Latin *caput*) or origin of many
other sins. They can be listed as follows:

1. Pride
2. Envy
3. Anger
4. Avarice (a.k.a. greed)
5. Lust
6. Gluttony
7. Sloth

We will define each of these in more detail later. For now, it is worth noting that there are different ways of counting and identifying the capital sins. Already in the seventh century, the famous Eastern Christian writer John Climacus pointed out that while some claimed there were "eight deadly sins," in his view, "in fact the number is seven."[5] This debate over how to count the capital sins happens in part because some writers distinguish between two kinds of pride (pride and vainglory), whereas others distinguish between two kinds of sloth (sloth and acedia). In this chapter, I will follow the list given above, which has become standard in Western Christianity.[6]

Here and in the chapters to follow, we will explore the capital sins of pride, envy, anger, avarice, lust, gluttony, and sloth—along with their remedies. For now, we need to begin by asking one preliminary question: Where in the Bible do Christian spiritual writers get the idea of seven capital sins?

THE SEVEN SINS IN JEWISH SCRIPTURE

In contrast to the two lists of the Ten Commandments (Exodus 20; Deuteronomy 5), the Jewish Scriptures contain no explicit list of the seven capital sins. However, the book of Proverbs lays the biblical foundation for later tradition in two key ways: by speaking of "seven abominations" that dwell in the human heart (Proverbs 26:25) and by explicitly teaching against each of the seven capital sins.

The Seven Abominations of the Heart

Remarkably, the book of Proverbs refers to "seven abominations" (Hebrew *sheba' to'ēbōth*) that dwell in a sinful human heart. Consider both the original Hebrew text and the ancient Greek translation of Proverbs:

> He who hates, dissembles with his lips
> 　　and harbors deceit in his heart;
> when he speaks graciously, believe him not,
> 　　for there are *seven abominations in his heart.*
> (Proverbs 26:24–25)

> 　If your enemy begs you with a great voice, do not be persuaded;
> 　　for *seven vices are in his soul.*
> 　(Proverbs 26:25 LXX)[7]

In the Hebrew Scriptures, the word "abomination" (Hebrew *to'ebah*) is frequently used to refer to something either ritually or morally offensive to God.[8] In context, Proverbs here is using the moral sense of the word to refer to seven sins within the heart. This, at least, is how the ancient Greek translation of Proverbs interpreted the expression. There are "seven vices" or "seven evils" (Greek *hepta ponēriai*) within the human "soul" (Proverbs 26:25 LXX).[9] Significantly, it is precisely this passage from Proverbs that led the fourth-century Christian writer John Cassian to speak of the "sevenfold source of vice" in the human soul.[10]

The Seven Sins in Proverbs

Remarkably, the book of Proverbs also contains detailed teaching about all seven of the principal vices—as well as their opposing virtues. Consider the following chart:

The Seven Capital Sins and Seven Opposing Virtues in Proverbs	
1. Pride (Proverbs 6:16–17; 21:24)	**1. Humility** (Proverbs 15:33; 29:23)
2. Envy (Proverbs 24:19–20; 27:4)	**2. Mercy** (Proverbs 14:21, 31; 19:17)[11]
3. Anger (Proverbs 15:18; 19:19; 27:4)	**3. Meekness** (Proverbs 16:32; 19:11; 29:8, 11)
4. Avarice (Proverbs 11:1; 15:27; 20:10, 23; 25:14)	**4. Generosity** (Proverbs 19:6, 17; 28:27)
5. Lust (Proverbs 6:24–29)	**5. Chastity** (Proverbs 5:15–20)
6. Gluttony (Proverbs 20:1; 23:19–21, 29–35)	**6. Temperance** (Proverbs 23:1–3, 6–8)
7. Sloth (Proverbs 6:9–11; 24:30–34; 26:13–16)	**7. Diligence** (Proverbs 6:6–8; 10:4–5; 13:4–5; 28:19; 31:27)

We will look at each of these vices and virtues in more detail in the chapters to come. For now, the main point is that the identification of these particular vices as sinful is deeply biblical.

JESUS AND THE SEVEN SINS

When we turn from the Jewish Scriptures to the teaching of Jesus, we discover that he, too, never gives an exact list of the seven capital sins. However, two aspects of his teaching also lay the foundation for the later spiritual tradition.

The Parable of the Seven Evil Spirits

In one of his most mysterious parables, Jesus himself speaks of "seven" evil spirits that can dwell in a person's soul:

> When the unclean spirit has gone out of a man, he passes through waterless places seeking rest, but he finds none. Then he says, "I will return to my house from which I came." And when he comes he finds it empty, swept, and put in order. *Then he goes and brings with him seven other spirits more evil than himself, and they enter and dwell there;* and the last state of that man becomes worse than the first.
>
> (Matthew 12:43–45; cf. Luke 11:24–26)

In this parable, Jesus is describing the soul of a person as a "house" that can either be cleansed of sin by repentance ("swept and put in order") or inhabited by unclean spirits (that fill it with "evil"). For our purposes here, what matters most is this: just as Proverbs spoke of "seven evils" dwelling within the human "soul" (Proverbs 26:25 LXX), so, too, Jesus speaks of "seven" spirits of "evil" that can dwell in the "house" of a person's soul (Matthew 12:44-45).

Once again, it is precisely the Parable of the Seven Evil Spirits that led ancient Christian writers to speak of "seven vices"[12] or the "sevenfold source of vice."[13] Notice here that Jesus' words can be used to support either the number seven or the number eight, depending on whether one puts the emphasis on Jesus' enumeration of "seven" evil spirits (= seven capital sins) or on the combination of the seven with the original "unclean spirit" (seven +

one = "eight vices").[14] Either way, Jesus describes the human tendency to sin as much more than just bad choices. Instead, temptation is part of an invisible spiritual battle for the soul and whether it will allow itself to become the "house" of evil spirits.

Jesus and the Seven Capital Sins

Jesus never gives an explicit list of seven capital sins. Like the book of Proverbs, however, he does give parables and sayings that address each of the seven capital sins—as well as their opposing virtues. Consider the following chart:

1. Pride (Mark 7:22; Luke 18:9–14)	**1. Humility** (Matthew 5:3; 18:1–4; Luke 14:7–11)
2. Envy (Luke 15:25–32)	**2. Mercy** (Matthew 5:7; Luke 6:32–36)
3. Anger (Matthew 5:21–26)	**3. Meekness** (Matthew 5:5; 5:38–40)
4. Greed (Matthew 6:19–24; Luke 12:13–21)	**4. Generosity** (Matthew 5:42; Luke 6:30–31; 14:12–14; Acts 20:35)
5. Lust (Matthew 5:27–30)	**5. Chastity** (Matthew 5:8; cf. 5:28)
6. Gluttony (Matthew 24:45–51; Luke 16:19–31; 21:34–35)	**6. Temperance** (Matthew 5:6; 6:25–33)
7. Sloth (Matthew 25:14–30)	**7. Diligence** (Matthew 24:44–46; Mark 13:33–36)

However one interprets the Parable of the Seven Evil Spirits, one thing is crystal clear: on multiple occasions, Jesus explicitly teaches against pride, envy, anger, greed, lust, gluttony, and sloth. We will spend the next several chapters looking closely at what Jesus has to say about each of these capital vices.

THE SEVEN SINS IN CHRISTIAN TRADITION

For now, we can end this brief introduction to the seven capital sins with three key insights from the later Christian tradition.

The Gateway to a Multitude of Vices

First, the reason identifying and understanding the seven capital sins is so important is because they are the *root causes* of many other specific vices.[15] They are gateways to a multitude of sins. Consider the classic words from Gregory the Great in the late sixth century:

> [These] *seven principal vices* produce from themselves *so great a multitude of vices,* when they reach the heart, they bring, as it were, the bands of an army after them.[16]

For example, the sin of envy gives birth to other vices, such as hatred, gossip, and slander. Likewise, the sin of avarice gives birth to fraud, perjury, and the violence often associated with theft. Finally, the sin of lust gives birth to selfishness, infidelity, and even hatred of God.[17] In the following chapters, we will look at specific examples of the kinds of vices each of the seven capital sins leads to. For now, the main point is this: if the seven capital sins really are the root of the vices, then by focusing on uprooting *them,* we will be able to root out other more specific sins that flow directly from them.

The Predominant Fault

Second, not everyone is affected by these capital sins in the same way. Most of us have what the spiritual writers refer to as a predominant fault—that is, one of the capital sins that we are most inclined to commit. Consider the words of the ancient Christian writers John Cassian and John Climacus:

> Although these . . . vices, then, disturb the whole human race, nonetheless *they do not assail everyone in the same way.* In one person the spirit of lust is *dominant,* in another wrath rides roughshod, . . . and in still another pride holds sway. And although it is evidence that we are all attacked by all of these, yet we each suffer in different ways and manners.[18]

> Keep a special watch for *the one spirit that unfailingly attacks you* whether you stand, walk, sit, stir, get up, pray, or sleep.[19]

As we work through each of the capital sins in the coming chapters, I invite you to ask yourself: Which of these capital sins am I most inclined to commit? Which of these is my principal fault? Be sure to pay close attention to what happens in your heart as you read about each of the seven capital sins. If you feel especially uncomfortable or convicted while reading a particular chapter, that may be a sign that you need to focus more on that particular vice. If by the end of our study you still cannot identify your predominant fault (for we are often blind to it), it may be advisable to ask family or friends who know you best—especially those who live with you—what they think. The identification of our predominant fault is a crucial step in beginning to root out our vices and starting to grow in virtue.

The Seven Opposing Virtues

Third and finally, as we begin to recognize and begin to root out our predominant fault, it is also crucial to identify and cultivate the opposing virtue. Here we can put into practice the extremely valuable advice of Ignatius of Loyola and Francis de Sales:

> In order to better understand the faults committed that come under the Seven Capital Sins, let the contrary virtues be considered. So also, to better avoid these sins, *one should resolve to endeavor by devout exercises to acquire and retain the seven virtues contrary to them.*[20]

> When attacked by some vice *we must practice the contrary virtue as much as we can* and refer all the others to it. By this means we will vanquish our enemy and at the same time advance in all the virtues.[21]

In other words, it is not enough to try to empty our hearts of whatever vice it is that we struggle with most. We also need to begin filling it with the opposing virtue. With this in mind, we can now begin our study of each of the capital sins and their contrasting virtues. We will begin with the chief sin of all—pride.

11

$\backsim$

PRIDE VS. HUMILITY

Every one who exalts himself will be humbled.
—Jesus of Nazareth (Luke 18:14)

IN ORDER TO UNDERSTAND THE FIRST CAPITAL SIN—PRIDE—IT IS important to begin by saying what it is not. In English, we often use the word "pride" to describe admiration for the accomplishments of a loved one (for example, "I'm proud of my wife") or affection for one's homeland or people (for example, "I'm proud to be an American"). In the Bible and the Christian spiritual tradition, pride has nothing to do with either of these definitions.

Instead, "pride" can be defined as a *disordered self-love* or *irrational desire for self-exaltation*. In ancient Greek, the word "pride" (Greek *hyperēphania*) comes from a verb meaning to "out-shine" or "over-shine" (Greek *hyper-phainō*) others.[1] Likewise, in ancient Latin, the word "pride" (Latin *superbia*) can be translated as "arrogance" or "superiority."[2] Seen in this light, it involves a longing to be exalted above others. Ultimately, the sin of pride stems from loving ourselves more than we love our neighbor, and even more than we love God.

Over the centuries, the Christian spiritual writers have left no room for doubt that pride is the first and the worst of all the capital sins. The following quotes are just a tiny sampling:

There is no other vice . . . which so reduces to naught every virtue and so despoils and impoverishes a human being of all righteousness and holiness as does the evil of pride.

—John Cassian (5th century)[3]

Pride, the queen of sins, . . . is the beginning of all sin.

—Gregory the Great (6th century)[4]

Pride . . . is the beginning and the end of all evil.

—John Climacus (7th century)[5]

No matter what your state in life, it is essential to kill this selfish love in yourself.

—Catherine of Siena (14th century)[6]

These are strong words. If pride is indeed the "queen of sins," then we need to take a very close look at exactly what the Bible says about it, why Jesus goes to such lengths to warn his disciples against it, and what remedies there are to heal it.

PRIDE IN JEWISH SCRIPTURE

When we open the pages of Jewish Scripture, there are at least three major passages that help to develop a biblical understanding of the sin of pride: the sin of Adam and Eve (Genesis 3), the fall of Lucifer (Isaiah 14), and the book of Proverbs' description of pride as an "abomination" (Proverbs 16). Let's take a few moments to look at each.

The Pride of Adam and Eve

Although the word "pride" is never used in the biblical account of the fall of Adam and Eve, it lies at the very heart of the story. After

Eve tells the serpent that God has forbidden them to eat of the forbidden fruit of the tree on pain of death, we read,

> But the serpent said to the woman, "You will not die. For God knows that when you eat of it your eyes will be opened, and *you will be like God,* knowing good and evil."
> (Genesis 3:4–5)

Notice here the sinful desire for self-exaltation. When the serpent says they will be like "God" (Hebrew *'elohim*), the original Hebrew can mean either "be like God" (singular) or "be like gods" (plural). Either way, it describes the temptation to be exalted to *divine status* by disobeying God's command.[7] Notice also that this desire for divine status is irrational. According to Genesis, God creates man and woman in his "image" and "likeness" (Genesis 1:26) and makes them "very good" (Genesis 1:31). However, they are still just creatures. It makes no sense for Adam and Eve to believe the serpent's claim that they could become divine by disobeying the Creator.[8]

In other words, the very first sin, the fall of Adam and Eve, takes place because of an irrational desire to be like God—but apart from God and in place of God. Seen in this light, the pride of Adam and Eve is a kind of idolatry. Later in the Bible, when God gives the Ten Commandments to Moses, the very first commandment will state, "I am the LORD your God. . . . You shall have no other gods before me" (Exodus 20:2–3). In Adam and Eve's attempt to become like gods by disobeying God, they effectively break the first commandment precisely by putting *themselves* in the place of God. At its heart, pride is self-worship.

The Pride of Lucifer
The second major example of pride in the Jewish Scriptures comes from an oracle of the prophet Isaiah about the fall from heaven of a mysterious figure called the "Day Star," also known as "Lucifer":

How you are fallen from heaven,
   O Day Star, son of Dawn! . . .
You said in your heart,
   "I will ascend to heaven;
   above the stars of God
   I will set my throne on high; . . .
I will ascend above the heights of the clouds,
   I will make myself like the Most High."
   (Isaiah 14:12–14)

In its original context, this oracle is explicitly spoken against "the king of Babylon" (Isaiah 14:4). However, since ancient times, it has been interpreted with reference to the fall of an *angel* named "Day Star" (Latin *Lucifer*) (Isaiah 14:12 Vulgate).[9] One reason for this angelic interpretation is that in Jewish Scripture, evil pagan kings are often described as being under the power of wicked "gods" or evil angels.[10] Moreover, the oracle describes things the king of Babylon himself never actually did—like fall from heaven.

For such reasons, Christian writers long have interpreted this passage as a description of the fall of the angel Lucifer, who sought to exalt himself above all the other angels ("the stars of God") and even above God himself (Isaiah 14:13-14). From this point of view, the sin of pride is not only the reason for the fall of the first humans. It is also the reason for the fall of Satan.[11]

The Sin of Pride in Proverbs

The third and final example of pride in Jewish Scripture comes from two rather shocking sayings:

Every one who is arrogant is an abomination to the LORD;
   be assured, he will not go unpunished.
   (Proverbs 16:5)[12]

Pride goes before destruction,
>   and a haughty spirit before a fall.
>   (Proverbs 16:18)

According to Jewish Scripture, pride isn't just unattractive; it is an "abomination." The exact same Hebrew word is used to describe idolatry, which is also "an abomination to the LORD" (Deuteronomy 7:25). It means something morally repugnant to God.[13] Like the sin of idolatry, pride is an abomination precisely because it—like idolatry—puts a creature in the place of the Creator.

JESUS AND PRIDE

When we turn from Jewish Scriptures to Jesus, we find the same radical opposition to the sin of pride. As we've already seen, Jesus repeatedly warns his disciples *not* to perform spiritual exercises "in order to be seen" by others (Matthew 6:1-2, 5, 16, 18). The reason is simple but important: if a person prays, fasts, or gives to the poor *for the sake of being exalted* in other people's eyes, then he ends up committing the sin of pride in the very act of doing works that are supposed to be remedies for sin.

In addition to this basic warning, there are two key passages in the Gospels in which Jesus explicitly identifies pride as a sin.

The Evil of Pride

To begin with, when Jesus gives a list of major vices, pride is right there at the center:

> From within, *out of the heart of man,* come evil thoughts, fornication, theft, murder, adultery, coveting, wickedness, deceit, licentiousness, envy, slander, *pride,* foolishness. All these *evil things* come from within, and they defile a man.
>   (Mark 7:20–23)[14]

We'll come back to this list more than once in our study of the capital sins. For now, the main point is that, according to Jesus, pride isn't just a personality flaw. It is a disordered self-love that comes out of the human heart and morally defiles a person. For Jesus, pride isn't just unattractive. Pride is evil.

The Pharisee and the Tax Collector

With that said, no teaching of Jesus better illustrates the sin of pride than his famous Parable of the Pharisee and the Tax Collector:

> [Jesus] also told this parable to some who *trusted in themselves* that they were righteous and *despised others:* "Two men went up into the temple to pray, one a Pharisee and the other a tax collector. *The Pharisee stood and prayed thus with himself,* 'God, I thank you that I am not like other men, extortioners, unjust, adulterers, or even like this tax collector. I fast twice a week, I give tithes of all that I get.' But the tax collector, standing far off, would not even lift up his eyes to heaven, but beat his breast, saying, 'God, be merciful to me a sinner!' I tell you, this man went down to his house justified rather than the other; for every one who *exalts himself* will be humbled, but he who *humbles himself* will be exalted."
>
> (Luke 18:9–14)

In order to understand this parable, it is crucial to emphasize three points. First, contrary to what many Christian readers of the New Testament might assume, at the time of Jesus, the Pharisees were widely respected for their integrity in keeping the commandments and for practicing "the highest ideals," such as regular fasting and tithing. Thus, in a first-century Jewish context, the Pharisee would ordinarily have been seen as a *positive*, not a negative figure.[15] By contrast, tax collectors were widely despised

as thieves and extortionists who regularly broke the commandment "You shall not steal" (Exodus 20:15). Second, although
many English translations say the Pharisee prayed "with himself,"
the Greek literally says he prayed "*to* himself" (Greek *pros heauton*)
(Luke 18:11).[16] Third and finally, notice that the Pharisee praises
himself while praying about two things—fasting and almsgiving—
that Jesus insists his disciples do in secret, so as to avoid praise
(see Matthew 6:1–18).

With these points in mind, we can see that Jesus is using this
parable to overturn ordinary expectations about virtue and vice
and to give an example of spiritual pride. By focusing on the difference between the prayers of the two men, he shows one to be
proud and the other to be humble:

The Pharisee's Prayer	The Tax Collector's Prayer
1. Self-focused ("prayed to himself")	1. God-focused (prays to "God")
2. Judges others ("extortioners, unjust, adulterers")	2. Judges himself ("be merciful to me")
3. Blind to his sin ("I am not like other men")	3. Sorry for his sin (he "beat his breast")
4. Proud ("exalts himself")	4. Humble ("humbles himself")
5. Not forgiven (not "justified")	5. Forgiven ("went down to his house justified")
(Luke 18:11, 14)	(Luke 18:13–14)

Recall the definition of pride with which we began this c͏
sinful desire for self-exaltation. That is precisely why Jesu͏
the parable by warning that everyone who "exalts" or "lift͏
(Greek *hypsoō*) himself will be humbled, while whoever "huml͏
or "lowers" (Greek *tapeinoō*) himself will be exalted (Luke 18:i͏
One can hardly think of a clearer example of someone puttin͏
himself in the place of God than Jesus' description of the Pharisec͏
as *praying "to himself."* Indeed, everything Jesus says here is a warning to those who trust "in themselves" rather than the grace of
God (Luke 18:9)—which is a kind of idolatry.[17]

THE REMEDY FOR PRIDE: HUMILITY

So, what do we do about this tendency to love ourselves above all
others and even more than God? What remedy is there for us if
the vice of pride is our predominant fault?

Humility Toward God

First and foremost, we need to make a conscious and concerted
effort to cultivate humility toward God. As the letter of James
says:

> "*God opposes the proud,* but gives grace to the humble." Sub-
> mit yourselves therefore to God. . . . *Humble yourselves before*
> *the Lord* and he will exalt you.
> (James 4:6–7, 10)

One way to cultivate such humility is to get down on our knees in
prayer on the "ground" (Latin *humus*)—from which we get the
word "humility"—and recognize that God is God and we are not.

Another way is to strive with all our might to avoid breaking
the commandments of God. For example, in his *Spiritual Exercises*,

"e kinds of humility," of which keep-
 the most fundamental:

mility. This is necessary for salvation. It
   .at as far as possible, I so subject and hum-
     .o obey the law of God our Lord in all things, so
      .n were I *made lord of all creation, or to save my life
      .arth, would I consent to violate a commandment,* whether
       .e or human, that binds me under pain of mortal sin.[18]

che Bible, this awe and reverence for God is known as "the fear
of the LORD," which is "the beginning of knowledge" (Proverbs
1:7).[19] To humble ourselves before God by refusing to break the
commandments is the first battle in the war against pride.

Humility Toward Our Neighbor

In addition to showing humility toward God, we also need to
show humility toward our neighbor. Practically speaking, humility means developing the habit of not placing ourselves above
others and deliberately looking for the good in every person we
meet. In the words of Thomas à Kempis:

> *Do not esteem yourself as better than others,* for you may be ac-
> counted as worse in the sight of God who knows all human
> hearts. . . . If you have anything good, believe that others
> have better; in this way, you remain humble. *It will do you no
> harm to consider yourself the worst of all, but it will hurt you to
> prefer yourself to anyone else.* The humble live in continual
> peace.[20]

While it might be somewhat easier to be humble toward God—
after all, he is the Creator of the universe—it can be very difficult

to practice humility toward our neighbor. However, it is the only path to peace and happiness.

Happy Are the Poor in Spirit

Finally, we need to ask God to give us the virtue of humility. This virtue is so fundamental that at the very beginning of the Sermon on the Mount, it is the first thing Jesus speaks of:

> He went up on the mountain. . . . And he opened his mouth and taught them, saying: *"Blessed are the poor in spirit, for theirs is the kingdom of heaven."*
>
> (Matthew 5:1–3)

In order to understand this beatitude, it's important to realize that the word translated as "blessed" literally means "happy" (Greek *makarios*).[21] Moreover, when Jesus speaks of being "poor in spirit," this is an ancient Jewish way of referring to humility.[22] Consider the following:

> It is better to be of *a lowly spirit* with *the poor*
> than to divide the spoil with *the proud*.
> (Proverbs 16:19)

> A man's *pride* will bring him low,
> but he who is *lowly in spirit* will obtain honor.
> (Proverbs 29:23)

In other words, Jesus begins the Sermon on the Mount by teaching his disciples that the virtue of humility—the opposite of pride—is not only necessary for entering the kingdom of heaven but is also *the key to happiness*.[23] Although the prideful think they will be happy by exalting themselves over others and before God, they are sadly mistaken. In the end, pride isolates us from God and from others and makes us miserable.[24] Thus, to cultivate the virtue of humility is one of the first steps on the spiritual path that Jesus gave to his disciples when he taught them how to be happy.

Unfortunately, the sin of pride is not content to remain alone. Disordered self-love often gives birth to other vices, other sins. In the next chapter, we will look closely at the spiritual disease of the heart known as envy.

12

ENVY VS. MERCY

> From within, out of the heart of man, come evil
> thoughts, . . . coveting, . . . envy.
> —Jesus of Nazareth (Mark 7:21–22)

THE SECOND CAPITAL SIN—ENVY—CAN BE DEFINED AS *AN IRRATIO-nal sadness over someone else's good fortune* and *a covetous desire to possess what rightly belongs to someone else.* Envy is a hidden grief that fills one's heart with sorrow because of the false belief that another person's happiness somehow threatens our own. It is a sinful craving to rob one's neighbor of what is rightfully his. It is a spiritual disease that slowly devours the soul from within.

In the history of Christian spirituality, various writers have described envy as an especially destructive sin—a kind of self-inflicted wound. Consider the following words of ancient, medieval, and modern authors:

> As rust wears away iron,
> so envy corrodes the soul it inhabits.
> —Basil the Great (4th century)[1]

No joy of its own pleases the pining soul, wounded by its own pain; someone else's happiness torments it. . . . Once envy has infected the mind, it wipes out all the good works it finds.

> —Gregory the Great (6th century)[2]

Envy is pain over the good fortune of others.
—John Damascene (8th century)[3]

Envy . . . is clean contrary to charity, which,
as Saint Paul says, rejoices in goodness.
—John of the Cross (16th century)[4]

Are the spiritual writers correct? Is envy really so deadly? Why do human beings often respond to other people's happiness or prosperity by growing sad and seeking to take what doesn't belong to them?

In this chapter, we will answer these questions by looking at what the Bible has to say about envy. As we will see, one reason envy is so serious is because it not only leads to misery but also is the direct opposite of love of neighbor.

ENVY IN JEWISH SCRIPTURE

When it comes to the sin of envy, several passages in Jewish Scripture show it to be a particularly destructive capital sin.

The Envy of Cain

The first example of envy in the Bible comes from the famous account of Cain and Abel:

> Now Adam knew Eve his wife, and she conceived and bore Cain, saying, "I have gotten a man with the help of the LORD." And again, she bore his brother Abel. Now Abel was a keeper of sheep, and Cain a tiller of the ground. In the course of time Cain brought to the LORD an offering of the fruit of the ground, and Abel brought of the firstborn of his flock and of their fat portions. *And the LORD had regard for*

*Abel and his offering, but for Cain and his offering he had no re-
gard. So Cain was very angry, and his face fell.* The LORD said
to Cain, "Why are you angry, and *why has your face fallen? If
you do well, will you not be accepted? And if you do not do well,
sin is crouching at the door; its desire is for you, but you must master it.*"

Cain said to Abel his brother, "Let us go out to the field."
And when they were in the field, Cain rose up against his
brother Abel, and killed him.

(Genesis 4:1–8)[5]

Why does God accept Abel's offering and not Cain's? Genesis
does not say. The most probable explanation is that Abel gives his
best sheep to God (the "firstborn"), while Cain just gives "*an*
offering"—not his firstfruits (Genesis 4:3–4).[6] With that in mind,
notice Cain's response: he grew "very angry" and his "face fell"
(Genesis 4:5). We will look at Cain's anger in the next chapter.
Here our focus is on Cain's sadness.

If we define envy as an irrational "sadness at the sight of another's goods and the immoderate desire to have them for oneself,"[7] then Cain is the perfect biblical example. For one thing, in
context, Cain's sadness is totally irrational. Abel has not actually
done anything to harm Cain. God's displeasure with Cain has
nothing to do with Abel. As God says, if Cain had done well and
presented God with an acceptable offering, God would have been
pleased (Genesis 4:7). Moreover, Cain's sadness stems from his
pride—his unwillingness to blame himself for his own failure to
please God. He grows angry with Abel because Abel's goodness
makes Cain look bad. Instead of feeling sadness over his own sin,
which would have led to repentance, Cain feels sadness over
Abel's good fortune—the very definition of envy. Finally, Cain's
sadness leads him to *covet* the praise that Abel possesses. If Cain
can't have God's praise, then he will rob Abel of it by taking his

brother's life. In the end, Cain's envy leads directly to hatred of Abel—a hatred that results in the first murder in the Bible. For such reasons, since ancient times, Christian interpreters have recognized that "it was envy that corrupted Cain" and led him to kill the one "he hated for being better than himself."[8]

The Commandment Against Coveting

The second key teaching on envy in the Jewish Scriptures comes from the final words of the Ten Commandments. There God forbids his people to covet one another's spouses or possessions:

> *You shall not covet* your neighbor's house; *you shall not covet your neighbor's wife,* or his manservant, or his maidservant, or his ox, or his ass, or anything that is your neighbor's.
>
> (Exodus 20:17)

In this commandment, the word "covet" or "desire" (Hebrew *chamed*) refers to an "inordinate, ungoverned, selfish desire to acquire" what rightfully belongs to someone else.[9] Notice that coveting is an interior sin. All the other commandments involve external actions, such as idolatry, blasphemy, murder, and so forth. By contrast, the commandment against coveting focuses on what happens in the heart. While envy can lead to external actions such as adultery or theft, it begins as a desire that comes from within.

Perhaps that is one reason the book of Proverbs describes "jealousy" toward others as a kind of disease that causes the bones to rot:

> A tranquil mind gives life to the flesh,
> > but *jealousy makes the bones rot.*
> > (Proverbs 14:30)[10]

In the ancient Latin translation of Proverbs, the word "jealousy" (Hebrew *qin'ah*) was translated as "envy" (Latin *invidia*) (Proverbs 14:30 Vulgate). It was this very verse that led one ancient Christian writer to describe envy as an interior disease of the soul: "Solomon said it right, 'A healthy heart means the life of the flesh, but envy means rotten bones.'"[11]

The Devil's Envy

The third and final example of envy in the Old Testament comes from the Wisdom of Solomon. Although this book is not in contemporary Jewish or Protestant Bibles, since ancient times, it has been recognized as Scripture by Catholic and Orthodox Christians. As we saw in the last chapter, according to Isaiah, it was pride that led "Lucifer" to fall from heaven (Isaiah 14). According to the book of Wisdom, it was "envy" (Greek *phthonos*) that led the devil to tempt Adam and Eve:

> God created man for incorruption,
> and made him in the image of his own eternity,
> but *through the devil's envy death entered the world,*
> and those who belong to his party experience it.
> (Wisdom of Solomon 2:23–24)

With these words, the Wisdom of Solomon reflects the ancient Jewish tradition that the devil envies Adam and Eve because they possess the state of "righteousness" and "incorruption" that he himself has lost.[12] Although the devil can no longer possess it for himself, he still covets the gifts of God's grace that Adam and Eve have received. As with Cain, this spiritual envy leads the devil to commit murder—by bringing about the spiritual death of the first man and woman.

JESUS AND ENVY

When we open the Gospels in search of what Jesus says about envy, two passages stand out: his inclusion of "envy" and "coveting" in the list of evils that come from a person's heart (Mark 7:21-23), and the story of the elder brother's envy in the second half of the Parable of the Prodigal Son (Luke 15:25-32). Let's take a few moments to look at each.

The Evil of Envy

As with pride, so, too, with envy: Jesus includes it in a short list of especially evil vices:

> From within, *out of the heart of man,* come evil thoughts, fornication, theft, murder, adultery, *coveting,* wickedness, deceit, licentiousness, *envy,* slander, pride, foolishness. All these *evil things* come from within, and they defile a man.
>
> (Mark 7:21–23)

In this passage, the word "coveting" (Greek *pleonexia*) can be defined as "the state of desiring to have more than one's due."[13] The word "envy" literally means an "evil eye" (Greek *ophthalmos ponēros*)—an ancient Jewish expression referring to "an attitude of envy, jealousy, or stinginess."[14] Both terms are closely related to avarice (a.k.a. greed), which we will discuss in a later chapter. For now, the main point is that Jesus, like the Jewish Scriptures before him, identifies both "coveting" and "envy" as especially interior sins, which come out of a person's heart. Envy is not just harmful; it is evil.

The Envy of the Elder Son

Just as the premier example of envy in Jewish Scripture involves a story of two brothers—Cain and Abel—so, too, in Jesus' Parable of the Prodigal Son. In chapter 4, we focused on the first half of the parable, which tells how the younger son took his share of his father's property and squandered it on "loose living" before repenting and coming home (see Luke 15:11–24). We now turn to the second half, which describes the response of the elder son:

> Now his *elder son* was in the field; and as he came and drew near to the house, he heard music and dancing. And he called one of the servants and asked what this meant. And he said to him, *"Your brother has come, and your father has killed the fatted calf, because he has received him safe and sound." But he was angry and refused to go in.* His father came out and entreated him, but he answered his father, *"Lo, these many years I have served you, and I never disobeyed your command; yet you never gave me a kid, that I might make merry with my friends.* But when this son of yours came, who has devoured your living with harlots, you killed for him the fatted calf!" And he said to him, "Son, you are always with me, and all that is mine is yours. *It was fitting to make merry and be glad, for this your brother was dead, and is alive; he was lost, and is found."*
>
> (Luke 15:25–32)

Any first-century Jew hearing this parable of Jesus would easily pick up on the echoes of the story of Cain and Abel: an *older brother* who grows *angry* with his *younger brother* because the younger brother *receives favor* from their father.[15] Small wonder that in Jesus' parable, the elder son's response exemplifies the sin of envy in several ways.

For one thing, the elder son refuses to rejoice over the good fortune of his brother's repentance. Just like Cain, instead of being happy, he is "angry" with his younger brother (Luke 15:28). He is envious over the killing of the fatted calf and the celebration made by the father. Moreover, also as with Cain, the elder son's envy is irrational. After all, the younger son took only "the share of property" that was rightfully his (Luke 15:12). He did not take anything that belonged to the older brother. Nevertheless, the elder son sees his father's favor toward the younger son as a threat to him—even though it, too, takes nothing from him. As his father says, "All that is mine is yours" (Luke 15:31). Finally, note how the elder son's envy is rooted in pride. He is totally focused on himself, his accomplishments, and his wants. He exalts himself above his younger brother by touting how much better he is: how "many years" he has served and "never disobeyed" his father (Luke 15:29). He does not even care that his own brother—who was spiritually dead and lost in sin—has been restored to life. He is totally turned in on himself. Envy has filled his heart with anger and bitterness.

In sum, according to the Jewish Scriptures and Jesus, the sin of envy or covetousness, although deeply hidden inside a person's heart, is just as deadly and destructive as other, more visible, violations of the Ten Commandments. What starts out as sadness over someone else's good fortune can eventually turn into hatred—the desire for bad things to happen to him or her. Likewise, the ugly vices of gossip, slander, and detraction—revealing another person's faults unnecessarily—are often rooted in envy. Finally, when the good fortune of others makes us sad or angry rather than joyful, the only "pleasure" we are left with is our ability to inflict pain on them by destroying their reputations.[16]

THE REMEDY FOR ENVY: MERCY

But how do we get rid of envy? If we've already caught this disease of the heart, then what is the cure? When it comes to the vice of envy, what is the opposing virtue?

Here the answer is somewhat less straightforward than it was with pride. On the one hand, some Christian spiritual writers identify charity—that is, love of neighbor—as contrary to envy.[17] This is certainly true. However, one could make a case that love is opposed to *all* the capital sins. For this reason, we will focus here on another suggestion: the virtue of *mercy*.[18] Whereas envy consists of sorrow over another person's good fortune, mercy consists of compassion toward another person's misfortune. The former is rooted in pride, and the latter in love. Consider the following:

Envy	Mercy
Grieves over another person's good fortune	Grieves over another person's misfortune
Rooted in love of self	Rooted in love of neighbor

For this reason, as the medieval spiritual writer Thomas Aquinas puts it, "The envious have no mercy . . . nor is the merciful man envious."[19] (Think here of the elder son, who certainly showed no mercy toward his younger brother.) With this basic idea in mind, we can now ask the question, What do we do if our predominant fault is envy?

Get Rid of All Envy

The first thing to do if we struggle with sadness over other people's good fortune is, as with all the vices, to make a conscious and concerted effort to drive envy out of our hearts.

For example, the apostle Peter commands Christians to completely "put away all . . . envy" (1 Peter 2:1). The Greek verb for "put away" here can also be translated as "get rid of."[20] It implies the *complete removal* of something from one's life. The reason for radically uprooting envy from the heart is simple: the apostle Paul lists "envy" (Greek *phthonos*) as one of the "works of the flesh" that will exclude a person from "the kingdom of God" (Galatians 5:19, 21). As with the other Ten Commandments, when envy involves grave matters—like coveting one's neighbor's spouse or livelihood—it is a mortal sin. What starts out as sadness over someone else's good fortune (envy) can easily turn into the desire for bad things to happen to that person (hatred).

Happy Are the Merciful

Equally necessary, we need to ask God to help us cultivate the virtue of mercy. Once again, Jesus highlights the importance of this virtue at the very beginning of the Sermon on the Mount, in the fifth beatitude:

> Blessed are the merciful, for they shall obtain mercy.
>
> (Matthew 5:7)

In this verse, the word "merciful" (Greek *eleēmōn*) can be defined as "compassionate."[21] As we saw in an earlier chapter, this word comes from the same root as "almsgiving" (Greek *eleēmosynē*). In other words, Jesus is not speaking here about just feeling compassion for those who are in need; he is speaking about doing something for them. As he says elsewhere,

> If you *love* those who love you, what credit is that to you? For even sinners love those who love them. And if you *do good* to those who do good to you, what credit is that to you? For even sinners do the same. And if you *lend* to those from whom you hope to receive, what credit is that to you? Even sinners lend to sinners, to receive as much again. *But love your ene-*

mies, and do good, and lend, expecting nothing in return; and your
reward will be great, and you will be sons of the Most High; for he
is kind to the ungrateful and the selfish. *Be merciful, even as*
your Father is merciful.

(Luke 6:32–36)

Notice here that for Jesus, love is not about *feeling* good toward
others but about *doing* good to them—whether they deserve it or
not. Notice also Jesus' emphasis on performing acts of charity—
lending without expecting in return. Thus, in one breath, Jesus
uproots both the hatred and the covetousness that flow directly
from the vice of envy.

Seen in this light, the virtue of mercy—especially mercy toward
our enemies—is the ultimate antidote to envy. As soon as we feel
the first movements of sadness in our hearts because of others'
good fortune, we should immediately stop and ask God to bless
them even more. If, through God's grace, we can develop the habit
of showing mercy to others, especially by almsgiving, we will eventually draw the deadly poison of envy out of our hearts.

With all this in mind, we can now examine the third capital sin,
which is closely tied to envy. We need to look at the sin of anger.

13

ANGER VS. MEEKNESS

Every one who is angry with his brother
shall be liable to judgment.
—Jesus of Nazareth (Matthew 5:22)

IN ORDER TO UNDERSTAND THE THIRD CAPITAL SIN—ANGER—IT'S important to state upfront that not all anger is wrong. In itself, anger is just a *feeling* of resistance against an offense or injustice. As an emotion, it can be either good or evil.[1] For this reason, the Bible describes both good and bad forms of anger. *Righteous anger* (sometimes called "zeal") is a reasonable resistance to evil, injustice, or sin. It desires to correct an offense not in order to do harm but for the sake of preserving justice. It flows out of love and the desire for good. It does not overreact or punish unfairly. *Sinful anger* (sometimes called "wrath"), by contrast, is an irrational reaction to a perceived offense. It desires to injure the offender and to do harm for the sake of vengeance. It flows out of pride and impatience. It overreacts and punishes excessively.[2]

With this distinction between righteous and sinful anger in mind, spiritual writers from ancient to modern times are very clear that the latter has no place in the heart of a Christian:

The anger aroused by impatience is one thing, but the anger formed by zeal is something else. The former is the offspring of vice, the latter that of virtue.
—Gregory the Great (6th century)[3]

The deadly poison of anger . . . must be totally uprooted from the depths of our soul.
—John Cassian (5th century)[4]

There is no greater obstacle to the presence of the Spirit in us than anger.
—John Climacus (7th century)[5]

I state absolutely and make no exception, do not be angry at all if that is possible. Do not accept any pretext whatever for opening your heart's door to anger. . . . Those who appear in public as angels but are devils in their own homes fail greatly.
—Francis de Sales (17th century)[6]

In this chapter, we will explore what the Bible teaches about anger, how to tell the difference between just and unjust anger, and what the antidote is for the "deadly poison" of sinful anger.

ANGER IN JEWISH SCRIPTURE

As we saw with both pride and envy, sinful anger is described in the first pages of Genesis, linked with one of the Ten Commandments, and warned against in the book of Proverbs. Let's take a few moments to look at what Jewish Scripture teaches about this vice.

The Wrath of Cain

The first example of sinful anger in the Jewish Scriptures comes once again from the story of Cain and Abel:

> The LORD had regard for Abel and his offering, but for Cain and his offering he had no regard. *So Cain was very angry,* and his face fell. The LORD said to Cain, *"Why are you angry,* and why has your face fallen? If you do well, will you not be accepted? *And if you do not do well, sin is crouching at the door; its desire is for you, but you must master it."*
>
> Cain said to Abel his brother, "Let us go out to the field." And when they were in the field, *Cain rose up against his brother Abel, and killed him.*
> (Genesis 4:4–8)

This is a perfect portrait of sinful anger. For one thing, Cain's response is excessive. While the English says Cain was "very angry," the Hebrew literally says he "burned [Hebrew *charah*] greatly" (Genesis 4:5).[7] In other words, Cain isn't just upset; he is *fuming* with rage. Moreover, Cain is out of control. That is why God compares Cain's sin to a beast that he must strive to master. Once the fire of anger is kindled, like a wild beast, it easily gets out of hand. Finally, Cain's response is both irrational and unjust. After all, Abel has not actually done anything to harm him. Yet Cain "punishes" Abel with a violent death. In this way, the wrath of Cain leads to the first violation of the law that God will later give to Moses in the Ten Commandments: "You shall not kill" (Exodus 20:13).

The Sin of Anger in Proverbs

When we move from Genesis to the book of Proverbs, we discover further insights into the nature of sinful anger. Consider the following teachings of Scripture:

He who is slow to *anger* has great understanding,
   but he who has *a hasty temper* exalts *folly.*
   (Proverbs 14:29)

A hot-tempered man stirs up strife,
   but he who is slow to anger quiets contention.
   (Proverbs 15:18)

Wrath is cruel, *anger is overwhelming.*
   (Proverbs 27:4)

Notice here that sinful anger is linked to a hasty temper and folly. In other words, it is quick to kindle and often reckless. When people give in to rage, they temporarily "lose it" and do things they would never do if they were calm. This is much clearer in ancient Hebrew, in which the word for "anger" (Hebrew *'aph*) is the same word as "nostril" (Hebrew *'aph*) (Proverbs 14:29; 15:18). This vivid imagery flows from the fact that once people begin to flare their nostrils in the heat of anger, they are probably already starting to lose control.[8]

Notice also that anger inevitably leads to "strife" or "quarreling" (Proverbs 15:18). This is a very serious charge, not to be taken lightly. For elsewhere Proverbs teaches that a person who "sows strife" between brothers is an "abomination" to God (Proverbs 6:16, 19). In other words, sinful anger is repulsive to God—like the abomination of idolatry. Angry people are constantly at war with everyone around them—often including their own families. In the end, just as Cain ends up "a fugitive and a wanderer on the earth" because of his anger (Genesis 4:14), so, too, those who abuse their families or neighbors by reacting to the smallest offense with wrath will eventually end up isolated and alone with their rage.

JESUS AND ANGER

When we turn from Jewish Scripture to the life of Jesus, we immediately encounter examples of righteous anger (which Jesus himself displays) and sinful anger (which Jesus completely rejects).

The Righteous Anger of Jesus

On several occasions, *Jesus himself displays righteous anger.* The most obvious example of this is his famous act of overturning the tables of the money changers in the Jerusalem Temple (see John 2:13–17). Here Jesus' action is driven by his "zeal" (Greek *zēlos*) for the Temple as his "Father's house" (John 2:16–17). He is offended on behalf of God by the sacrilegious presence of traders in the Temple, and he seeks to right this wrong by driving them out. Another example is Jesus' act of healing the man with a withered hand on the Sabbath (see Mark 3:1–5). In this case, the Gospel of Mark explicitly states that Jesus feels "anger" (Greek *orgē*) at the "hardness of heart" of those who do not want him to heal the man (Mark 3:5).[9] In both cases, the anger of Jesus is neither irrational, excessive, nor unjust. Unlike sinful anger, which flows from pride and seeks to do harm, the anger of Jesus flows from his love of God and neighbor and seeks to heal.

Sinful Anger and the Prison of Gehenna

With that said, when it comes to sinful anger, Jesus makes absolutely clear that it has no place in the hearts of his disciples. In the Sermon on the Mount, Jesus forbids not only murder but also anger itself:

> You have heard that it was said to the men of old, "You shall not kill; and whoever kills shall be liable to judgment." *But I say to you that every one who is angry with his brother shall be li-*

able to judgment; whoever insults his brother shall be liable to the council, and whoever says, "You fool!" shall be liable to the Gehenna of fire.

(Matthew 5:21–22)[10]

In order to properly interpret this passage, three points are essential.

First, Jesus begins his teaching against "being angry" (Greek *orgizō*) by quoting the Ten Commandments: "You shall not kill" (Exodus 20:13). This quotation shows that, in context, Jesus is talking about *sinful* anger—the kind that leads to murder—and not the righteous zeal he himself displays elsewhere.

Second, Jesus forbids his disciples to use angry words. Even insults, such as "empty head" (Greek *raka*) and "moron" or "fool" (Greek *mōros*), have no place on the lips of his disciples (Matthew 5:22).[11]

Third, and perhaps most striking of all, Jesus teaches that whoever does insult his neighbor will be liable not just to judgment by God but also to "the Gehenna of fire" (Matthew 5:22). In order to understand this saying, it's important to recall that the word "Gehenna" originally referred to the "valley of Hinnom" (Hebrew *gē-hinnom*), located just outside Jerusalem and known for having been a place of idolatry and human sacrifice (see 2 Kings 23:10; Jeremiah 32:35). By the time of Jesus, "Gehenna" had become a common name for the otherworldly realm of the dead, in which sinners are punished by fire. Although the word "Gehenna" never occurs in the Old Testament, in ancient Jewish writings outside the Bible, it is described as a place of *permanent* punishment for some and *temporary* punishment for others.[12]

Jesus seems to use "Gehenna" in both ways. In some places, he speaks of Gehenna as a place of permanent punishment (see Matthew 10:28; Mark 9:43–48). Here in his teaching on anger, however, Jesus seems to describe Gehenna as a debtor's "prison" from which a person will be *released* when he has paid the debt of his sin. Right after declaring that those who use angry words will be liable to Gehenna, Jesus states:

> So if you are offering your gift at the altar, and there remember that your brother has something against you, leave your gift there before the altar and go; *first be reconciled to your brother,* and then come and offer your gift. Make friends quickly with your accuser, while you are going with him to court, lest your accuser hand you over to the judge, and the judge to the guard, and *you be put in prison; truly, I say to you, you will never get out till you have paid the last penny.*
>
> (Matthew 5:23–26)

In other words, Jesus exhorts his disciples to reconcile *now* with anyone they have offended through anger or insults. Otherwise, they will not get out of the prison of Gehenna until they have paid for "every careless word" (Matthew 12:36). According to Jesus, it is not enough to avoid violence or murder. He wants to root out all anger from his disciples' *hearts,* which first means getting it out of their *mouths.*

THE REMEDY FOR ANGER: MEEKNESS

So what are we to do with this sinful tendency to overreact to offenses and lose control of ourselves? What remedy is there for us if the vice of anger is our predominant fault?

Do Not Let the Sun Set on Your Anger

The first thing to do is to make a conscious and consistent effort to root out all sinful anger from our hearts and from our lives. As the apostle Paul warns the people of Ephesus:

> Be angry but do not sin; *do not let the sun go down on your anger,*
> and give no opportunity to the devil. . . . *Let all bitterness and*
> *wrath and anger and clamor and slander be put away from you,*
> with all malice, and be kind to one another, tenderhearted,
> forgiving one another, as God in Christ forgave you.
>
> (Ephesians 4:26–27, 31–32)

Notice here that Paul does not forbid all anger ("Be angry")—only
sinful anger ("but do not sin"). How can we tell the difference? If
the day has ended and we're *still* fuming, then it's probably the
sinful kind. If it leads to bitterness and the "clamor" of arguing,
then it's definitely evil.

Be Slow to Anger

So what is the remedy? Choosing to forgive those who have injured us—just as God forgave us in Christ.[13] Indeed, who are we to
burn with anger at others when God himself has been patient
with us and has forgiven us so many times? As the letter of James
teaches:

> Let every man be quick to hear, slow to speak, *slow to anger,*
> for the anger of man does not work the righteousness of God.
> Therefore *put away all vulgarity and excessive malice* and re-
> ceive with meekness the implanted word, which is able to
> save your souls.
>
> (James 1:19–21)[14]

Like the other capital sins, anger is a doorway to other vices, such
as quarreling, cursing, verbal abuse, physical abuse, and even
bloodshed.[15] Anyone who has experienced abuse at the hands of
someone consumed by wrath will know all too well the damage
done by this particular sin.

Happy Are the Meek

Another thing we need to do is *ask God to give us the virtue of gentleness,* also known as "meekness."[16] Once again, it is Jesus himself who places meekness at the forefront of the Sermon on the Mount:

> *Blessed are the meek,* for they shall inherit the earth.
>   (Matthew 5:5)

In order to understand this beatitude, three points are in order. First, as noted above, the word commonly translated as "blessed" literally means "happy" (Greek *makarios*). Second, the word "meek" (Greek *praus*) does not mean "weak."[17] It refers instead to the "gentle"—that is, those who refuse to be overcome by anger because they trust in God. Consider, for example, how the book of Psalms describes the meek:

> *Refrain from anger, and forsake wrath!* . . .
> For the wicked shall be cut off;
>   but those who wait for the LORD *shall possess the land.*
>
> Yet a little while, and the wicked will be no more . . .
> But *the meek shall possess the land.*
>   (Psalm 37:8–11)

Third, when Jesus says that the meek shall inherit "the earth"—or "the land" (Greek *gē*)—he is not talking about the earthly promised land. Instead, he is speaking about the heavenly promised land of the new creation (see Matthew 19:28).

In other words, Jesus begins the Sermon on the Mount by showing his followers that the virtue of meekness—the opposite of anger—is another key to happiness in this world and eternal life in the next. Although the angry think they will be satisfied by inflicting punishment on those who have injured them, the reality is that anger only breeds more of itself. By contrast, those who refuse to give in to sinful anger in this world will one day taste the peace of the life of the world to come. To begin rooting out the vice of anger and cultivating the virtue of gentleness is yet another crucial step on the spiritual path that Jesus gave to his disciples and to us.

Now that we've looked at the three capital sins that are rooted in a disordered desire for power—pride, envy, and anger—we can next turn our attention to the capital sin rooted in a disordered desire for possessions—avarice.

14

Avarice vs. Generosity

You cannot serve God and mammon.
—Jesus of Nazareth (Matthew 6:24)

THE FOURTH CAPITAL SIN—AVARICE (A.K.A. GREED)—CAN BE DE-
fined as *an irrational or immoderate desire to acquire money or possessions.* Avarice is a disordered craving that turns a person away
from heaven and toward the things of the earth. When avarice
fills the human heart, it eventually drives out love of God and love
of neighbor. When it leads to theft, fraud, or bearing false witness, it becomes a mortal sin. According to Jesus, avarice is one of
the most spiritually dangerous of all the vices.

It would be easy to fill a small library with the many sermons,
treatises, and books that have been written about avarice, covetousness, and greed.[1] Here are just a few quotations from spiritual
writers over the course of the last two thousand years:

> Avarice, which we can call the love of money . . . turns into
> "the root of all evils," sprouting the shoots of many vices.
> —John Cassian (5th century)[2]

> Avarice is a worship of idols and is the offspring
> of unbelief.
> —John Climacus (7th century)[3]

> Covetousness [Latin *avaritia*] . . . is defined as
> "immoderate love of possessing."
> —Thomas Aquinas (13th century)[4]

> Avarice is a raging fever. . . . You are truly avaricious if you
> longingly, ardently, anxiously desire to possess goods that
> you do not have, even though you say that you would not
> want to acquire them by unjust means.
> —Francis de Sales (17th century)[5]

Isn't this putting it a bit too strongly? After all, don't human beings need money and possessions in order to survive? Why is avarice so dangerous? And is it really akin to idolatry and "the root of all evils"?

In this chapter, we will answer these questions by looking briefly at what the Jewish Scriptures, the teaching of Jesus, and the letters of the apostles have to say about the dangers of wealth and the love of money. As we will see, the reason avarice is so spiritually dangerous is because of how it affects the human heart.

AVARICE IN JEWISH SCRIPTURE

In order to understand the teaching of Jesus about the dangers of wealth and the sin of avarice, it is important for us to look at three passages from the Jewish Scriptures.

The Commandment Against Coveting

The first of these is the Ten Commandments. Although the word "greed" does not occur in the Decalogue, it is implicitly prohibited by the commandment against coveting one's neighbor's possessions:

> *You shall not covet* your neighbor's house; you shall not covet
> your neighbor's wife, or his manservant, or his maidservant,
> or his ox, or his ass, *or anything that is your neighbor's.*
>
> (Exodus 20:17)

Recall that the word "covet" (Hebrew *chamad*) can be defined as an
"inordinate, ungoverned, selfish desire."[6] Elsewhere, the term is
specifically used to describe a person's covetous desire for treasure or money (see Joshua 7:21; Job 20:20). As we will see in a moment, it is this disordered desire for possessions that is at the root
of the sin of avarice.

Avarice and the Evil Eye

The second key passage is the biblical commandment to give
money to the poor and the needy (Deuteronomy 15:7–11). We
looked at this passage earlier in our study of almsgiving (see
chapter 8). For now, we simply want to focus on its use of the
image of the "evil eye":

> Take heed lest . . . *your eye be evil* to your poor brother, and
> you give him nothing, and he cry to the Lord against you, *and
> it be sin in you.*
>
> (Deuteronomy 15:9)[7]

Although some translations speak of a "hostile" eye (RSV), the
Hebrew literally says "evil eye" (Hebrew *ra'ah 'ayin*). In some modern European languages, "the evil eye" is an expression used to
refer to curses or hexes, but that is not how it is used in Jewish
Scripture. In the Bible, the "evil eye" can be used to describe either
(1) an *envious* person who looks with a covetous "eye" at what belongs to others, or (2) a *greedy* person who turns his "eye" away
from the poor and refuses to give them anything. Here in Deuter-

onomy, the latter kind of greed is not just unattractive; it is explicitly called a sin.

Avarice Never Gets Enough

The third passage, from the book of Proverbs, also uses the image of the "evil eye" to describe someone whose avarice drives him to spend his life chasing after money and neglecting his own family:

> *A man with an evil eye hastens after wealth,*
>> and does not know that want will come upon
>> him. . . .
> *He who robs his father or his mother*
>> and says, "That is no transgression,"
>> is the companion of a man who destroys.
> *A greedy man stirs up strife,*
>> but he who trusts in the LORD will be enriched.
>> (Proverbs 28:22, 24–25)

In Hebrew, the word "wealth" (Hebrew *hōn*) is the same as the word "enough" (Hebrew *hōn*) (Proverbs 30:15-16), and the word for "greedy" literally means "wide of appetite."[8] In other words, avaricious people are insatiable: they never get enough. Their desire to possess is almost infinite; it can never be satisfied by any material gain. Moreover, if greed leads people to fail to provide for their own father or mother, they are no better than "a man who destroys"—that is, a murderer. In the end, by putting their trust in money, the avaricious fail in both love of God and love of neighbor.

Jesus and Avarice

When we open the pages of the Gospels, we find two classic passages in which Jesus addresses the sin of avarice: his teaching on money in the Sermon on the Mount (Matthew 6:19–24) and the Parable of the Rich Fool (Luke 12:13–21). Let's take a few moments to look at each.

The Evil Eye and Love of Mammon

Many are familiar with Jesus' saying about storing up "treasures" in heaven and serving God rather than "mammon." What sometimes gets overlooked, however, is that—right in between these two famous sayings—Jesus uses the Jewish metaphor of the "evil eye" to illustrate how greed casts the soul into spiritual darkness:

> *Do not lay up for yourselves treasures on earth,* where moth and rust consume and where thieves break in and steal, but *lay up for yourselves treasures in heaven,* where neither moth nor rust consumes and where thieves do not break in and steal. *For where your treasure is, there will your heart be also.*
>
> The eye is the lamp of the body. *So, if your eye is sound,* your whole body will be *full of light;* but *if your eye is evil,* your whole body will be *full of darkness.* If then the light in you is darkness, how great is the darkness!
>
> No one can serve two masters; for either he will *hate* the one and *love* the other, or he will be *devoted* to the one and *despise* the other. *You cannot serve God and mammon.*
>
> (Matthew 6:19–24)[9]

For years, when I read these words, I would simply skip over Jesus' puzzling saying about the "eye" as "the lamp of the body." However, once I discovered that the "evil eye" was an ancient Jewish metaphor for greed, I realized that all three teachings go together.[10] In the first saying, Jesus is warning his disciples against storing up money and possessions ("treasures on earth"). The reason is not because they are bad in themselves but rather because humans are inclined to love whatever we consider precious. "Where your *treasure* is, there will your *heart* be also" (Matthew 6:21). In the second saying, Jesus uses the Jewish metaphor of the "evil eye" to show how loving possessions fills the soul with darkness. Consider the following chart:

1. Good eye	1. Evil eye
(= Generosity)	(= Greed)
2. Fills the body with light	2. Fills the body with darkness
(= Interior goodness)	(= Interior evil)

In his third saying, Jesus reveals why the love of "mammon" (an Aramaic word for "money") is so dangerous. *Avarice drives love of God out of the heart.* According to Jesus, a person will either love money and hate God or be devoted to God and despise money. There is no middle ground. That is why Jesus elsewhere explicitly lists "coveting" or "avarice" (Greek *pleonexia;* Latin *avaritia*) as one of the "evil things" that come out of the human heart and defile it (Mark 7:22–23). We cannot love God and love money. Period.

The Parable of the Rich Fool

Jesus also uses the Parable of the Rich Fool to illustrate just how irrational and spiritually dangerous greed is:

> [Jesus] said to [his disciples], "Take heed, and *beware of all covetousness; for a man's life does not consist in the abundance of his possessions."* And he told them a parable, saying, "The

land of a rich man brought forth plentifully; and he thought to himself, 'What shall I do, for I have nowhere to store my crops?' And he said, 'I will do this: I will pull down my barns, and build larger ones; and there I will store all my grain and my goods. And I will say to my soul, Soul, you have ample goods laid up for many years; take your ease, eat, drink, be merry.' But God said to him, *'Fool! This night your soul is required of you; and the things you have prepared, whose will they be?' So is he who lays up treasure for himself, and is not rich toward God."*

(Luke 12:15–21)

It is important to note that the word "covetousness" (Greek *pleonexia*) refers to an *insatiable* desire to acquire possessions.[11] It was eventually translated into Latin as "avarice" (Latin *avaritia*)—the standard name for the fourth capital sin. In context, it also refers to an irrational desire to accumulate earthly wealth. That is why God calls the rich man a "fool" or "unwise" (Greek *aphrōn*) (Luke 12:20). Even from an earthly point of view, it makes no sense to devote himself to storing up so much wealth when his life could end at any moment. From an eternal perspective, his avarice is even more foolish, since by storing up earthly treasure "for himself," he has failed to be "rich toward God" (Luke 12:21).[12] When it comes to his heavenly "bank account"—which is nothing other than the "treasure" box of his "heart" (Luke 12:34)—the rich man is spiritually bankrupt.

THE REMEDY FOR AVARICE: GENEROSITY

So how do we heal the disease of avarice? What are we to do if a disordered desire for possessions is our predominant fault?

The Love of Money

The first thing to do is to completely uproot any love for money or possessions from our hearts. As the apostle Paul says, "*Put to death* therefore what is earthly in you: . . . *covetousness,* which is idolatry" (Colossians 3:5).[13]

Notice that for Paul, the greedy break commandments against idolatry and coveting simultaneously by making things into God. That is why Paul includes the "greedy" in his list of those who "will not inherit the kingdom of God" (1 Corinthians 6:9–10). No matter how much money they have stored up on earth, according to Paul, they have no "inheritance in the kingdom of Christ" (Ephesians 5:5). As he famously states elsewhere,

> *For the love of money is the root of all evils;* it is through this craving that some have wandered away from the faith and pierced their hearts with many pangs.
>
> (1 Timothy 6:10)

Notice that Paul speaks here of the "*love* of money" (Greek *philargyria*)—not just desire for it—as the root of all evils. If this seems exaggerated, ask yourself, How many murders have been committed because people loved money more than they loved their fellow human beings? What about the tsunami of robbery, corruption, lying, extortion, blackmail, slavery, human trafficking, and war that has crashed onto the shores of human history?[14] Sadly, Paul's words are all too true. Moreover, they show us that the sin of avarice is really a heart problem. It's a question of disordered *love.* No amount of finite wealth, however vast, will ever fully satisfy the human heart's desire for the infinite love of God.

So how do we know if we've allowed the love of money to worm its way into our hearts? One easy way to tell is if we get angry or upset when we *lose* money through no fault of our own. Consider the words of Francis de Sales:

> If you find your heart very desolated and afflicted at the loss of property, believe me, . . . *you love it too much*. The strongest proof of love for a lost object is suffering over its loss.[15]

No matter who we are or what our state of life is—clergy or laity, married or single, young or old—we must never allow money or possessions to have any place in our *hearts*.

Happy Are Those Who Give

Another thing to do if we struggle with avarice is to ask God to give us *the virtue of generosity*. We've already looked briefly at how to cultivate the habit of generosity in our chapter on almsgiving. However, it is important to note that Jesus also speaks of it in another of his beatitudes. In this case, the beatitude is not found in the Sermon on the Mount but rather at the end of Paul's farewell speech to the church at Ephesus, when he reminds them of "the words of the Lord Jesus," who said:

> *It is more blessed to give* than to receive.
> (Acts 20:35)

As with the other beatitudes, the word for "blessed" here is "happy" (Greek *makarios*). Thus, Jesus is teaching his disciples that the path to true happiness is not through accumulating stuff but through generosity. So, if we struggle with a disordered desire for money or possessions—and we all do because we are fallen human beings—the best way to root it out is to develop the habit of *giving them away*. In doing so, not only will we avoid succumbing to the vice of avarice and ending up like the rich fool, but we also will have discovered yet another of Jesus' secrets to happiness in this world and heavenly treasure in the next.

With all this in mind, we can now turn our attention to those capital sins rooted in a disordered desire for physical pleasure. We begin with what might be the most infamous of all the vices—lust.

15

LUST VS. CHASTITY

Every one who looks at a woman lustfully has already
committed adultery with her in his heart.
—Jesus of Nazareth (Matthew 5:28)

THE FIFTH CAPITAL SIN—LUST—CAN BE DEFINED AS *A DISORDERED
desire for sexual pleasure*. According to the Bible, in itself, the pleasure of marital union is good. After all, the very first words spoken by God to man and woman are "Be fruitful and multiply"
(Genesis 1:28). Moreover, the "one flesh" union of husband and
wife is part of creation—before the first sin is ever committed
(Genesis 2:24).

However, after the Fall, this originally good desire for marital
union—just like other good human desires—becomes disordered,
inclined to sin, and difficult to control. By definition, lust is the
desire to misuse or abuse the sexual pleasure that God created for
the union of husband and wife and the procreation of children
(Genesis 1:28).[1] As we will see, Jesus himself describes "sexual immorality" (Greek *porneia*) as one of the "evil things" that comes
out of the human "heart" (Mark 7:21, 23). In the final analysis,
lust is not just a physical problem. Like other sins, at its deepest
level, lust is a heart problem.

When we look at what Christian spiritual writers on the capital
sins have to say, we discover that they are very realistic about the
universal human experience of disordered sexual desire and the

difficulty involved in avoiding the vice of "sexual immorality" (Greek *porneia*) or "fornication" (Latin *fornicatio*). Consider the following:

> Our second struggle . . . is against the spirit of fornication. This savage war is longer than the others.
> —John Cassian (5th century)[2]

> All demons try to darken our minds. . . . But the demon of fornication tries harder than all the others.
> —John Climacus (7th century)[3]

> It is vanity to indulge the desires of the flesh, and to involve yourself in things for which you will later be grievously punished.
> —Thomas à Kempis (15th century)[4]

Is lust really so serious? Do we really need to wage "war" against it? And if so, what are the remedies for this particular vice?

In this chapter, we will look carefully at what the Jewish Scriptures, the teaching of Jesus, and the writings of the apostles have to say about lust. As we will see, one of the reasons lust is so spiritually damaging is because it corrupts and distorts our ability to rightly love our neighbor.

LUST IN JEWISH SCRIPTURE

In order to understand the teaching of Jesus regarding lust, at least three key passages from Jewish Scripture demand our attention: the laws against adultery and coveting in the Ten Commandments, the story of King David's adultery with Bathsheba, and the teaching of Proverbs. Let's take a few moments to look at each.

Two of the Ten Commandments

Although there are only Ten Commandments, two of the ten—that is, 20 percent—are focused on the issue of illicit sexual desire:

> You shall not commit *adultery*.
> (Exodus 20:14)

> You shall not *covet* your neighbor's . . . wife.
> (Exodus 20:17)

Notice here that the commandment against "adultery" prohibits the *physical* act of having relations with another person's spouse, while the commandment against "coveting" prohibits the *interior* act of desiring to commit adultery.[5] Although the latter is addressed to men, Jewish Scripture elsewhere clarifies that it also applies to women (see Leviticus 20:10). Both of these laws belong to the second of the two tablets of the Ten Commandments. Thus, although coveting and adultery are often justified as acts of "love," from an ancient Jewish perspective, they are both violations of the love of neighbor.[6]

The Lust of King David

Another passage from Jewish Scripture involves what is arguably the most famous example of lust in the Bible: King David's act of adultery with Bathsheba:

> In the spring of the year, the time when kings go forth to battle, David sent Joab, and his servants with him, and all Israel; and they ravaged the Ammonites. . . . But David remained at Jerusalem.
>
> It happened, late one afternoon, when David arose from his couch and was walking upon the roof of the king's house, that he saw from the roof a woman bathing; and the woman

was very beautiful. And David sent and inquired about the woman. And one said, "Is not this Bathsheba, the daughter of Eliam, the wife of Uriah the Hittite?" *So David sent messengers, and took her; and she came to him, and he lay with her.*

(2 Samuel 11:1–4)

Note well that David does not just stumble into the act of adultery. There are several preliminary steps:

(1) **Step 1: Idleness.** The account begins with David having sent his armies out to war while he himself remains in Jerusalem. In ancient Israel, it was customary for the king to lead his troops into battle.[7] Yet what is David doing? Lounging about and sleeping well into the afternoon. The sloth of David is the first step toward his sin of lust.

(2) **Step 2: Refusal to Look Away.** Next, from his rooftop, David sees Bathsheba bathing—probably in an open-air courtyard. At this time, David is a married man and Bathsheba is a married woman (see 2 Samuel 6; 11:3). Yet David chooses not to look away from his neighbor's wife.

(3) **Step 3: Covetous Curiosity.** To the contrary, David begins to inquire about the identity of the woman he is gazing at. This is not idle curiosity. There is a covetous desire driving David's inquiry and an adulterous purpose behind it.

(4) **Step 4: Adultery.** Finally, David acts on his desires. He summons Bathsheba and commits the physical act of adultery with her. As a result, Bathsheba conceives, and David ends up plotting the murder of her husband, Uriah, so that his sin will not be exposed (2 Samuel 11:5–27). In the end, the lust of David leads him to violate not one, not two, but *three* of the Ten Commandments. That is how lust is. It quickly gets out of control. What starts with David breaking the commandment against coveting ends with David committing adultery and murder (see Exodus 20:13–14, 17).

The Fire of Lust

As a book of instruction for spiritual beginners, one of the primary aims of Proverbs is to warn its readers against coveting and adultery.[8] Consider just one example:

> *Can a man carry fire in his bosom*
> *and his clothes not be burned?*
> Or can one walk upon hot coals
> and his feet not be scorched?
> *So is he who goes in to his neighbor's wife;*
> *none who touches her will go unpunished. . . .*
> *He who commits adultery has no sense;*
> *he who does it destroys himself.*
> (Proverbs 6:27–29, 32)

When it comes to lust, the book of Proverbs—like the Ten Commandments—warns against both the disordered desire (the "fire" of lust) and the external action (he who "commits adultery"). Those who think they can commit adultery without any negative consequences have "no sense." For this reason, as with other sins, *lust is irrational.* It doesn't make sense. It's often rooted in fantasy that is unrealistic about the consequences of human actions. For in the end, the adulterer "destroys himself." As one commentator put it, "Adultery kills."[9] This is, of course, exactly what happens to King David. Although David repents and is forgiven by God (see Psalm 51), his sin still has murderous consequences for Uriah and tragic consequences for himself and his family (see 2 Samuel 12:5–18). According to Jewish Scripture, we cannot play with the "fire" of lust without getting burned.

JESUS AND LUST

With all this in mind, we are in a better position to understand what Jesus has to say about lust in two key passages: his description of "sexual immorality" as evil (Mark 7:21) and his warning against committing "adultery" in one's heart (Matthew 5:27–30).

The Evil of Porneia

To begin with, Jesus includes illicit sexual actions in his list of vices that spiritually defile a person:

> What comes out of a man is what defiles a man. For from within, out of the heart of man, come evil thoughts, *sexual immorality,* theft, murder, adultery, coveting. . . . *All these evil things come from within, and they defile a man.*
> (Mark 7:20–23)[10]

Although some English translations have the word "fornication" here (e.g., RSV) instead of "sexual immorality," the original Greek word is *porneia*—from which we get the English word "pornography."[11] In ancient Greek, *porneia* has a much broader meaning than just illicit relations between unmarried people. In a first-century Jewish context, *porneia* can refer to *any* sexual act apart from the procreative union of a married man and woman.[12] In other words, while the Ten Commandments explicitly prohibit only "adultery" (Greek *moicheia*), Jesus goes further: he describes *all acts of porneia* as morally "evil" acts that spiritually "defile" the human heart (Mark 7:23).

The Lustful Gaze and Adultery in the "Heart"

Even more striking, Jesus not only condemns lustful acts. He even condemns lustful looks:

You have heard that it was said, "You shall not commit adultery." *But I say to you that every one who looks at a woman in order to covet her has already committed adultery with her in his heart.* If your right eye causes you to sin, pluck it out and throw it away; it is better that you lose one of your members than that your whole body be thrown into Gehenna. And if your right hand causes you to sin, cut it off and throw it away; it is better that you lose one of your members than that your whole body go into Gehenna.

(Matthew 5:27–30)[13]

In order to understand this saying correctly, four points are crucial.

First, Jesus begins his teaching against lustful looks by quoting the Ten Commandments: "You shall not commit adultery" (Exodus 20:14). This quotation shows that Jesus takes the illicit nature of "adultery" as a given. He is, after all, a Jew. It should not surprise us that the Ten Commandments establish the context for everything Jesus will say about lust in the heart.[14]

Second, some English translations refer to everyone who looks at a woman "lustfully" (Matthew 5:28, RSV) or "with lust" (NAB). However, in the original Greek, Jesus is actually quoting the commandment against *coveting*.[15] A more literal translation would be "Everyone who looks at a woman *in order to covet* [Greek *epithymēsai*] *her* has already committed adultery with her in his heart" (Matthew 5:28).[16] This is the same word used in the ancient Greek translation known as the Septuagint: "You shall not covet [Greek *epithymēseis*] your neighbor's wife" (Exodus 20:17 LXX). In other words—and this is important—Jesus is not talking about experiencing involuntary feelings of attraction because of another person's physical beauty. Rather, he is talking about *deliberately* looking at someone with the desire to commit sin with her. (Think here of David's gazing at Bathsheba.)

Third, should there be any doubt about this, we need only look at Jesus' image of committing "adultery" in the "heart" (Matthew 5:28). In the Jewish Scriptures, the "heart" is more than just the seat of human emotion. It is *the place of decision*, where a person chooses to do good or evil.[17] The heart decides who or what we are going to love. As the Bible says, "You shall love the LORD your God with all your heart" (Deuteronomy 6:5). Thus, Jesus is speaking not about *feeling* a disordered desire for illicit pleasure but about choosing to *consent* to it. It is precisely because lust so easily gets inside the human heart that Jesus insists it have absolutely no place in the lives of his disciples: they must completely "pluck out" and "cut off" anything in their lives that causes them to sin through lust (Matthew 5:29-30). Otherwise, according to Jesus, they risk being forever separated from God in Gehenna. In short, Jesus takes the sin of lust very, very seriously.

THE REMEDY FOR LUST: CHASTITY

So, what is a person to do? What is the remedy for lust? How can anyone win the battle against this vice, when the desires that motivate it are so strong and so difficult to control?

Lust and Holiness Are Incompatible

The first order of business is to avoid putting ourselves in situations of temptation.[18] We will never cultivate the virtue of chastity if we make no effort to eliminate occasions of lust from our lives. We must refuse the temptation to say to God, as Augustine of Hippo did when he was younger, "Grant me chastity and continence, but not yet!"[19]

Along these lines, the apostle Paul lists "sexual immorality" (Greek *porneia*) as one of the "works of the flesh" that will prevent a person from inheriting "the kingdom of God" (Galatians 5:19,

21). In other words, all sexual acts outside the marital union of a husband and wife are gravely sinful.[20] According to Paul, lust and holiness are incompatible:

> This is the will of God, your holiness: that you abstain from sexual immorality; that each one of you know how to control his own body in holiness and honor, not in the passion of lust like heathen who do not know God.
>
>   (1 Thessalonians 4:3–5)[21]

As we saw earlier, holiness means being set apart *from* sin and being set apart *for* God. According to the New Testament, every single person is called to holiness. For this reason, neither external acts of "sexual immorality" (Greek *porneia*) nor internal acts of "lust" (Greek *epithymia*) have any place in the life of a follower of Jesus.[22] We cannot serve both God and *porneia*. We will either love one and hate the other or be devoted to one and despise the other.

The Three Stages of Temptation

On the other hand, it is also essential to understand the difference between simply feeling temptation (which is not sinful) and delighting in it or consenting to it (which are sinful).[23] Since ancient times, Christian commentators on Jesus' words in the Sermon on the Mount have distinguished *three steps* of sexual temptation: suggestion, pleasure, and consent.[24] Consider the explanation of these given by Francis de Sales:

1. *Temptation:* "sin is proposed to the soul" (not sinful)
2. *Delight:* "[the soul] is either pleased or displeased"
3. *Consent:* "either [the soul] gives consent or it refuses."[25]

As Francis goes on to explain, the mere temptation to "any sin whatsoever," no matter how strong, is not in itself sinful, "provided we do not take pleasure in it and give consent to it."[26] As we saw earlier, Jesus himself was tempted in the desert with "every temptation" (Luke 4:13), yet he remained without sin (see Hebrews 4:15).[27] The reason: because Jesus neither delighted in nor consented to the temptations being proposed to him. The same is true for us in the battle against lust. "No matter how long a temptation lasts it cannot harm us so long as it displeases us" and we refuse to give in.[28]

Happy Are the Pure in Heart

In addition—and this is crucial—it is necessary *to ask God to give us the gift of chastity.* As Jesus' warnings against committing "adultery" in the "heart" make clear, the virtue of chastity does not merely consist of abstaining from certain bodily acts (Matthew 5:28). True chastity is found in the human heart. Once again, as Jesus says in the Sermon on the Mount:

> *Blessed are the pure in heart,* for they shall see God.
> (Matthew 5:8)

Although the word "pure" (Greek *katharos*) can have a variety of meanings, the most famous example of "purity of heart" in Jewish Scripture comes from Psalm 51, the prayer attributed to King David after he had committed adultery with Bathsheba:

> Wash me thoroughly from my iniquity,
>   and cleanse me from my sin! . . .
> *Create in me a pure heart,* O God,
>   and put a new and right spirit within me.
> (Psalm 51:2, 10)[29]

Notice here that David realizes that a "pure heart" (Greek *kardian katharan*) is something only *God* can "create"; David cannot achieve it on his own power alone. Only God can give the freedom and happiness that comes with the gift of chastity.

Fasting, Meditation, and Manual Labor

Last, but certainly not least, as later Christian spiritual writers will emphasize, there are certain practical ways to counter the vice of lust that can be practiced by every Christian. In the words of John Cassian:

> *Fasting* alone is not sufficient to procure and possess the purity of perfect chastity; . . . there must be *constant meditation on Scripture* . . . as well as toilsome *manual labor,* which restrains and recalls the feckless wanderings of the heart; . . . before all else there must have been laid a foundation of *true humility,* without which there can never be a victory over any vice.[30]

If through fasting we can learn to control our cravings for food, we will also learn to control our cravings for other physical pleasures.[31] If we discipline our bodies through regular physical labor, we will grow in self-control and self-mastery in other areas. If we struggle with lustful thoughts and images in our minds, then we need to fill our imagination with the beauty of Scripture by memorizing it and meditating on it daily.[32] As the book of Psalms says,

> *How can a young man keep his way pure?*
> By guarding it according to your word. . . .
> *I have laid up your word in my heart,*
> that I might not sin against you.
> (Psalm 119:9, 11)

In the end, none of us can win the battle against lust by our own power. We need the humility to ask God—the maker of hearts—to create in us a "clean heart" (Psalm 51:10).

As we just saw, lust is not the only capital sin rooted in a disordered desire for physical pleasure. There is another vice that is often not spoken of, or even thought of as sinful. I am speaking here of gluttony. To it we now turn our attention.

16

GLUTTONY VS. TEMPERANCE

Watch yourselves, lest your hearts be weighed down
with indulgence and drunkenness.
—Jesus of Nazareth (Luke 21:34)[1]

THE SIXTH CAPITAL SIN—GLUTTONY—CAN BE DEFINED AS A *DIS-ordered or immoderate desire for the pleasure of food or drink.* In order to understand gluttony correctly, it is important to emphasize that food and drink, in themselves, are good. For example, according to the book of Genesis, God creates all the plants and fruits of the earth and gives them to man and woman "for food" (Genesis 1:29). He also explicitly permits them to "freely eat of every tree of the garden"—with the sole exception of the forbidden fruit (Genesis 2:16–17).

However, after the fall of Adam and Eve, the originally good desire for food becomes disordered, inclined to sin, and difficult to control. Human beings now experience cravings to *abuse* food and drink. Like other sinful desires, these cravings tend to be both irrational and excessive. Gluttony craves more food or drink than is necessary for the sake of sustaining life, purely for increasing pleasure. In its most serious form, gluttony leads to overeating and drunkenness—even to the point of harming one's health or losing self-control. Gluttony, like other sins, is a self-inflicted wound, which physically abuses the body and spiritually injures the soul. As a rule, gluttony weakens the human heart, making it incapable of prayer and powerless in the face of temptations.

When we turn to Christian writings on the capital sins, we discover that gluttony was widely regarded as one of the first that needed to be fought against:[2]

> Unless we first tame the enemy dwelling within us, namely our gluttonous appetite, we have not even stood up to engage in the spiritual combat.
> —Gregory the Great (6th century)[3]

> Control your appetites before they control you.
> —John Climacus (7th century)[4]

> Gluttony denotes, not any desire of eating and drinking,
> but an inordinate desire.
> —Thomas Aquinas (13th century)[5]

In this chapter, we will look briefly at what the Bible teaches about gluttony. As we will see, although nowadays the abuse of food and drink is often viewed as an issue of merely physical health, according to Jesus, gluttony and drunkenness are both matters of spiritual life and death.

GLUTTONY IN JEWISH SCRIPTURE

In order to understand the biblical teaching on the vice of gluttony, it's important to begin by pointing out that in the Jewish Scriptures, gluttony and drunkenness are almost always treated *together,* as two sides of the same coin.

A Glutton and a Drunkard

When we turn to the Law of Moses, we discover that it treats both gluttony and drunkenness with the utmost seriousness. For example, in ancient Israel, when these vices got so out of control that they posed a threat to the family, they could actually rise to the level of a capital crime:

> If a man has a stubborn and rebellious son, who will not obey the voice of his father or the voice of his mother, and, though they chastise him, will not give heed to them, then his father and his mother shall take hold of him and bring him out to the elders of his city . . . , and they shall say to the elders of his city, *"This our son is stubborn and rebellious, he will not obey our voice; he is a glutton and a drunkard."* Then all the men of the city shall stone him to death with stones; so you shall purge the evil from your midst; and all Israel shall hear, and fear.
>
> (Deuteronomy 21:18–21)

In context, the twofold description of the rebellious son as a "glutton and a drunkard" does not refer to liking a good meal or a glass of wine from time to time. The word "glutton" (Hebrew *zōlel*) refers to someone who squanders his money in a life of partying. (Think here of the Parable of the Prodigal Son.) Likewise, the word "drunkard" (Hebrew *sōbe'*) refers to someone who drinks excessively to the point of losing control.[6] According to the Law of Moses, both of these are "evil" (Deuteronomy 21:21), especially when they lead someone to violate the commandment "Honor your father and your mother" (Exodus 20:12)—as they so often do. It is frequently one's closest family members who are the first to be injured by the vices of gluttony and drunkenness.

Gluttony and Drunkenness in Proverbs

This is precisely why the book of Proverbs repeatedly warns beginners in the way of righteousness against associating with people who abuse food and drink:

> Hear, my son, and be wise,
>   and direct your heart in the way.
> *Be not among drunkards,*
>   *or among gluttonous eaters of meat;*
> for *the drunkard* and *the glutton* will come to poverty,
>   and slumber will clothe a man with rags.
> (Proverbs 23:19–21)[7]

Notice how gluttony and drunkenness once again go together. Both stem from an excessive craving for physical pleasure. Significantly, the word "glutton" literally means "one who squanders flesh" (Hebrew *zalal basar*) (Proverbs 23:20). In other words, gluttony involves the wasting of food. As Proverbs says elsewhere: although at first, wine "goes down smoothly," when it is abused, "it bites like a serpent, and stings like an adder" (Proverbs 23:31-32). Like all sin, the vice of gluttony starts with pleasure but ends with pain. For this reason, according to Proverbs, one of the first steps in the journey of the spiritual "way" or "path" involves turning away from both of these vices.[8]

JESUS AND GLUTTONY

When we turn from the Jewish Scriptures to the teachings of Jesus, three passages involving gluttony and drunkenness stand out.

Jesus Is Accused of Being "a Glutton and a Drunkard"

For one thing, during his public ministry, Jesus himself is falsely accused of both vices:

> [Jesus said,] "John came neither eating nor drinking, and they say, 'He has a demon'; *the Son of man came eating and drinking,* and they say, 'Behold, *a glutton and a drunkard,* a friend of tax collectors and sinners!'"
>
> (Matthew 11:18–19; cf. Luke 7:34)

In a first-century Jewish context, the dual charge of being "a glutton and a drunkard" is directly evocative of the biblical description of the "rebellious son" that we just read about (Deuteronomy 21:18-21). In other words, because Jesus spent time eating and drinking with sinners in order to share the gospel of repentance with them, some people actually charged *him* with violating the Law of Moses.

Jesus Warns His Disciples Against Getting Drunk

Of course, the charges are false. To be sure, there is no doubt that Jesus drank wine. Think here of Jesus' miraculous transformation of water into wine during the wedding at Cana (John 2:1-11) or his use of wine at the Last Supper (Matthew 26:26-28).[9] On the other hand, Jesus elsewhere solemnly warns his disciples against abusing alcohol:

> Heaven and earth will pass away, but my words will not pass away. *But watch yourselves lest your hearts be weighed down with indulgence and drunkenness and cares of this life,* and that day come upon you suddenly like a snare; for it will come upon all who dwell upon the face of the whole earth.
>
> (Luke 21:33–35)[10]

Notice here that Jesus does not forbid alcohol; he forbids "drunkenness" (Greek *methē*).[11] Notice also the link Jesus draws here between drunkenness, heaviness of heart, and the cares of this life. He knows full well that people often get drunk not just for the sake of pleasure but in order to *self-medicate*. Both drunkenness and overeating seem to offer escapes from interior suffering and the burdens of life. As with the other capital sins, therefore, at its deepest level, gluttony is not just a physical problem. Disordered cravings flow from the pain of the broken human heart.

The Parable of Lazarus and the Rich Man

Finally, there is no clearer example of gluttony in the teaching of Jesus than the famous Parable of Lazarus and the Rich Man.[12] Here we will focus on the first half of the parable while keeping in mind the biblical teaching on gluttony:

> *There was a rich man, who was clothed in purple and fine linen and who feasted sumptuously every day. And at his gate lay a poor man named Lazarus, full of sores, who longed to be fed with what fell from the rich man's table;* moreover the dogs came and licked his sores. *The poor man died and was carried by the angels to Abraham's bosom. The rich man also died and was buried; and in Hades, being in torment,* he lifted up his eyes, and saw Abraham far off and Lazarus in his bosom. And he called out, "Father Abraham, have mercy upon me, and send Lazarus to dip the end of his finger in water and cool my tongue; for I am in anguish in this flame." But Abraham said, "Son, remember that you in your lifetime received your good things, and Lazarus in like manner evil things; but now he is comforted here, and you are in anguish. And besides all this, between us and you a great chasm has been fixed, in order that

those who would pass from here to you may not be able, and
none may cross from there to us."

(Luke 16:19–26)[13]

The heart of this parable revolves around what happens to Lazarus and the rich man after they die. On the one hand, Lazarus is
carried away by angels to rest in the peace of "Abraham's bosom."
This expression reflects the biblical image of death as being "gathered" to one's ancestors.[14] By contrast, the rich man goes to
"Hades"—a place of fire and torment. By the time of Jesus, the
Greek word *Hadēs* was often used to describe the otherworldly
realm of punishment for sinners (e.g., Sirach 21:9–10). As Jesus
himself says elsewhere, it is the opposite of heaven: "And you,
Capernaum, will you be *exalted to heaven*? You shall be *brought
down to Hades*" (Luke 10:15).

   With this in mind, the reason the rich man is condemned to
Hades is not because he explicitly broke any of the Ten Commandments. Jesus never describes him as an idolater or thief or
murderer. Instead, all we know is that he was a "rich man," wore
expensive clothes, and "feasted sumptuously" every single day
(Luke 16:19). No—*the rich man goes to Hades because his life of gluttony
led him to neglect the suffering and hunger of his neighbor.* Indeed, when
Jesus says that Lazarus "longed to be fed," he uses the same Greek
expression used for the prodigal son, who "longed to be fed" with
the pigs' food (Luke 15:16).[15] In other words, Lazarus is starving
to death on the doorstep of the rich man, while the latter feasts
every single day. What is the result of the rich man's gluttony?
Eternal separation from God and his neighbor, as well as the pain
of flames that burn his tongue—the very part of his body that fed
his gluttony and his failure to love his neighbor who was in need.

THE REMEDY FOR GLUTTONY: TEMPERANCE

So, what are we to do? How do we fight against the temptations to abuse food or drink? What is the remedy for gluttony?

Drunkenness, Revelry, and Ancient Paganism

The first thing every follower of Jesus must do is to completely uproot any tendencies for or habits of abusing food or drink. Consider the words of the apostle Peter:

> *Let the time that is past suffice for doing what the Gentiles like to do,* living in licentiousness, passions, *drunkenness, revels, drinking parties,* and lawless idolatry. *They are surprised that you do not now join them in the same debauchery,* and they abuse you; but they will give account to him who is ready to judge the living and the dead.
>
> (1 Peter 4:3–5)[16]

It's important to remember here that many early Christians were converts from Gentile paganism. In contrast to the Jewish Scriptures, which describe gluttony and drunkenness as gravely sinful (Deuteronomy 21:18-21), the Gentile world by and large had no such inhibitions. Pagan festivals often involved overeating and drunkenness—as well as the many other sins that take place once people get drunk.[17] In fact, the Gentiles even had specific deities dedicated to the very vices Jews regarded as sinful—such as Dionysus, the god of wine, and Komos, the god of revelry.[18]

According to Peter, although Christians may have engaged in such actions in the "past," they no longer have any place in their new lives (1 Peter 4:3). Followers of Christ are to forego such activities—even if it means being judged by the very friends they used to party with. The reason for this is simple: according to the New Testament, to deliberately get drunk is a mortal sin. As the apostle Paul teaches, those who engage in drunkenness and revelry will "not inherit the kingdom of God" (Galatians 5:19, 21). Because drunkenness involves a loss of self-control, it often leads to other physically and morally depraved actions, which Peter refers to as "debauchery" (1 Peter 4:4). Like the other capital sins, it has no place in the life of a Christian.

Happy Are Those Who Hunger and Thirst

Another thing to do in the battle against gluttony is to *ask God for the virtue of temperance*—that is, the strength to control our appetites for the pleasure of food and drink.[19]

As we discussed earlier, the chief way to develop the virtue of temperance is by beginning to practice fasting (see chapter 7). In addition to voluntarily abstaining from food or drink, however, it is also important to cultivate an "appetite" for spiritual nourishment. Once again, Jesus gives a powerful testimony to this point in the Sermon on the Mount:

> *Blessed are those who hunger and thirst for righteousness,* for they shall be satisfied.
>
> (Matthew 5:6)

Recall once again that the word "blessed" literally means "happy" (Greek *makarios*). One of the great ironies of gluttony and drunkenness is that, in the end, neither actually satisfies. Neither vice has ever made anyone happy. The fleeting pleasure they provide quickly subsides, often to be replaced by an even stronger craving for more—no matter what the cost. When this craving turns into an addiction, we end up slaves to our own impulses, resulting in all kinds of self-inflicted physical and spiritual damage.

In the fourth beatitude, Jesus gives us a spiritual key to breaking the cycle of addiction, by turning our hearts away from worldly pleasure and teaching them to hunger and thirst for God. In the words of the ancient Christian writer John Cassian:

> We shall never be able to spurn the pleasures of eating here and now if our mind is not fixed on divine contemplation and if it does not take delight, instead, in the love of virtue and the beauty of heavenly things.[20]

In other words, to win the battle against gluttony, it is not enough to empty our stomachs. We also have to fill our hearts with truth, goodness, and beauty. We need to read the Bible every day and develop a "taste" for the writings of the great saints and the spiritual classics. When we do this—when we direct our desires away from earthly things and toward God—we will begin to discover the truth that Jesus uttered in the midst of his own battle with temptation: "Man shall not live by bread alone, but by every word that proceeds from the mouth of God" (Matthew 4:4).

With that said, we might be tempted to think we have exhausted our treatment of the capital sins rooted in the "lust of the flesh." But we have not yet discussed the seventh capital sin—one that many people may not even regard as a sin—sloth.

17

SLOTH VS. DILIGENCE

Why do you sleep?
Rise and pray that you may not enter into temptation.
—Jesus of Nazareth (Luke 22:46)

THE SEVENTH CAPITAL SIN—SLOTH—CAN BE DEFINED AS A *DIS-ordered inclination to apathy or laziness in fulfilling one's duties.* When it involves physical idleness, the neglect of worldly duties, and refusal to work, it is often referred to simply as "sloth." When it involves spiritual idleness, laxity in prayer, and the neglect of religious duties, it is commonly referred to as "acedia"—from the Greek word meaning "weariness" or "apathy" (Greek *akēdia*).[1]

One reason this distinction between physical sloth and spiritual sloth is important is because it is entirely possible for a person to be very diligent about earthly labor and yet very negligent about spiritual exercises—and vice versa. In essence, sloth entails *avoiding the effort* required by physical or spiritual labor. It habitually cuts corners in prayer, flees from the difficulty of work, and always chooses the easy path. At all costs, sloth avoids doing anything that might interfere with the pleasures of comfort, ease, and entertainment. Sloth flows from pride and a sense of entitlement to enjoying the fruits of other people's labor. As we will see, according to Jesus, when sloth leads someone to neglect grave spiritual obligations to God or neighbor, it can be a mortal sin.

In the history of Christian spirituality, the sin of sloth has been the subject of numerous treatises.[2] The following quotes are just a sample:

> Once [*akēdia*] has seized possession of a wretched mind . . . it renders him slothful and immobile in the face of all the work to be done.
>
> —John Cassian (5th century)[3]

> Despondency or *akēdia* . . . is a paralysis of the soul . . . a neglect of religious exercises.
>
> —John Climacus (7th century)[4]

> Sloth . . . is an oppressive sorrow, which . . . so weighs upon man's mind, that he wants to do nothing.
>
> —Thomas Aquinas (13th century)[5]

> With respect to spiritual sloth, beginners . . . find it irksome when they are commanded to do that wherein they take no pleasure. . . . They run fretfully away from everything that is hard.
>
> —John of the Cross (16th century)[6]

In other words, sloth—whether physical or spiritual—is not just an unfortunate character flaw. It is a "disease" of the will that slowly renders a person incapable of persevering in the "difficult" and "narrow" spiritual path of Jesus (Matthew 7:13–14).[7]

In this chapter, we will take a brief look at what the Bible teaches about sloth and acedia. As we will see, understanding and avoiding both forms of sloth is an absolutely crucial step to making spiritual progress.

SLOTH IN JEWISH SCRIPTURE

Perhaps the most famous example of sloth in Jewish Scripture is the idleness of King David, which—as we saw in chapter 15—was the first step on his path to adultery (see 2 Samuel 11:1–27). However, no book of Jewish Scripture devotes more attention to teaching against sloth than the book of Proverbs.

The Way of the Sluggard

The word "sluggard" or "lazy person" (Hebrew *'atzel*) occurs fourteen times in the book of Proverbs—and nowhere else in the Hebrew Scriptures.[8] Clearly, the exhortation to avoid sloth is especially important for spiritual beginners. Over and over again, Proverbs warns against the temptation to idleness, especially in the form of oversleeping:

> *How long will you lie there, O sluggard?*
>> When will you arise from your sleep?
>> (Proverbs 6:9)

> *The way of a sluggard is overgrown with thorns,*
>> but the path of the upright is a level highway.
>> (Proverbs 15:19)

> As a door turns on its hinges,
>> *so does a sluggard on his bed.*
> *The sluggard buries his hand in the dish;*
>> it wears him out to bring it back to his mouth.
> *The sluggard is wiser in his own eyes*
>> than seven men who can answer discreetly.
>> (Proverbs 26:14–16)

Several aspects of these sayings are worth highlighting. First, notice the close link between sloth and *sleep*. Like a door slowly swinging on its hinges, the sluggard turns over in bed, refusing to rise because he is unwilling to face the day's labor.[9] He even eats in a lazy fashion—barely able to bring his hand up to his mouth! Second, Proverbs paints a stark contrast between two spiritual paths. The path of the slothful person is overgrown with briars and therefore impossible to make progress on, while the path of the virtuous is straight and level. Finally, Proverbs draws a direct link between the vice of sloth and pride. Despite his inactivity, "in his own eyes," the sluggard is wiser than anyone else. Entitled to his leisure, he sees himself as so smart that he does not have to expend the effort involved in learning.[10]

JESUS AND SLOTH

When we turn from Jewish Scripture to the life and teachings of Jesus, two passages shed light on the vice of sloth: the Parable of the Talents (Matthew 25:14–30) and the sleepiness of the apostles in Gethsemane (Mark 14:32–42). Let's take a few moments to look closely at each.

The Parable of the Talents

Although the Parable of the Talents is a bit long, it is worth reading carefully, since it is the principal place where Jesus explicitly addresses the seriousness of sloth:

> [The kingdom of heaven] will be as when a man going on a journey called his servants and entrusted to them his property; *to one he gave five talents, to another two, to another one, to each according to his ability.* Then he went away. He who had

received the five talents went at once and traded with them; and he made five talents more. So also, he who had the two talents made two talents more. But he who had received the one talent went and dug in the ground and hid his master's money. Now after a long time the master of those servants came and settled accounts with them. And he who had received the five talents came forward, bringing five talents more, saying, "Master, you delivered to me five talents; here I have made five talents more." His master said to him, *"Well done, good and faithful servant; you have been faithful over a little, I will set you over much; enter into the joy of your master."* And he also who had the two talents came forward, saying, "Master, you delivered to me two talents; here I have made two talents more." His master said to him, *"Well done, good and faithful servant; you have been faithful over a little, I will set you over much; enter into the joy of your master."* He also who had received the one talent came forward, saying, "Master, I knew you to be a hard man, reaping where you did not sow, and gathering where you did not winnow; so I was afraid, and I went and hid your talent in the ground. Here you have what is yours." But his master answered him, *"You wicked and slothful servant!* You knew that I reap where I have not sowed, and gather where I have not winnowed? Then you ought to have invested my money with the bankers, and at my coming I should have received what was my own with interest. So take the talent from him, and give it to him who has the ten talents. For to every one who has will more be given, and he will have abundance; but from him who has not, even what he has will be taken away. *And cast the useless servant into the outer darkness, where there will be weeping and gnashing of teeth."*

(Matthew 25:14–30)[11]

In order to feel the force of this parable, three points are necessary.

First, at the time of Jesus, a "talent" (Greek *talanton*) was a gold or silver coin worth about 6,000 days' wages—or fifteen years of labor![12] In other words, the master in the parable entrusts his servants with an unbelievably valuable gift. To one he gives five talents (30,000 days' wages), to another two talents (12,000 days' wages), and to the last, one talent (6,000 days' wages). Although the servants are not entrusted with the same amounts, they all receive an incredible amount of money.

Second, the master freely gives the talents to the servants. They do nothing to earn them. However, the gift is not unconditional. *The servants are obligated to use the gifts they have been freely given.*[13] Sure enough, the first servant doubles his gift to ten talents (= 60,000 days' wages). Likewise, the second doubles his gift to four talents (= 24,000 days' wages). By contrast, the third servant refuses to make the effort to multiply the gift he has been given. Instead, he simply buries it and offers it back on the day of reckoning. This leads to a stark contrast between the master's response to each servant:

First Servant	Second Servant	Third Servant
5 · 10 talents	2 · 4 talents	1 · 1 talent
Well done / good	Well done / good	Wicked
Faithful	Faithful	Slothful
Enters into master's joy	Enters into master's joy	Cast into outer darkness

As this chart shows, it is not enough to receive the gift. The master expects the servant to multiply what he has received so that the master can get a return on his investment when he comes to "settle accounts."

With all this in mind, remember that the Parable of the Talents, like most of Jesus' parables, is really about the kingdom of heaven. The master represents God, while the servants represent us. The talents are the incredibly costly gifts of graces that we have received, and the day of settling accounts is the Last Judgment. *Although we do not have to do anything to earn the initial gifts of grace, once they are ours, God requires us to work at multiplying them.* If we refuse to do so because we are "lazy" or "slothful," we will be cast out of the kingdom and into the "outer darkness" (Matthew 25:30).[14] According to Jesus, if we are slothful—for example, if we do not multiply the spiritual gifts we have been given by sharing the gospel with others—then we, too, will have to render an account on the day of judgment for why we did nothing with what we were given.

The Apostles in Gethsemane

Another key passage illustrating the danger of sloth involves the failure of the apostles to keep watch during Jesus' agony in Gethsemane:

> They went to a place which was called Gethsemane; and he said to his disciples, "Sit here, while I pray." And he took with him Peter and James and John, and began to be greatly distressed and troubled. And he said to them, "My soul is very sorrowful, even to death; *remain here, and watch.*" And going a little farther, he fell on the ground and prayed. . . . *And he came and found them sleeping,* and he said to Peter, *"Simon, are you asleep? Could you not watch one hour? Watch and pray that you may not enter into temptation; the spirit indeed is*

willing, but the flesh is weak." And again he went away and prayed, saying the same words. *And again he came and found them sleeping, for their eyes were very heavy; and they did not know what to answer him.* And he came the third time, and said to them, "Are you still sleeping and taking your rest? It is enough; the hour has come; the Son of man is betrayed into the hands of sinners."

(Mark 14:32–35, 37–41)

In order to understand how this passage relates to the sin of sloth, it is crucial to recognize that when Jesus tells the disciples to "watch" or "keep awake" (Greek *grēgoreō*) (Mark 14:34), he is referring to the Jewish custom of staying awake to pray on Passover night: "This . . . is *a night of watching* kept to the LORD by all the people of Israel throughout their generations" (Exodus 12:42). In other words, the disciples fail to put out the physical and spiritual effort necessary to keep vigil with Jesus.[15] That is why Jesus upbraids them when he finds them asleep and says, "*Keep awake and pray* that you may not enter into temptation; the spirit indeed is willing, but the flesh is weak" (Mark 14:38).[16] With these words, he is summoning the disciples to fight against the weakness and weariness of their flesh. Unfortunately, in addition to falling asleep again, even worse, after Jesus is arrested, they "forsook him, and fled" (Mark 14:50). What starts as mere laziness and laxity in prayer ends in the betrayal and abandonment of Jesus. Sloth, like the other capital sins, is a slippery slope.

THE REMEDY FOR SLOTH: DILIGENCE

So, what are we to do? What is the remedy for the capital sin of sloth?

Do Not Lead Lives of Idleness

First and foremost, any habits of physical idleness (sloth) and spiritual laxity (acedia) must find no place in the life of a follower of Jesus.[17] With regard to sloth, it is the apostle Paul who pens the classic Christian teaching:[18]

> Even when we were with you, we gave you this command: *If any one will not work, let him not eat. For we hear that some of you are living in idleness, mere busybodies, not doing any work.* Now such persons we command and exhort in the Lord Jesus Christ to do their work in quietness and to earn their own living.
>
> (2 Thessalonians 3:10–12)[19]

It is important to stress that Paul is *not* talking here about refusing to give alms to unemployed beggars.[20] He is talking about people within the church who are able to work but refuse to do so.[21] These are Christian parasites who feed off the labor of the congregation without contributing anything themselves. With that said, it is important to note that these sluggards are not *totally* inactive. They waste the time they should be using to fulfill their obligations to God and neighbor by following their idle curiosity and poking into matters that do not concern them. Paul solemnly warns these "busybodies" or "meddlers" to work quietly and earn their own living. As Christians, their duty is to *work* and not grow weary in doing good.

Happy Are the Diligent

Another thing that needs to be done is to *ask God for the virtue of diligence,* both in daily labor and in daily prayer.

Unlike the other virtues, Jesus does not appear to speak about diligence in the beatitudes of the Sermon on the Mount. However, in the twin parables of the Master's Return and the Faithful Steward (Luke 12:35–48), he gives two additional beatitudes for disciples who are vigilant in prayer and diligent in duty:

> *Blessed are those servants* whom the master finds *awake* when he comes.
>
> (Luke 12:37)

> *Blessed is that servant* whom his master when he comes will *find so doing.*
>
> (Luke 12:43)

Once again, the virtue of diligence isn't just about avoiding divine judgment. It is yet one more secret given by Jesus to those who wish to be "blessed" or "happy" (Greek *makarios*).

Manual Labor and Lectio Divina

Perhaps that is why the sixth-century father of Western Christian monasticism, Benedict of Nursia, specifies manual labor and meditation on Scripture as the twofold remedy for sloth:

> *Idleness is the enemy of the soul.* Therefore the brethren should be occupied at certain times in *manual labor,* and again at fixed hours in *sacred reading.*[22]

Notice here that Benedict insists on certain *fixed times* for work and for prayer. This is absolutely crucial. Make no mistake: we will never make progress in the spiritual life if we do not consistently set aside time for both. "We cannot pray 'at all times' if we do not pray at specific times, consciously willing it."[23] Notice also that when Benedict speaks of vigilant prayer, he focuses in particular on "sacred reading" (Latin *lectio divina*)—that is, meditation on Scripture.[24] We will look more closely at *lectio divina* in chapter 20. For now, the point is that meditation on Scripture requires both time and effort.

In sum, the battle against sloth means choosing each day to rise from sleep and work quietly, faithfully, and without complaining. It also means absolute fidelity to spending time each day in both vocal prayer and meditation. If, through God's grace, we continue to work and pray diligently—even when we are weary—then we, too, will one day hear the words "Well done, good and faithful servant" (Matthew 25:21).

18

SORROW VS. PATIENCE

Blessed are those who mourn, for they shall be comforted.
—Jesus of Nazareth (Matthew 5:4)

IN WESTERN CHRISTIANITY, THE MEDIEVAL LIST OF THE SEVEN
capital sins often ends with sloth.[1] However, this was not always
the case. As I mentioned earlier, in ancient times, some Christian
writers spoke of *eight* capital sins, including one that we have not
yet discussed—sorrow (a.k.a. "sadness").[2] In honor of this ancient
Christian tradition, we will close our discussion of the vices and
virtues by looking at an eighth capital sin—"sorrow" (Greek *lypē*;
Latin *tristitia*). Although many people do not even think of sorrow
as a sin—much less a capital sin—as we will see, according to the
Bible, sinful sorrow can in fact be spiritually deadly.

In order to understand this particular vice, it is crucial to start
by emphasizing that *not all sorrow is sinful*. Like other emotions, in
itself, sorrow is just a feeling. On the level of mere emotion, it is
neither good nor evil. The Bible, however, draws a clear distinction between two kinds of sorrow: (1) "godly sorrow," which is
good, and (2) "worldly sorrow," which is evil (2 Corinthians 7:10).[3]

On the one hand, *godly sorrow* is a reasonable response to evil,
suffering, or loss—especially the evil of sin. It desires to change
things for the sake of conforming to God's will. It is rooted in
love for God and neighbor. It does not exaggerate but faces evil or
loss directly and realistically. Godly sorrow leads to repentance,

trust in God, and eternal life. On the other hand, *worldly sorrow* is an irrational response to evil, suffering, or loss. It is rooted in pride and a disordered love for the things of this world. It over-reacts to the loss of earthly goods and the frustration of worldly desires. It does not lead to repentance but to regret that things have not gone according to our will.[4] When worldly sorrow turns into despair—the complete loss of trust in God's providence—it can be a mortal sin. As the apostle Paul says, "worldly sorrow" leads to "death" (2 Corinthians 7:10).

With this distinction in mind, consider what various spiritual writers have said about sinful sorrow over the course of Christian history:[5]

> Sadness is to be equally rejected as this-worldly and death-dealing, and it is to be immediately cast out from our hearts.
> —John Cassian (5th century)[6]

> Sorrow of the heart surpasses every outward wound. . . .
> Of all the soul's passions, sorrow is most harmful.
> —Thomas Aquinas (13th century)[7]

> Evil sorrow disturbs and upsets the soul, arouses
> inordinate fears, creates disgust for prayer.
> —Francis de Sales (17th century)[8]

In this chapter, we will look at what the Bible has to say about sinful sorrow. As we will see, on the one hand, Jesus himself experiences sorrow when he mourns over sin and death. At the same time, the Bible clearly warns against the kind of sorrow that flows from a disordered love of this passing world and leads to the refusal to follow Jesus, no matter what it costs.

SORROW IN JEWISH SCRIPTURE

Although Paul is the first biblical writer to explicitly distinguish godly sorrow and worldly sorrow, the Jewish Scriptures contain important examples of both kinds in the story of Job and the book of Proverbs.

The Sorrow of Job and His Wife

The book of Job begins by describing him as a man who is "blameless and upright" and tremendously blessed (Job 1:1–3). For one thing, God has given Job seven sons and three daughters. Moreover, Job is the owner of thousands of sheep, camels, oxen, and donkeys, as well as the master of many servants. He is so wealthy that he is called "the greatest of all the people of the east" (Job 1:3). However, at the prompting of an angel named "Satan," God permits Job to lose almost everything he has. First, his oxen are slain by raiders, his sheep are killed by a storm, and his camels and servants are put to the sword. Next, while feasting together, all of Job's children are killed in a storm. Finally, Job himself is struck with an illness that covers his body with "loathsome sores from the sole of his foot to the crown of his head" (Job 1:13–2:7).

Imagine losing almost all your possessions. If you are a parent, imagine losing not just one of your children but all of them—on the same day. Finally, imagine living with the constant pain of boils covering your entire body. How would you respond? Here is how Job and his wife respond:

> *Then Job arose, and rent his robe, and shaved his head, and fell upon the ground, and worshiped.* And he said, "Naked I came from my mother's womb, and naked shall I return; *the* LORD *gave, and the* LORD *has taken away; blessed be the name of the* LORD."

In all this Job did not sin or charge God with wrong.
(Job 1:20–22)

Then his wife said to him, "Do you still hold fast your integrity? *Curse God, and die.*" But he said to her, ". . . Shall we receive good at the hand of God, and shall we not receive evil?" In all this Job did not sin with his lips.
(Job 2:9–10)

Notice here that Job does experience profound sorrow. In Jewish Scripture, the tearing of one's garments and the shaving of one's head are customary signs of extreme grief.[9] At the same time, Job's sorrow does not lead him to sin. He never accuses God of doing anything "wrong" (Job 1:22). Instead, Job's sorrow leads him to pray. Job thanks God for his blessings and humbly accepts the suffering God has permitted. In stark contrast, the sorrow of Job's wife leads her to blasphemy. Her infamous words—"Curse God, and die" (Job 2:9)—may be the clearest description of sinful sorrow anywhere in the Bible.[10] Job's wife is not only overcome with grief; she has also given up on God. Her sorrow has led her to despair and to hate God.

Sinful Sorrow in Proverbs

Once the biblical distinction between godly sorrow and evil sorrow is clear, we can better understand why the book of Proverbs warns against the latter:

A glad heart makes a cheerful face,
    but *by sorrow of heart the spirit is broken.*
(Proverbs 15:13)

A cheerful heart is a good medicine,
    but *a broken spirit dries up the bones.*
(Proverbs 17:22)

Like a moth on a garment and a worm in a tree,
   so *sorrow harms the heart.*
(Proverbs 25:20 LXX)[11]

In the second proverb, the word "broken" or "sorrowful" (Hebrew *nakeʾ*) will later be translated as "grief" (Greek *lypē*) or "sorrow" (Latin *tristitia*)—the classic name for this capital sin. According to Proverbs, evil sorrow breaks a person's spirit and eats away at the heart like a worm inside a tree. It is not healthy but harmful. Eventually, sinful sadness kills a person from within.

JESUS AND SORROW

When we turn to the life and teaching of Jesus in the Gospels, two key examples of the difference between godly sorrow and worldly sorrow stand out: the sorrow of Jesus in Gethsemane (Matthew 26:36–44) and the sorrow of the rich young man who chose not to follow Jesus (Mark 10:19–22).

The Godly Sorrow of Jesus in Gethsemane

During his agony in Gethsemane, Jesus experiences sorrow in the face of his own suffering and death:

> Jesus went with them to a place called Gethsemane, and he said to his disciples, "Sit here, while I go there and pray." And taking with him Peter and the two sons of Zebedee, *he began to be sorrowful and troubled.* Then he said to them, "*My soul is very sorrowful, even to death;* remain here, and watch with me." *And going a little farther he fell on his face and prayed, "My Father, if it be possible, let this cup pass from me; nevertheless, not as I will, but as you will."* And he came to the disciples and found them sleeping; and he said to Peter, "So, could you

not watch with me one hour? Watch and pray that you may not enter into temptation; the spirit indeed is willing, but the flesh is weak." Again, for the second time, he went away and prayed, "My Father, if this cannot pass unless I drink it, your will be done." And again he came and found them sleeping, for their eyes were heavy. So, leaving them again, he went away and prayed for the third time, saying the same words.

(Matthew 26:36–44)

When Jesus says that his soul is "sorrowful [Greek *perilypos*], even to death" (Matthew 26:38), it is very close to the word that will later be used for the capital sin of "sorrow" (Greek *lypē*). So, why is the sorrow of Jesus not sinful? Because of how Jesus responds— by praying. Contrast this with the actions of the disciples in Gethsemane: they were "sleeping for sorrow" (Greek *lypē*) (Luke 22:45). While Jesus' sorrow drives him to pray so fervently that he sweats blood, the disciples' sorrow overcomes them so that they fail to pray.[12] Moreover, despite his sorrow, Jesus humbly accepts whatever suffering is necessary for the sake of salvation: "My Father, if this cannot pass unless I drink it, your will be done" (Matthew 26:42). In this way, *Jesus' sorrow actually draws him closer to the Father*.

The Worldly Sorrow of the Rich Young Man

Contrast the prayerful sorrow of Jesus with the worldly sorrow of the rich young man. The two are completely different. In an earlier chapter, we examined the first half of Jesus' encounter with this young man as he instructs him on the necessity of keeping the Ten Commandments (see Matthew 19:17–19; cf. Mark 10:17–19). Now consider the second half:

And he said to [Jesus], "Teacher, all these I have observed from my youth." And Jesus looking upon him loved him, and said to him, "You lack one thing; go, sell what you have, and give to the poor, and you will have treasure in heaven; and come, follow me." *Disheartened by the saying, he went away sorrowful; for he had great possessions.*

(Mark 10:20–22)[13]

Observe the dramatic change that takes place when Jesus invites him to give up his possessions. The young man not only becomes "disheartened" or "gloomy," but he turns and goes away "sorrowful" or "grieving" (Greek *lypoumenos*) (Mark 10:22). Why? Because he had "great possessions." This is a perfect example of how worldly sorrow is rooted in a disordered love for the things of this world.[14] In other words, the reason the young man is sad is because *he loves his possessions more than he loves Jesus.* Like the other capital sins, sorrow is a problem of the heart. In the end, it leads the rich young man to turn away and refuse to follow Jesus. Tragically, it makes him incapable of journeying where Jesus wants to lead him—to "eternal life" (Mark 10:17).

THE REMEDY FOR SORROW: PATIENCE

So, what are we to do? What is the remedy for sinful sorrow?

You Will Be Sorrowful

The first thing that all followers of Jesus must do is to realize that they *will* experience sorrow. In this valley of tears, sorrow is inescapable. No one makes it out of this world alive, and no one leaves without getting wounded. As Jesus himself says to his disciples:

> Truly, truly, I say to you, *you will weep and lament,* but the world will rejoice; *you will be sorrowful,* but your sorrow will turn into joy.
>
> (John 16:20)

The question, of course, is how we respond: we can choose either the "godly sorrow" that leads to "salvation" or the "worldly sorrow" that leads to "death" (2 Corinthians 7:10). How can we tell the difference? If a spirit of sadness comes over us that leads us to stop praying, then it is definitely the sinful kind. In the words of Francis de Sales:

> *If you are ever caught by this evil kind of sorrow*, . . . prayer is a sovereign remedy, for it lifts up the soul to God who is our only joy and consolation. . . . Although it may seem that everything you do at this time is done coldly, sadly, and sluggishly, *you must persevere*.[15]

Whenever we stand before the precipice of suffering or experience the total collapse of how we *thought* our lives were going to be, we should take the words of Jesus when he was sorrowful and make them our own: "Father, if it be possible, let this cup pass from me; nevertheless, not as I will, but as you will" (Matthew 26:39).

The Virtue of Patience

The second thing to do is *to ask God for the virtue of patience*—by which we bear the sufferings and evils of this life without giving in to bitterness.[16] Since ancient times, Christian spiritual writers have identified "the virtue of patience" as being directly opposed to sorrow.[17] In fact, the word "patience" (Latin *patientia*) comes from the same root as "suffer" (Latin *pati*).[18] Because patience protects the heart from abandoning God, it has been called "the root and guardian of all the virtues."[19] Perhaps more than any other virtue, the spiritual writers insist that patience must be given by God; it is not something we can achieve on our own power.[20]

With this in mind, it is no coincidence that the New Testament points to Job as a model of this virtue:

As an example of suffering and patience, brethren, take the prophets who spoke in the name of the Lord. Behold, we call those happy who were steadfast. You have heard of *the steadfastness of Job.*

(James 5:10–11)

The happiness of Job did not come from the absence of pain but from his trust in "the purpose of the Lord" (James 5:11). In other words, true patience is ultimately rooted in love. As Augustine of Hippo once wrote, "The greater the charity of God that the saints possess, the more do they endure all things for Him whom they love."[21] Or, as Paul said, *"Love is patient.* . . . Love bears all things, believes all things, hopes all things, endures all things" (1 Corinthians 13:4, 7).

They Shall Be Comforted

Finally, when we experience sorrow, it is crucial to keep our eyes fixed on the hope of eternal life. Once again, Jesus says in the Sermon on the Mount,

Blessed are those who mourn, for *they shall be comforted.*

(Matthew 5:4)

At first glance, this may be the most paradoxical of all Jesus' beatitudes. How can those who mourn be "happy" (Greek *makarios*)? The answer: because they see their sufferings from an eternal perspective. Because they know that one day, they *will* be comforted. In the words of John Cassian:

> *We shall be able to overcome every kind of sadness* . . . *when we are ever rejoicing at the sight of things eternal* . . . and when we remain steadfast and are neither cast down by present events nor carried away by good fortune, viewing both as empty and soon to pass.[22]

It is no coincidence that it was the *rich* young man who went away from Jesus sad. The reason is because he loved the things of this world more than he loved the God who gave them to him. He failed to realize that everything he possessed was nothing in comparison to "eternal life" (Mark 10:17).

A Prayer for Patience

Thus, in order to overcome sinful sadness, we must remember that everything in this life, however good it may be, will inevitably pass away. Consider the famous and beautiful prayer of Teresa of Avila:

> Let nothing trouble you
> Let nothing frighten you
> Everything passes
> God never changes
> Patience
> Obtains all
> Whoever has God
> Wants for nothing
> God alone is enough.[23]

Only when we fall in love with *the God who does not pass away* will we be able to bear all things, believe all things, hope all things, and endure all things—with patience.

MAKING PROGRESS

19

EXAMINATION OF HEART

Each tree is known by its own fruit.
—Jesus of Nazareth (Luke 6:44)

NOW THAT WE HAVE COMPLETED OUR SURVEY OF VICES AND VIR-
tues, what do we do with what we have learned? Each of us experiences temptations to all the capital sins at one time or another.
However, they do not affect everyone in the same way or to the
same degree. In one person, pride or anger might predominate,
whereas in another, lust or gluttony might be strongest. The purpose of the last eight chapters was to deepen our understanding
of each of the capital sins and their opposing virtues so that we
might be able to see them more clearly in ourselves, identify our
predominant fault, and grow in self-knowledge. In these final
chapters, we will focus on several key steps to making progress in
the spiritual life. The first step is *the regular examination of the incli-
nations to vice or virtue in our hearts.*

Throughout Church history, several spiritual classics have
used the image of a tree and its fruits to depict the human heart
and its desires for vice or virtue. Consider the words of the following ancient, medieval, and modern Christian writers:

These [capital sins] must be fought against. . . . For a tree
whose width and height are harmful will more easily wither

up if the roots which support it are exposed and cut before-hand.

—John Cassian (5th century)[1]

Think of the soul as a tree made for love and living only by love. . . . This tree, so delightfully planted, bears many-fragranced blossoms of virtue.

—Catherine of Siena (14th century)[2]

Our hearts are trees, affections and passions are branches,
and works or actions are fruits.

—Francis de Sales (17th century)[3]

In other words, just as a tree rooted in poor soil with sickly branches is going to produce rotten fruits, so, too, a heart rooted in pride that cultivates evil desires is going to produce vices. And just as a tree rooted in rich soil with strong branches is going to produce good fruits, so, too, a heart rooted in the love of God and neighbor that cultivates good desires is going to produce virtues.

In this chapter, we will briefly explore the biblical roots of this ancient tradition of comparing the soul and its vices or virtues to a tree and its fruits. The ultimate goal is to provide a helpful and scripturally based method of examination of conscience, in order to help us root out sin and grow in love. As we will see, the imagery of two trees—one good, one evil—comes straight from Jewish Scripture. In fact, Jesus himself uses the two trees to teach his disciples about the necessity of self-knowledge and the examination of one's heart.

The Two Trees in Jewish Scripture

In order to understand Jesus' comparison of the heart and its works to a tree and its fruits, it is important to begin with two key sections from the Old Testament: the account of the two trees in Eden (Genesis 2:7–9) and the description of wisdom as a "tree of life" (Proverbs 3:18; 11:30).

The Two Trees in Eden

In Jewish Scripture, the history of salvation begins with an account of two trees—one good, one evil—in the Garden of Eden:

> Then the LORD God formed man of dust from the ground, and breathed into his nostrils the breath of life; and man became a living being. And the LORD God planted a garden in Eden, in the east; and there he put the man whom he had formed. And out of the ground the LORD God made to grow every tree that is pleasant to the sight and good for food, the *tree of life* also *in the midst of the garden*, and *the tree of the knowledge of good and evil.*
>
> (Genesis 2:7–9)

Compare and contrast the key features of these two trees:

Good Tree	Evil Tree
1. Tree of "life"	1. Tree of "knowledge"
2. Adam permitted to eat its fruit	2. Adam forbidden to eat its fruit
3. Whoever eats will "live for ever"	3. Whoever eats will "die"
(Genesis 2:9, 16; 3:22)	(Genesis 2:9, 17)

These are no ordinary trees, for the choice between them is a matter of supernatural life and death. According to Genesis, the tree of life does not just give ordinary bodily nourishment. Whoever eats its fruit will live forever. Likewise, the tree of knowledge does not just bring physical death. Whoever eats its fruit will be separated from God and lose the immortality that could have been gained by tasting the fruit of the tree of life.[4] Because Adam and Eve choose to eat the forbidden fruit, they are driven away from God's presence in Eden. Instead of becoming wise like God, they have simply become aware of their own sin. Having once known what it was to be "good"—for that is how God created them (Genesis 1:31)—they now gain a firsthand knowledge of evil, precisely by breaking God's command and acting as if they have the power to *decide for themselves* what is good and what is evil.[5]

The Tree of Life in Proverbs

Outside the book of Genesis, the tree of knowledge is not mentioned in Jewish Scripture. The book of Proverbs, however, does mention the tree of life, when it uses it as a symbol for wisdom and understanding:

> Happy is the man who finds *wisdom,*
>> and the man who gets *understanding.* . . .
> *She is a tree of life to those who lay hold of her;*
>> those who hold her fast are called happy.
> (Proverbs 3:13, 18)

> *The fruit of the righteous is a tree of life,*
>> but lawlessness takes away lives.
> (Proverbs 11:30)

According to Proverbs, just like Adam and Eve, all human beings have a choice between good and evil. If they choose to follow their desires for good and walk the path of wisdom, they will taste the fruits of peace and happiness. If, however, they choose to follow their desires for evil and walk the path of foolishness, they will reap the fruits of lawlessness and death:

Good Tree	Evil Tree
1. Tree of life = Wisdom	1. Tree = Folly (implied)
2. Branches = righteous desires	2. Branches = lawless desires
3. Fruit = life	3. Fruit = death

According to Proverbs, then, wisdom is not just a virtue. It is a new "tree of life" (Proverbs 3:18).[6] In other words, the practice of virtue is *a way of returning to Eden*. Likewise, good works are not just about following rules or fulfilling duties. They are the "fruit" of wisdom, which give peace and happiness to those who partake of it. Through the image of the tree of life, Proverbs reveals that the secret to a happy life is to choose virtue over vice, good rather than evil.

JESUS AND THE TWO TREES

With this Jewish context in mind, we can better understand Jesus' use of the imagery of two trees to illuminate the mystery of the human heart and its inclination to vice or virtue. He does this in three key passages.

The Tree of the Heart

In the so-called Sermon on the Plain (Luke 6:17–49), Jesus uses the imagery of a tree and its fruit to describe the human heart:

No *good tree* bears *bad fruit,* nor again does *a bad tree* bear *good fruit;* for *each tree is known by its own fruit.* For figs are not gathered from thorns, nor are grapes picked from a bramble bush. The *good person* out of the good treasure of *his heart* produces good, and *the evil person* out of his evil treasure produces evil; for out of the abundance of *the heart* his mouth speaks.

(Luke 6:43–45)[7]

This is no mere metaphor. Jesus' contrast between the fruit of a good and evil tree clearly echoes the two trees in Eden. Even his reference to figs and thorns recalls the fig leaves that Adam and Eve use to cover themselves and the thorns that spring up after the Fall (see Genesis 3:7, 18). By means of these allusions to Genesis, Jesus reveals that the choice between good and evil ultimately takes place within the deepest part of a person: the "heart" (Greek *kardia*). Thus, when Jesus says that "each tree is known by *its own fruit*" (Luke 6:44), he is emphasizing the necessity of recognizing the movements of one's own heart toward vice or virtue.[8] In short, he is using the imagery of the two trees to speak about spiritual self-knowledge.

The Power to Choose Good or Evil

Likewise, in his warning to those who accused him of being possessed (Matthew 12:22–34), Jesus also uses the two trees to emphasize that each individual has the power to freely choose good or evil:

Either make the tree good, and its fruit good; or make the tree bad, and its fruit bad; for the tree is known by its fruit. *You brood of vipers!* how can you speak good, when you are evil? For out of the abundance of *the heart* the mouth speaks.

(Matthew 12:33–34)

Here, too, there are echoes of Eden. Not only does Jesus speak once again of a good tree and a bad tree, but he even uses the imagery of a "brood of vipers." This calls to mind the mysterious oracle in Genesis about the future war between the serpent's "seed" or "offspring" and the "seed" of the "woman" (Genesis 3:15).[9] According to Jesus, like Adam and Eve, each human being has the power to freely choose—from the heart—either to do good or to do evil.

You Will Know Them by Their Fruits

Finally, in the Sermon on the Mount, Jesus uses the image of the two trees to emphasize the necessity of recognizing virtue and vices in others. Specifically, he warns against being deceived by people who seem outwardly virtuous but who are inwardly vicious:

> Beware of false prophets, who come to you in sheep's clothing but inwardly are ravenous wolves. *You will know them by their fruits.* Are grapes gathered from thorns, or figs from thistles? So, *every sound tree bears good fruit, but the bad tree bears evil fruit.*
>
> (Matthew 7:15–17)

At first glance, it might seem that Jesus is contradicting himself with these words. Just a few verses earlier, he famously commands his disciples, *"Judge not,* that you be not judged," and warns them against seeing the "speck" in their "brother's eye" while failing to notice the "log" in their own (Matthew 7:1–5).

In reality, however, the two teachings dovetail perfectly. For it is precisely those who *lack* self-knowledge who are often quick to condemn others and be easily duped by spiritual charlatans. On the one hand, it is important for followers of Jesus not to despise others for minor faults (the "speck") while failing to see the major vices (the "log") in their own hearts. That is what Jesus is referring to when he tells his disciples not to "judge" (Greek *krinō*)—a word that in context is a synonym for "condemn" (Greek *katakrinō*).[10] On the other hand, it is equally important not to be deceived by frauds and predators who appear to be outwardly virtuous ("sheep's clothing") but are inwardly evil ("ravenous wolves"). Jesus wants his disciples to avoid both the spiritual pride and the spiritual naivete that often stem from the failure to see clearly the good and evil in their own hearts.

EXAMINATION OF THE HEART

With all this in mind, we can now gather up the fruits of our study and apply them to how we, too, might grow in self-knowledge, especially through the practice known as the "examination of conscience."[11] In light of the words of Jesus about the "tree" of the human heart, we might also refer to this as the "examination of the heart." With regard to this practice, several points are important.

The Examination of Conscience

The first thing that needs to be said is that the basic practice of self-examination, especially before partaking of the Lord's Supper, goes back to New Testament times.[12] For example, the apostle Paul warns:

> Whoever, therefore, eats the bread or drinks the cup of the Lord in an unworthy manner will be guilty of profaning the body and blood of the Lord. *Let a man examine himself, and so eat of the bread and drink of the cup.*
>
> (1 Corinthians 11:27–28)

Following Paul's lead, Christian spiritual writers throughout history have insisted that followers of Jesus develop the habit of frequently examining their consciences.[13] Consider the following words from ancient, medieval, and modern times:

> By *examining our conscience,* scrutinizing our thinking, and considering what we have done right on this day and what on that day . . . [we will discover] how much improvement we have achieved in our passions.
> —John Chrysostom (4th century)[14]

> *In the morning make a resolution and in the evening examine how you did.* Look at what you said, did, or thought, to discover if you have offended God or your neighbor.
> —Thomas à Kempis (15th century)[15]

> Ask [the Holy Spirit] for light and sight that you may attain a perfect knowledge of yourself. . . . *Knowledge of our spiritual progress depends on examination of this kind.*
> —Francis de Sales (17th century)[16]

In sum, according to both Scripture and Christian tradition, the regular examination of one's conscience, especially before partaking of the Lord's Supper, is a basic part of the life of any disciple who wants to make progress on the spiritual path.

The Two Trees of Vices and Virtues

But exactly how does one go about this? As one might expect, there are a variety of methods.[17] Perhaps most common is the practice of examining one's conscience according to the Ten Commandments. However, because the Commandments focus on especially grave sins like idolatry, murder, and adultery, it can sometimes be difficult to apply them directly to our everyday lives. Thus, it is important to note that spiritual writers like Ignatius of Loyola also recommend examining one's conscience according to the capital sins and their opposing virtues:

> *In order to understand better the faults committed that come under the Seven Capital Sins, let the contrary virtues be considered. So* also, the better to avoid these sins, one should resolve to endeavor by devout exercises to acquire and retain the seven virtues contrary to them.[18]

As an aid to this kind of examination, the seven vices and their opposing virtues (along with the eighth added by some spiritual writers) are depicted in the diagram of the "Two Trees."[19]

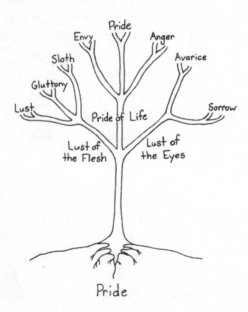

The Evil Tree

Notice in this diagram that the three main branches of *the evil tree* are identical to the three disordered desires of the triple lust. If we choose to cultivate our disordered desires for self-exaltation, we will bear the fruits of envy, anger, and pride. If we cultivate our disordered cravings for physical pleasure, we will bear the fruits of lust, gluttony, and sloth. Finally, if we cultivate our disordered desires for worldly possessions, we will bear the fruits of avarice and sorrow.

Notice also that the three main branches of *the good tree* are identical to the three spiritual exercises given by Jesus in the Sermon on the Mount: prayer, fasting, and almsgiving. If we persevere in secret prayer to the Father, we will grow in the virtues of humility, mercy, and meekness. If we practice detachment from possessions by discreetly giving to the poor, we will grow in the

The Good Tree

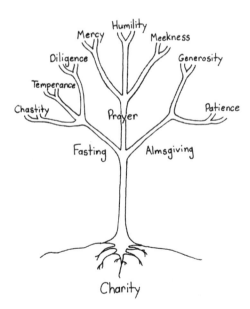

virtues of generosity and patience. Finally, if we practice self-control through private fasting, we will grow in the virtues of chastity, temperance, and diligence.

In sum, when we examine our hearts according to the capital sins and their opposing virtues, we will likely find that we have plenty of work to do in cutting off the bad branches and their fruits and cultivating the good branches and theirs.

Focus on One Fault and Its Opposing Virtue

Finally, when practicing the examination of conscience, it is helpful to be especially attentive to which of the capital sins is our predominant fault. This can sometimes be ascertained by which of the vices we fall into most easily and most frequently. Once our predominant fault is identified, we should focus our energies on rooting out this particular vice and growing in its opposing virtue. In the words of Francis de Sales:

> Consider from time to time *which passions are most predominant in your soul.* When you have discovered them *adopt a way of life that will be completely opposed to them* in thought, word, and action.[20]

One reason for focusing on our predominant fault is so that we do not become discouraged or overwhelmed by trying to do everything at once. In addition, the spiritual classics agree that growth in even one of the virtues leads to growth in them all. In the words of John of the Cross:

> *Through the practice of one virtue all the virtues grow,* and similarly, through an increase of one vice, all the vices and their effects grow.[21]

According to Jesus, our hearts are like "trees." But what kind have we planted? What fruits are we cultivating? It is only by becoming aware of our faults that we can make a deliberate effort to fight against them. If we are blind to sin in our lives, we are never going to make progress in virtue. However, by regularly examining our hearts, we will gradually begin to *grow in self-knowledge* and realize the truth of Jesus' teaching that "each tree is known by its own fruit" (Luke 6:44).

20

Lectio Divina and Jacob's Ladder

You will see heaven opened, and the angels of God ascending and descending upon the Son of man.
—Jesus of Nazareth (John 1:51)

A SECOND KEY TO MAKING PROGRESS IN THE SPIRITUAL LIFE IS THE
regular practice of meditation on Scripture, known in the West as
lectio divina (Latin for "divine reading").[1] When it comes to the
process of spiritual growth, throughout history, Christian writers
have agreed on two points.

The first is that the practice of praying with Scripture is essential for making spiritual progress. Consider the following quotes
from ancient, medieval, and modern writers:

You must strive in every respect to give yourself assiduously
and even constantly to sacred reading.
—John Cassian (5th century)[2]

The perfection of the blessed life is contained in
these four steps [of *lectio divina*].
—Guigo the Carthusian (12th century)[3]

Meditation is the basis for acquiring all the virtues, and to
undertake it is a matter of life and death for all Christians.
—Teresa of Avila (16th century)[4]

The second point of agreement is that the biblical story of Jacob's ladder (see Genesis 28:10–17) is the standard image for the spiritual progress made by the soul in its journey to heaven.[5] Consider the following:

> Jacob's ladder was a figure of . . . the ascent through virtue, little by little . . . by the emending and correcting of one's habits.
> —John Chrysostom (4th century)[6]

> These [steps of *lectio divina*] make a ladder for monks by which they are lifted up from earth to heaven.
> —Guigo the Carthusian (12th century)[7]

> This ladder of contemplation . . . is prefigured by that ladder which Jacob saw as he slept.
> —John of the Cross (16th century)[8]

By far the most famous example is the ancient Christian writer John Climacus—that is, "John of the Ladder" (Greek *klimakos*). His classic work on the spiritual life, *The Ladder of Divine Ascent*, consists of thirty-three "steps" based on the biblical image of Jacob's ladder.[9]

At first glance, the connection between *lectio divina* and the story of Jacob's ladder may not be apparent. However, when we interpret this mysterious episode in its ancient Jewish context and in light of the words of Jesus, we will discover a profound link between the two. As we will see, Jesus' own interpretation of Jacob's ladder will lay the foundation for the Christian practice of meditation on Scripture and provide us with a helpful illustration of the steps involved in learning how to practice *lectio divina*.

JACOB'S LADDER IN JEWISH SCRIPTURE

One of the most memorable episodes in the Old Testament comes from the account of the mysterious vision that the patriarch Jacob has one night:

> Jacob . . . came to a certain place, and stayed there that night, because the sun had set. Taking one of the stones of the place, he put it under his head and lay down in that place to sleep. *And he dreamed that there was a ladder set up on the earth, and the top of it reached to heaven; and behold, the angels of God were ascending and descending on it! And behold, the* LORD *stood above it* and said, "I am the LORD. . . . *Behold, I am with you.* . . ." Then Jacob awoke from his sleep and said, "Surely the LORD is in this place; and I did not know it." And he was afraid, and said, "How awesome is this place! This is none other than *the house of God,* and this is *the gate of heaven.*"
>
> (Genesis 28:10–13, 15–17)

Several aspects of this story are important to highlight.

Jacob and the Stairway to Heaven
The first thing that needs to be said is that the "ladder" Jacob sees is probably not the kind of ordinary ladder with rungs that we are familiar with today but rather a stairway (Genesis 28:12).[10] Such stairways were used by priests to go up and down ancient temple-mountains known as *ziggurats*.[11] Thus, you can picture it as follows:

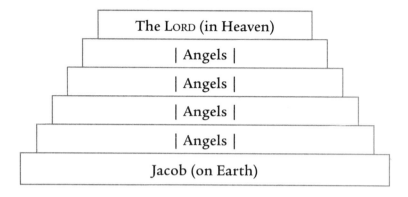

| The LORD (in Heaven) |
| Angels |
| Angels |
| Angels |
| Angels |
| Jacob (on Earth) |

That is why Jacob names the place "house of God" (Genesis 28:17)—a standard name for the Temple. It is also why when Jacob looks up, he sees "the LORD" himself standing at the top of the stairway (Genesis 28:13). Jacob is not just having a vision of heaven; he is having a vision of *God*. Finally, when Jacob awakens, he is so overcome by his encounter that he also names the place the "gate of heaven" (Genesis 28:17). In short, Jacob's vision is of a sacred stairway that not only connects heaven and earth but also allows him to experience a personal encounter with the God of the universe.

JESUS AND JACOB'S LADDER

With this biblical background in mind, we can turn to how Jesus interprets the story of Jacob's ladder. Although it is easy to miss if you're not reading closely, in the Gospel of John, Jesus reveals that he himself—the "Word" made "flesh" (John 1:14)—is the true stairway to heaven.

Nathanael, the Fig Tree, and Jacob's Ladder

Many are familiar with the famous exchange between Jesus and Nathanael in the Gospel of John:

> Jesus saw Nathanael coming to him, and said of him, "Behold, an Israelite indeed, in whom is no guile!" Nathanael said to him, "How do you know me?" Jesus answered him, "Before Philip called you, *when you were under the fig tree, I saw you.*" Nathanael answered him, "Rabbi, you are the Son of God! You are the King of Israel!" Jesus answered him, "Because I said to you, I saw you under the fig tree, do you believe? You shall see greater things than these." And he said to him, *"Truly, truly, I say to you, you will see heaven opened, and the angels of God ascending and descending upon the Son of man."*
>
> (John 1:47–51)

In order to understand this conversation, two points are crucial to emphasize.

First, in Jewish Scripture and tradition, the image of "sitting" beneath a "fig tree" was associated both with the coming of the Messiah[12] and with the practice of meditation on Scripture.[13] If this ancient Jewish tradition lies behind Nathanael's act of sitting "under the fig tree" (John 1:48), it may suggest that he, too, was *reading the Scripture* when Jesus saw him. If so, this would provide a plausible explanation for how Nathanael is able to go so quickly from skepticism to discipleship, identifying Jesus not only as his "Rabbi" but also as the "Son of God" and "King of Israel" (John 1:49). The answer: Nathanael's study of Scripture prepared him to receive the revelation of Jesus' identity.[14]

Jesus, the Living Ladder to Heaven

Second, Jesus responds to this confession of faith by declaring that Nathanael will see much greater things than this: he will see "heaven opened, and the angels of God ascending and descending upon the Son of man" (John 1:51).

When we recall the story of Jacob's ladder and the fact that Jesus often uses the expression "the Son of man" to refer to himself (John 9:35–37), the implication of these words is simply stunning. Just as Jacob saw the angels "ascending and descending" upon the stairway to heaven (Genesis 28:12, 17), so, too, Nathanael will one day see the angels "ascending and descending" upon *Jesus himself* (John 1:51). In other words, Jesus is revealing that he himself is the true "ladder" to heaven. You can picture it this way:

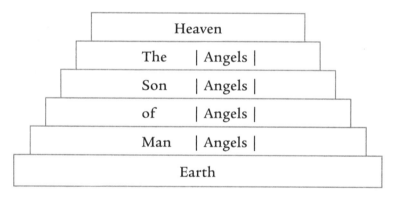

One reason Jesus' identification of himself as Jacob's Ladder is so important is because Jacob describes the place where he has the vision as the "house of God"—that is, the dwelling place of God on earth (Genesis 28:17). Another reason is because the Gospel of John tells us that Jesus is not just the Messiah but the "Word" (Greek *logos*) made "flesh" (John 1:14). In short, Jesus himself is the true Temple—the dwelling place of God on earth. He is the living ladder of Paradise.

THE FOUR STEPS OF *LECTIO DIVINA*

With all this in mind, we can now turn from the Bible to the later Christian tradition of *lectio divina*.[15] Although there are a variety of methods of meditating on Scripture, we will focus here on the famous description of the "four steps" of *lectio divina* in the brief but beautiful treatise known as *The Ladder of Paradise*.[16]

Lectio Divina *and Jacob's Ladder*

In the late twelfth century, a Carthusian monk named Guigo II wrote what is widely considered *the* classic medieval explanation of meditation on Scripture.[17] In it, he uses Jacob's ladder as an image for the four basic steps of *lectio divina:*

> One day when I was busy working with my hands I began to think about our spiritual work, and all at once four stages in spiritual exercise came to my mind: reading, meditation, prayer, and contemplation. *These make a ladder for monks by which they are lifted up from earth to heaven. It has few rungs, yet its length is immense and wonderful, for its lower end rests upon the earth, but its top pierces the clouds and touches heavenly secrets.*[18]

In the *Ladder of Paradise,* the four steps of *lectio divina* have the same power to lift up the soul into heaven as the ladder of Jacob does. You can picture it as follows:

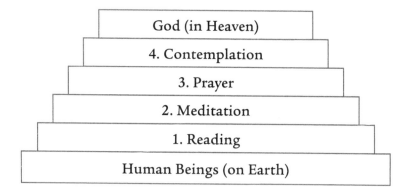

From this perspective, the Bible is much more than just an ancient holy book or a trustworthy guide for how to live a good life. Whenever followers of Jesus practice *lectio divina,* heaven is opened to them and the God of the universe speaks. In this way, Scripture itself becomes a true stairway to heaven.

The Four Steps Explained

But what exactly do each of these four steps entail? Thankfully, Guigo defines them (for clarity, I have enumerated them):

> (1) *Reading* is the careful study of the Scriptures, concentrating all one's powers on it. (2) *Meditation* is the busy application of the mind to seek with the help of one's own reason for knowledge of hidden truth. (3) *Prayer* is the heart's devoted turning to God to drive away evil and obtain what is good. (4) *Contemplation* is when the mind is in some sort lifted up to God and held above itself, so that it tastes the joy of everlasting sweetness.[19]

Let's take a few moments to explain each step:

Step 1: Reading: The first and most essential step of *lectio div-*

ina is "reading" (Latin *lectio*). This means opening up the Bible and reading its words slowly and carefully—not skimming or rushing.

Step 2: Meditation: Although *lectio divina* as a whole is a form of meditation, the second step—"meditation" (Latin *meditatio*)—refers specifically to the act of pondering what has been read. It involves using the mind to seek out the hidden truth contained in Scripture.

Step 3: Prayer: When it comes to the third step—"prayer" (Latin *oratio*)—once again, something very specific is meant. After reading the words of Scripture and thinking about them, the next step is to talk with God from the heart about them. In this way, prayer transforms meditation on Scripture into a *dialogue* between the soul and God. As one ancient Christian writer famously put it, "We speak to him when we pray, we listen to him when we read the divine oracles."[20]

Step 4: Contemplation: The fourth step is "contemplation" (Latin *contemplatio*). We've already read that contemplation can be defined as a special kind of prayer in which the "eyes" of the heart are fixed on God in a "gaze" of love (see chapter 3). The main thing we want to emphasize here is that in the first three steps of *lectio divina, we* act—by reading the Bible, thinking about it, and talking to God about it. In the fourth step, however, it is *God* who acts: by "lifting up" the soul to himself and allowing it to taste the "sweetness" of his presence. In other words, for this fourth step, we don't have to do anything except be still and "look" at God, quietly resting in his presence. Sometimes, in *lectio divina,* God through his grace can "lift" the soul on earth "above itself" so that it enjoys the sweetness of his heavenly presence.[21]

In sum, *lectio divina* involves four simple steps: reading the Bible, thinking about what we've read, talking to God about it, and quietly resting in his presence.

All Four Steps Go Together

In light of everything we've seen, it should be clear by now why Guigo claims that the "spiritual exercise" of a Christian should "revolve around" the four steps of *lectio divina*.[22] For one thing, all four steps work together to help our prayers avoid becoming fruitless, lukewarm, or even spiritually dangerous. As he states,

> Reading without meditation is *sterile,* meditation without reading is *liable to error,* prayer without meditation is *lukewarm,* and meditation without prayer is *unfruitful,* prayer when it is fervent wins contemplation, but *to obtain it without prayer would be rare,* even miraculous.[23]

In other words, if we only *read* the words of Scripture without ever *thinking* about them, our prayers will invariably end up dry and lifeless. On the other hand, if we spend all our time *thinking* about profound questions but never go to Scripture for answers, we will inevitably end up in all kinds of error. If all we do is *talk* to God without ever taking time to *think* about what he has said in his Word, then our prayers will likely end up being lukewarm monologues rather than a conversation from the heart. Finally, if we spend all our time pondering Scripture without ever *asking* God to give us the spiritual gifts we discover in its pages, then our meditation will never bear spiritual fruit.

In short, if our prayer life seems sterile, lukewarm, or unfruitful, then we need to practice *lectio divina*. If prayerful meditation on Scripture really is a "stairway" to heaven and a personal encounter with the Word made flesh, then it should be a daily part of every Christian's spiritual life.

Lectio Divina *and the Liturgy*

Finally, I would like to bring our chapter to a close by suggesting a parallel between the four steps of *lectio divina* and the liturgy.

Since ancient times, Christian worship has consisted of four basic parts: (1) the reading of Scripture, (2) the explanation of Scripture in a homily, (3) the Eucharistic prayer, and (4) communion. Consider, for example, one of the most ancient descriptions of early Christian worship we possess (for the sake of clarity, I have enumerated the steps):

> On the day we call the day of the sun, all who dwell in the city or country gather in the same place.
>
> (1) The memoirs of the apostles and the writings of the prophets are read, as much as time permits.
>
> (2) When the reader has finished, he who presides over those gathered admonishes and challenges them to imitate these beautiful things.
>
> (3) Then we all rise together and offer prayers for ourselves. . . .
>
> When the prayers are concluded we exchange the kiss.
>
> (4) Then someone brings bread and a cup of water and wine mixed together to him who presides over the brethren.
>
> He takes them and offers praise and glory to the Father of the universe, through the name of the Son and of the Holy Spirit and for a considerable time he gives thanks (in Greek: *eucharistian*) that we have been judged worthy of these gifts.
>
> When he has concluded the prayers and thanksgivings, all present give voice to an acclamation by saying: "Amen."
>
> When he who presides has given thanks and the people have responded, those whom we call deacons give to those present the "eucharisted" bread, wine and water and take them to those who are absent.
>
> —Justin Martyr (2nd century)[24]

With this basic fourfold structure in mind, consider the following parallels between Christian liturgy and *lectio divina:*

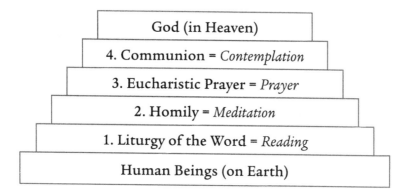

What remarkable parallels! If we stop to think about it, however, they shouldn't come as a surprise. After all, if Jesus really is the true "ladder" to heaven (see John 1:51) and if the "food" and "drink" he gives us really is "the living bread which came down from heaven" (John 6:51, 55), then it makes sense that the supreme act of *lectio divina* is that which takes place in the liturgy. Seen in this light, the practice of prayerful meditation on Scripture should naturally lead us to a deeper hunger for the spiritual nourishment given by Christ in the Eucharist.[25]

In sum, even if we've never practiced *lectio divina* in private, if we have attentively and prayerfully participated in the Eucharistic liturgy, then we have already begun to climb the Ladder of Paradise. Indeed, if both Jesus and Scripture are truly the Word of God, then every time we read and meditate on Scripture, we are *encountering the person of Christ himself*—the living stairway to heaven.

21

THE BATTLE OF PRAYER

He told them a parable, to the effect that they ought
always to pray and not lose heart.
—The Gospel of Luke (18:1)

IN ADDITION TO THE REGULAR EXAMINATION OF HEART AND DAILY
meditation on Scripture, a third key to making progress in the
spiritual life is *perseverance in prayer,* even in the midst of difficul-
ties and distractions. Over and over again, the spiritual classics
testify with one voice that prayer is both a gift of God's grace and
a battle that requires effort.[1] Consider the following:

Prayer is warfare to the last breath.
—Abba Agathon of Egypt (4th century)[2]

There can be no place for victory without the
adversity of a struggle.
—John Cassian (5th century)[3]

Is there any struggle greater than the effort to
overcome one's self?
—Thomas à Kempis (15th century)[4]

Why is prayer a battle? And who and what exactly is the struggle
against? Why is fighting this battle so important to making progress in the spiritual life?

We have already looked at the battle against vice in our study of the capital sins and their opposing virtues. In this chapter, we will focus on a different battle, in which the adversary is sometimes ourselves, sometimes the enemy, and sometimes—seemingly—God. Far from being free from all difficulty, as we will discover, "The 'spiritual battle' of the Christian's new life is inseparable from the battle of prayer. . . . *There is no holiness without renunciation and spiritual battle.*"[5]

THE BATTLE OF PRAYER IN JEWISH SCRIPTURE

When it comes to the theme of spiritual battle, the Jewish Scriptures are brimming with examples. For our purposes here, by far the most striking and significant example of the battle of prayer comes from the enigmatic and unforgettable story of Jacob's nocturnal wrestling match with a mysterious "man" who also seems to be God.

Jacob Wrestles with God

The episode takes place during Jacob's journey from his father-in-law Laban's house in Haran (located in modern-day Turkey) back home to the promised land of Canaan (see Genesis 31). Before crossing the Jabbok river, located east of Canaan, Jacob experiences a mysterious and life-changing struggle:

> The same *night* he arose and took his two wives, his two maids, and his eleven children, and crossed the ford of the Jabbok. He took them and sent them across the stream, and likewise everything that he had. *And Jacob was left alone; and a man wrestled with him until the breaking of the day.* When the man saw that he did not prevail against Jacob, he touched the hollow of his thigh; and Jacob's thigh was put out of joint as

he wrestled with him. Then he said, "Let me go, for the day is breaking." *But Jacob said, "I will not let you go, unless you bless me."* And he said to him, "What is your name?" And he said, "Jacob." Then he said, *"Your name shall no more be called Jacob, but Israel, for you have striven with God and with men, and have prevailed."* Then Jacob asked him, "Tell me, I pray, your name." But he said, "Why is it that you ask my name?" And there he blessed him. So Jacob called the name of the place *Peniel,* saying, "For *I have seen God face to face,* and yet my life is preserved." The sun rose upon him as he passed Penuel, *limping because of his thigh.*

(Genesis 32:22–31)

Several aspects of this passage are important.

First, notice the entire encounter takes place at night. Indeed, the impression is that Jacob spends the entire night wrestling with the man—right until the breaking of dawn. The struggle depicted between the two is extremely intense. In fact, the Hebrew word for "wrestle" (Hebrew *'abaq*) is the same word as "dust" (Hebrew *'abaq*), implying that they wrestled on the ground the entire night.[6]

Second, notice that the identity of the person with whom Jacob wrestles is ambiguous. On the one hand, Scripture says that it is "a man." On the other hand, Jacob himself identifies the person with whom he wrestles as "God" (Hebrew *'elohim*). That is why he calls the place *Peniel* (Hebrew for "face of God"), because he has "seen God face to face" (Genesis 32:30).[7] If so, this would help explain why Jacob's opponent demands he let him go before daybreak. As long as it is night, the face of Jacob's opponent is (at least somewhat) veiled. As God declares elsewhere, "man shall not see me and live" (Exodus 33:20). Still, Jacob does have a "face to face" experience, in that he encounters the presence of God.

Lastly, when God sees Jacob's stubborn refusal to let him go, God wounds him by putting his "thigh" out of joint.[8] Thus, Jacob leaves the encounter with God having received *a blessing and a wound.* The blessing seems to be that God has given him a new name.[9] Instead of being known as Jacob (Hebrew for "supplanter"), he will now be known as Israel (Hebrew for "he who strives with God").[10] In both ways, Jacob leaves the nighttime struggle with God a changed man. He has been exalted by the gift of the name and humbled by the permanent wound he has received, which leaves him limping for the rest of his life.

In sum, because Jacob is the father of the twelve tribes of Israel, he is also a model for the people of Israel who bear his name. In this light, it follows that those who bear his name—the Israelites—will likewise be defined in some way not only by the fact that they are chosen by God to receive divine blessing but also by the fact that they, too, will "strive with God" in prayer.[11] Indeed, the entire book of Psalms consists of prayer after prayer of the heart that strives after and often wrestles with God.

JESUS AND THE BATTLE OF PRAYER

As we've already seen, there are plenty of places in the Gospels in which Jesus describes the battle against sin and evil that his disciples will have to face. Here, however, we simply want to focus on one famous parable in which Jesus describes prayer itself as a kind of battle or struggle with a God who seems disinclined to answer.

The Parable of the Persistent Widow

If there is any parable that depicts the drama of prayer as a battle of faith, it is the famous Parable of the Persistent Widow:

He told them a parable, to the effect that they ought *always to pray* and *not lose heart.* He said, "In a certain city there was a judge who neither feared God nor regarded man; and there was a widow in that city who kept coming to him and saying, 'Vindicate me against my adversary.' For a while he refused; but afterward he said to himself, 'Though I neither fear God nor regard man, *yet because this widow bothers me,* I will vindicate her, *or she will wear me out by her continual coming.*' " And the Lord said, "Hear what the unrighteous judge says. *And will not God vindicate his elect, who cry to him day and night? Will he delay long over them? I tell you, he will vindicate them speedily.* Nevertheless, when the Son of man comes, will he find faith on earth?"

(Luke 18:1–8)

Several aspects of this parable need to be highlighted.

First, in this case, the evangelist Luke begins by telling us exactly what the upshot of the parable is about: prayer that is both continual and persistent. Followers of Jesus are to pray "always" or "at all times" (Greek *pantote*) and not "lose enthusiasm," "be discouraged," or "give up" (Greek *engkakeō*).[12]

Second, the parable revolves around two characters: an unrighteous judge who neither keeps the commandments nor shows any concern for others, and a persistent widow, who keeps coming to the judge to demand that he give her justice. In an ancient Jewish context, such a judge would be regarded as especially wicked, since he was breaking the Law of Moses, which commands care for widows: "You shall not afflict any widow or orphan. If you do afflict them, and they cry out to me, I will surely hear their cry" (Exodus 22:22–23).[13]

The Punching Widow

Third, although the unrighteous judge refuses to answer the widow's pleas "for a while" (Luke 18:4), he eventually relents. Although it is difficult to see in English, in the original Greek, it is not just the *persistence* of the widow that moves the unrighteous judge to act. It is also the possible threat of being *punched* by her. The Greek verb translated as "wear out" (RSV) literally means "to hit under the eye"—a term taken from ancient boxing.[14] Thus, a more literal translation would be this:

> Because this widow bothers me, I will vindicate her, *lest in the end she come and give me a black eye!*
> (Luke 18:5)[15]

Seen in this light, this story should perhaps be called the Parable of the *Punching* Widow! She is not merely persistent; she is pugilistic. She will stop at nothing, including striking the judge in the face, until her petition is granted.

And this, of course, is the point of the parable. Jesus is not just teaching his disciples to be persistent in prayer. He is not just teaching them to pray constantly. He is teaching them to pray with desperation and tenacity. He is teaching them to pray like the punching widow, who absolutely *refuses* to give up—no matter how powerless or fruitless her attempts may seem. He is teaching them, like Jacob, to refuse to let go of God in prayer until they receive a blessing, even if they get wounded in the process.

In order to do so, Jesus uses a standard ancient Jewish argument of "from less to greater."[16] If even a wicked judge will give justice to the persistent prayer of a lowly widow, then how much more will the good God hear the prayers of his beloved people, who "cry to him day and night" (Luke 18:7)? Indeed, from an ancient Jewish perspective, if God did not answer the prayers of a widow, he would be violating his own law about caring for widows in their affliction. Thus, Jesus declares, "I tell you, he will vindicate them speedily" or "soon" (Luke 18:8).[17]

With that said, Jesus does end on a somewhat ominous note when he states, "Nevertheless, when the Son of man comes, will he find faith on earth?" (Luke 18:8). These words reveal that the entire Parable of the Persistent Widow is ultimately about *the virtue of faith*. Although we tend to use the word "faith" in English to refer primarily to "belief" that something is true, in ancient Greek, "faith" (Greek *pistis*) also means "fidelity."[18] In other words, Jesus is using the widow as a model for *fidelity* to prayer—even when it seems as though God, like the judge, is deaf or indifferent.

THE BATTLE OF PRAYER

Both Jewish Scripture and Jesus are quite clear that insofar as prayer involves a relationship with God, it involves much more than just words, gestures, or even experiences of consolation and illumination. At its heart, like all relationships, prayer is a struggle. It is a battle against ourselves and others, the collision of two wills who love each other but whose desires and plans do not always correspond exactly. With this in mind, we will bring this chapter to a close by highlighting several aspects of the battle of prayer that are crucial to making spiritual progress.

The Battle to Rise and Pray

It is no coincidence that Jacob wrestled with God during the night, when he was alone—not when he was with his family traveling on the way. The first battle that will have to be fought every day, day in and day out, involves the absolutely unfailing commitment to rise every morning at a fixed hour, no matter what, and spend time in prayer. In the words of John Climacus:

Give the first fruits of your day to the Lord, for it will determine the rest of the day. An excellent servant of the Lord once said to me something well worth hearing: *"I can tell from my morning how the rest of the day will go."*[19]

Rest assured, this is the first fight to be fought. The only way to ever make progress in the spiritual life is to resolve to rise like Jacob and Jesus in the darkness, where we can be alone and wrestle with God. As Thomas à Kempis teaches, this means fighting against the temptation to waste time that we could be spending in prayer:

> If you avoid unnecessary conversation and idle visits, as well as a preoccupation with news and various reports, you will find sufficient and appropriate time for good meditations. . . . *Anyone who has set his heart on progressing spiritually will do well to spend time apart from the crowd, as Jesus did.*[20]

In other words, resolve every day to rise from sleep and make spending time alone with God a top priority. By doing so, we will learn, as Jacob did, just how weak and how strong we really are.[21]

The Struggle Against Distraction

Even if we win the battle to rise and pray, as soon as we do, another battle awaits us: the war against distraction. Anyone who has ever struggled with distraction during prayer will find the description of John Cassian very familiar:

> Whatever our soul was thinking about before the time of prayer inevitably occurs to us when we pray. . . . For the mind in prayer is shaped by the state that it was previously in, and, when we sink into prayer, the image of the same deeds, words, and thoughts plays itself out before our eyes.[22]

So, what are we to do? What *not* to do is to begin chasing down each distraction. Instead, all that we need to do is gently turn our hearts back to God. Take the advice of John Climacus:

> Fight always with your thoughts and call them back when they wander away. God does not demand of those under obedience that their thoughts be totally undistracted when they pray. And do not lose heart when your thoughts are stolen away. Just remain calm, and constantly call your mind back.[23]

From a certain point of view, some distractions during prayer can actually be *helpful,* since "a distraction reveals to us *what we are attached to.*"[24] Seen in this light, they can provide us with the opportunity to humbly ask God to turn our hearts away from worldly anxieties and trifles and toward the One whom we should love above all things. At the same time, we need to be sure not to invite distractions by trying to combine other tasks with our time of prayer.[25]

The Problem of "Unanswered" Prayer

The third and final battle of prayer involves the subject Jesus speaks of in the Parable of the Persistent Widow: the problem of unanswered prayer. This is the battle that takes place when we petition God over and over again for some seemingly good thing— whether it be the gift of some grace or deliverance from some suffering or evil—and the only response is . . . silence. The sometimes-crushing disappointment of not being answered according to our own will raises the perennial question, "What good does it do to pray?"[26] This is what some might call the "scandal" or "stumbling block" of prayer. As a result of feeling as if they are not being heard, many souls, tragically, stop praying altogether.

How do we win this battle? Why does God allow us to be like

the widow who cries out day and night but hears no answer and receives no justice? Consider the advice of the ancient Christian writer Evagrius of Pontus and Francis de Sales:

> Do not be troubled if you do not immediately receive from God what you ask him; *for he desires to do something even greater for you, while you cling to him in prayer.*[27]

> If it should happen that you find no joy or comfort in meditation . . . , I urge you not to be disturbed. . . . Repeat Jacob's words, *"Lord, I will not let you go until you bless me."*[28]

In other words, don't stop praying! Even if our exact petitions are never granted to us in this life, the very fact that unanswered prayer drives us to spend more time drawing close to God and begging him for deliverance is itself a gift of grace. By perseverance in prayer, our hearts become gradually more and more conformed to the will of God—whatever it may be. Like Jesus in the Garden of Gethsemane, who asked the Father to take the "cup" of suffering away from him if it were at all possible, unanswered prayer teaches us to learn to say with him, "Not my will, but yours, be done" (Luke 22:42). This is no small gift, for in these seven words are hidden the secret of holiness and happiness.

22

The Dark Night

In the night my hand is stretched out without wearying;
my soul refuses to be comforted.
—The Book of Psalms (77:2)

A FOURTH KEY TO MAKING PROGRESS IN THE FIRST STAGES OF SPIRI-
tual growth is to be aware of two very different but very common
spiritual experiences.

On the one hand, the spiritual classics agree that, after conversion, beginners often experience spiritual sweetness, light, and a
strong sense of God's presence during prayer. For example, one
ancient Christian writer describes the time just after conversion
as "that initial happy warmth."[1] Likewise, one medieval mystic
speaks of the "gift" of "sensible sweetness" or "spiritual consolation" that God often gives those just starting down the path.[2]
Finally, modern spiritual writers emphasize that "all those beginning to serve God" commonly experience "the sweet taste of sensible devotion" and "the pleasant light that invites them to hasten
forward in the path to God."[3]

On the other hand, the spiritual classics also agree that after a
soul has been faithfully living a life of prayer, examination of
heart, meditation, and avoiding vices, it ordinarily happens that
the spiritual lights "go out." At some point, these experiences of consolation are taken away and replaced with spiritual dryness, dark-

ness, and a feeling of God's absence during prayer.[4] Consider the following quotations:

> Sometimes he makes them dry and barren, sluggish at prayer, sleepy and unilluminated . . . making them think . . . that they are only regressing.
>
> —John Climacus (7th century)[5]

> When consolation is taken from you, do not immediately despair. . . . None of this is new or unknown to those who are experienced in the ways of God.
>
> —Thomas à Kempis (15th century)[6]

> *The night of sense is common and comes to many: these are the beginners.* . . . When they are going about these spiritual exercises with the greatest delight and pleasure, and when they believe that the sun of Divine favour is shining most brightly upon them, God turns all this light of theirs into darkness.
>
> —John of the Cross (16th century)[7]

In his classic work, *Dark Night of the Soul,* the great Spanish mystic John of the Cross refers to this experience as the *"dark night of the senses."*[8] He singles out three signs of this dark night: (1) dryness in prayer; (2) a desire to serve God but a lack of enjoyment in doing so; and (3) increasing difficulty in continuing to meditate.[9] Notice that this "night" is not the same as depression, illness, or tragedy. Nor should it be confused with that emptiness that comes from falling back into sin or growing lax in prayer because of acedia (see chapter 17). Rather, the dark night of the senses is something that happens when a Christian is faithfully living a spiritual life yet begins to lose all consolation in doing so.

Why does God allow this to happen? What is the purpose of

this "dark night"? And where do the spiritual writers find this idea in the Bible? In this chapter, we will take a closer look at what Scripture says about this common experience of spiritual desolation and how to conduct oneself in the midst of it.

THE DARK NIGHT IN JEWISH SCRIPTURE

If there is any place in Jewish Scripture where the experience of spiritual dryness, darkness, and absence of consolation is on full display, it is in the book of Psalms. For our purposes, two in particular—Psalm 77 and Psalm 143—stand out as premier examples of the dark night of the senses.

Psalm 77: The Dark Night of the Soul

The first of these two may be the most explicit description of the dark night of the senses in the entire Bible. Attributed to Asaph, one of King David's leading singers in the Temple (1 Chronicles 6:31–39), Psalm 77 describes the desolation of a soul that continues to pray and meditate but hears nothing from God:

> I cry aloud to God,
> aloud to God, that he may hear me.
> In the day of my trouble I seek the Lord;
>> *in the night my hand is stretched out without wearying;*
>> *my soul refuses to be comforted.*
>
> *I think of God, and I moan;*
>> *I meditate, and my spirit faints.* . . .
> *I commune with my heart in the night;*
>> *I meditate and search my spirit:*
> "Will the Lord spurn for ever,
>> and never again be favorable? . . .

> *Has God forgotten to be gracious?*
> *Has he in anger shut up his compassion?"* . . .

> I will meditate on all your work,
>   and muse on your mighty deeds.
>
> (Psalm 77:1–3, 6–9, 12)

Notice here the explicit language of a spiritual dark "night" (Hebrew *laylah*) of the "soul" (Hebrew *nephesh*) (Psalm 77:2). This may well be the origin of the title of John of the Cross's spiritual masterpiece.[10] Notice also that the psalmist's trouble is not focused on exterior trials and tribulations. Rather, his suffering is interior: his soul refuses to be comforted during his meditation.[11] He begs God for help, over and over again, but in the end, his spirit is still weak and faint. Although faithful to prayer, he feels as if he has been spurned by God, and he wonders whether God is angry with him. Despite all this, he does not stop crying out to God. His response to the experience of God's absence and the darkness of desolation is to keep praying.

Psalm 143: Spiritual Desolation and Dryness

The second key example of the dark night of the senses comes from Psalm 143.[12] This psalm, attributed to King David himself, vividly describes the experience of dryness and darkness during meditation:

> Hear my prayer, O LORD;
>   give ear to my supplications! . . .

> For the enemy has pursued me;
>   he has crushed my life to the ground;
>   *he has made me sit in darkness* like those long dead.

Therefore *my spirit faints within me;*
  my heart within me is desolate. . . .

  I meditate on all that you have done. . . .
I stretch out my hands to you;
  my soul thirsts for you like a parched land.

Make haste to answer me, O LORD! . . .
Hide not your face from me,
  lest I be like those who go down to the Pit.
Let me hear in the morning of your steadfast love,
  for in you I put my trust.
  (Psalm 143:1, 3–8)[13]

Notice once again that the "darkness" (Hebrew *machshak*) experienced by David is directly linked to his "meditation" (Hebrew *hagah*) (Psalm 143:3, 5). When he speaks of an "enemy" (Psalm 143:3), he does not seem to be referring to external persecution but rather to interior suffering—a "numbing of the heart" that leaves him spiritually crushed and in darkness.[14] Moreover, during this time, David also experiences such dryness that he compares his soul to a waterless desert. Finally, there is also the feeling of God's absence: it seems as though God has turned away his "face" (Hebrew *panim*) from David—a Hebrew word that also means "presence."[15] Despite all this, David does not stop praying. Instead, he puts his trust in God that the darkness will eventually give way to the light of "the morning" (Psalm 143:8).

JESUS AND THE DARK NIGHT

As far as I can tell, Jesus never directly describes the experience of spiritual dryness, darkness, and divine absence later known as the "dark night of the senses."[16] However, there is one parable of Jesus that describes *the kind of prayer* that is necessary to practice *during* the dark night of the senses. I am speaking here of the Parable of the Friend at Midnight (Luke 11:5-13). Let's take a few moments to look closely at this very important passage.

The Parable of the Friend at Midnight

In the Gospel of Luke, Jesus gives his disciples three principal parables on prayer: the Pharisee and the Tax Collector (Luke 18:9-14), the Persistent Widow (Luke 18:1-8), and the following:

> Which of you who has a friend will go to him *at midnight* and say to him, "Friend, lend me three loaves; for a friend of mine has arrived on a journey, and I have nothing to set before him"; and he will answer from within, "Do not bother me; the door is now shut, and my children are with me in bed; I cannot get up and give you anything"? *I tell you, though he will not get up and give him anything because he is his friend, yet because of his importunity he will rise and give him whatever he needs. And I tell you, Ask, and it will be given you; seek, and you will find; knock, and it will be opened to you.* For every one who asks receives, and he who seeks finds, and to him who knocks it will be opened. What father among you, if his son asks for a fish, will instead of a fish give him a serpent; or if he asks for an egg, will give him a scorpion? *If you then, who are evil, know how to give good gifts to your children, how much more will the heavenly Father give the Holy Spirit to those who ask him!*

> (Luke 11:5-13)

In order to understand how Jesus' words can be applied to the experience of the dark night of the senses, four points are necessary.

First, by setting the story at midnight, Jesus is once again alluding to the practice of secret prayer. For in Jewish Scripture, midnight is singled out as a special time of prayer, when the soul can be alone with God:

> At *midnight* I rise to praise you,
>> because of your righteous ordinances.
>
> (Psalm 119:62)

Just as the psalmist prays to God in the darkness of midnight, so, too, the friend in the parable makes his requests known in the privacy and intimacy of the night.[17]

Second, Jesus is teaching his disciples to shamelessly ask the Father for whatever they need. Although some English translations speak of the "persistence" (NAB) or "importunity" (RSV) of the friend at midnight, the Greek literally says that he is "without shame" (Greek *anaideia*) (Luke 11:8).[18] In making his request, he is not worried about how he looks but is entirely focused on getting what he needs.

Third, Jesus is teaching his disciples to pray with absolute confidence that the Father will hear and answer them. After using his standard formula for making a solemn declaration—"I tell you"—Jesus gives his disciples three commands (Luke 11:9):

1. *Ask:* "and it will be given you"
2. *Seek:* "and you will find"
3. *Knock:* "and it will be opened to you"

These are not suggestions. Jesus *commands* his disciples to pray with confidence in being heard. This confidence is not rooted in their own effort or worthiness but in Jesus' solemn promise and in the goodness of God. After all, if a sinful human being will give his friend whatever he needs because he wants to get back to sleep, and a sinful human father will give good gifts to his children, then how much more will the heavenly Father—who never sleeps and who is perfectly good—answer the prayers of disciples who pray with faith.

Finally—and this is important—Jesus ends by relating everything he has just said about prayer to "the supreme gift, the Holy Spirit."[19] Experience shows that human beings often ask God for material gifts—such as money, possessions, physical health, and success—that will not necessarily help them on the way to eternal life.[20] Jesus gives no guarantee that the Father will grant such worldly requests. He is not teaching his disciples that the Father will give them whatever they *want* but that he will give them whatever they *need*. No matter how deep the darkness may be, they can be completely confident that if they ask God for the gift of the Holy Spirit, they will assuredly receive it.[21] For Jesus, who does not lie, gives his solemn word: "*I tell you*, Ask, and it will be given you*" (Luke 11:9).

THE DARK NIGHT IN CHRISTIAN TRADITION

With all of this in mind, we bring this chapter to a close with a few practical but important points from later Christian tradition.

Do Not Be Surprised by Spiritual Dryness and Darkness
The first thing that needs to be said is that followers of Jesus who are striving to live lives of prayer should not be surprised *when*— not if—they begin to experience dryness and difficulty in prayer. As John of the Cross says:

> The night of sense is common and comes to many: these are the beginners. . . . *Ordinarily no great time passes after their beginnings before they enter this night of sense; and the great major-*

ity of them do in fact enter it, for they will generally be seen to fall into these aridities.[22]

In other words, the dark night of the senses is not a rare experience, reserved for the few. It is something common, experienced by many. Therefore, there is no reason it should catch us off guard.

Do Not Stop Praying

Equally important: if we begin to experience spiritual dryness and darkness during prayer, we must keep going down the spiritual path. *We must not turn back.* As Francis de Sales teaches:

> Devotion does not consist in the sweetness, delight, consolation, and sensible tenderness . . . [that take place] when we perform various spiritual exercises. . . . Many souls experience these tender, consoling feelings but still remain very vicious. . . . True devotion consists in a constant, resolute, prompt, and active will to do whatever we know is pleasing to God.[23]

In other words, *making spiritual progress is not about feeling good during prayer; it is about growing in virtue.* Too many people share the widespread misconception that spiritual consolations are the heart of prayer and worship. For this reason, as John of the Cross laments, many souls tragically abandon the spiritual path as soon as their prayer becomes dry:

> *These souls turn back at such a time if there is none who understands them; they abandon the road or lose courage;* or, at the least, they are hindered from going farther by the great trouble which they take in advancing along the road of meditation and reasoning.[24]

Like Asaph in the psalm, when prayer becomes dry and dark, we are quick to assume that something is wrong or, worse, that God has abandoned us. But nothing could be further from the truth. Like King David, we must keep praying, even in the midst of the night.

Be Still and Know That He Is God

Third, if we continue to experience increasing difficulty in meditation, we should not force it. In this regard, John of the Cross gives crucial instruction:

> The way in which they are to conduct themselves in this night of sense is to devote themselves not at all to reasoning and meditation, since this is not the time for it, but *to allow the soul to remain in peace and quietness, although it may seem clear to them that they are doing nothing and wasting their time,* . . . contenting themselves with merely a peaceful and loving attentiveness toward God.[25]

In other words, if we try to meditate but find it impossible, we should not insist on "doing something." Now is the time to allow God to do his work in the soul. As the book of Psalms says, *"Be still,* and know that I am God" (Psalm 46:10).

The Purpose of the Dark Night

Finally, and perhaps most important of all, the *reason* God allows the dark night of the senses to take place is *so that we can grow in virtue.*[26]

For example, the experience of dryness in prayer helps us grow in diligence by teaching us to pray not because it feels good or because we get something out of it but because we love God. Likewise, the experience of difficulty meditating helps us grow in diligence by teaching us to do what is right, even when it takes effort.

The experience of desolation helps us grow in patience as we willingly suffer and wait for God to deliver us.[27] Above all, the experience of spiritual darkness helps us grow in humility by making us realize how weak we really are and that everything we receive is a gift of God's grace.[28]

In fact, according to John of the Cross, it is precisely during the dark night of the senses that the soul "acquires the virtues opposed to" the capital sins[29] and begins to bear the "fruits of the Holy Spirit"[30] mentioned by the apostle Paul:

> The fruit of the Spirit is love, joy, peace, patience, kindness, goodness, faithfulness, gentleness, self-control.
>
> (Galatians 5:22–23)

In short, if we want the trees of our hearts to grow in the capital virtues and begin to bear the supernatural fruit of the Holy Spirit, we must be willing to let God transform us as we pass through the dryness and desolation of the dark night of the senses. Jesus has given us his solemn promise: if we, like the friend at midnight, are persistent in our prayer, God will give us whatever we need—above all, the gift of the Holy Spirit. For after the winter, the spring comes. After the darkness, the dawn breaks.

23
⌒

THE LIVING WATER

Sir, give me this water, that I may not thirst.
—The Samaritan Woman (John 4:15)

A FIFTH KEY TO MAKING PROGRESS ON THE SPIRITUAL JOURNEY—
and the one with which we will bring this book to a close—is the
realization that in the end, *even prayer itself is a gift from God.* As the
encounter of the human heart with the infinite God of the universe, prayer is not just something that we choose to do; it is
something that God does in us, through the grace of the Holy
Spirit.

Over the centuries, the saints and doctors of the spiritual life
have been keenly aware that prayer itself—especially contemplative prayer—is a gift. Consider, for example, the words of ancient,
medieval, and modern Christian writers:

> The word Spirit is the name which Paul gives to [this] kind
> of grace and to the soul who receives it. . . . The spiritual
> man . . . has the gift of prayer.
> —John Chrysostom (4th century)[1]

> When God gives you spiritual consolation, receive it with
> thanksgiving, but reflect that it is a gift of God, not the result
> of your merit.
> —Thomas à Kempis (15th century)[2]

God does not allow us to drink of this water of perfect contemplation whenever we like: the choice is not ours; this Divine union is something quite supernatural, given that it may
cleanse the soul.

—Teresa of Avila (16th century)[3]

How can this be? After all we've learned about the battle of prayer
and the effort required to make spiritual progress, how can it be
that prayer is also something God does in us?

In order to answer these questions, we will bring our study to
an end by returning to where we began: Jesus' encounter with the
Samaritan woman at the well. Throughout history, many spiritual writers have pointed to this passage as a kind of icon of
what happens in a soul during prayer.[4] As we will see, Jesus gives
us the key to understanding prayer as a gift of grace when he offers to give the Samaritan woman the mysterious "gift" of "living
water."

THE LIVING WATER IN JEWISH SCRIPTURE

In order to understand the words of Jesus, we first need to make
some brief points about the image of "living water" in the Old
Testament.

The Water That Cleanses from Sin

On a literal level, "living water" (Hebrew *mayim hayyim*) simply
means "flowing water"—as opposed to the stagnant water kept in
a cistern.[5] In Jewish Scripture, only living water could be used as
"the water for impurity, for the removal of sin" (Numbers 19:9).
Such water prepared a person to enter the dwelling place of God
and worship him in the Tabernacle:

For the unclean they shall take some ashes of the burnt sin offering, and *living water* shall be added in a vessel; then a clean person shall take hyssop, and dip it in the water, and sprinkle it upon the tent, . . . and upon the persons who were there.

(Numbers 19:17–18)[6]

Notice here the living water is combined with the ashes of a sacrifice in order for it to cleanse the people from sin. Notice also that a branch of "hyssop" is used to sprinkle the living water. This is the same kind of branch used to sprinkle the sacrificial blood of the Passover lamb when God redeems Israel (see Exodus 12:22). In other words, "living water" is sacrificial water that makes a sinful person capable of entering into God's presence.

The Living Water: God Himself

On more than one occasion in Jewish Scripture, God *himself* is described as "living water," who alone can quench the spiritual thirst of his people. Consider the following:

> As a deer longs
> for *flowing streams*,
> so longs my soul
> for you, O God.
> *My soul thirsts for God,*
> *for the living God.*
> (Psalm 42:1–2)[7]

Thus says the LORD: . . .
> *"[My people] have forsaken me,*
> *the fountain of living waters,*
> and hewed out cisterns for themselves,

> broken cisterns,
>> that can hold no water."
>> (Jeremiah 2:5, 13)

In both of these quotations, God himself is described as the only one who can ever quench the spiritual thirst of his people. The psalmist longs to satisfy his thirst for God by entering into his presence in "the house of God," that is, the Temple (Psalm 42:4).[8] And though the people of Israel try to slake their thirst with the lifeless water of "cisterns"—that is, with things other than God—in the end, these earthly realities cannot satisfy.[9]

The Water Flowing from the Temple

Lastly, in Jewish Scripture, the prophets describe the coming age of salvation as a time when a river of "living water" will flow out of the new Temple in Jerusalem to cleanse the world from sin and give life to all that it touches.

For example, the prophet Ezekiel has a vision of a river of water "flowing down from below the south end of the threshold of the temple, south of the altar" (Ezekiel 47:1). Although it starts out small, this stream quickly becomes a massive river that gives life to everything it touches (Ezekiel 47:3–12). Likewise, the prophet Zechariah foretells that on the same day that a mysterious figure is put to death, a fountain of "living waters" shall flow from Jerusalem:

> When they look on *him whom they have pierced,* they shall mourn for him. . . . On that day there shall be *a fountain* opened for the house of David and the inhabitants of Jerusalem *to cleanse them from sin and uncleanness.* . . . On that day *living waters shall flow* out from Jerusalem.
>> (Zechariah 12:10; 13:1; 14:8)

Though Zechariah does not use the word "Messiah," since ancient times, the one who was "pierced" has been identified as the long-awaited king.[10] Thus, according to Jewish Scripture, on the day that the future Davidic king is killed, an unceasing fountain of "living waters" shall flow from Jerusalem to cover the whole world and cleanse it from sin.

JESUS AND THE LIVING WATER

With this background in mind, we can now return to Jesus' offer of "living water" to the Samaritan woman and understand it in its ancient Jewish context:

> [Jesus] had to pass through Samaria. . . . Jacob's well was there, and so *Jesus, wearied as he was with his journey, sat down beside the well. It was about the sixth hour.*
>
> There came a woman of Samaria to draw water. *Jesus said to her, "Give me a drink."* . . . The Samaritan woman said to him, "How is it that you, a Jew, ask a drink of me, a woman of Samaria?" For Jews have no dealings with Samaritans. Jesus answered her, *"If you knew the gift of God, and who it is that is saying to you, 'Give me a drink,' you would have asked him, and he would have given you living water."* The woman said to him, "Sir, you have nothing to draw with, and the well is deep; where do you get that living water?" . . . Jesus said to her, *"Every one who drinks of this water will thirst again, but whoever drinks of the water that I shall give him will never thirst; the water that I shall give him will become in him a spring of water welling up to eternal life."* The woman said to him, *"Sir, give me this water,* that I may not thirst, nor come here to draw."
>
> (John 4:4, 6–7, 9–11, 13–15)

Many pages have been written about this rich and beautiful episode.[11] For our purposes here, a few observations will suffice.

The Living Water = the Holy Spirit

When Jesus promises to give the Samaritan woman "living water," he is not talking about ordinary flowing water. He is speaking about the *spiritual* water that wells up *inside* people and leads them to eternal life. As he says later, while speaking in the Temple,

> *If any one thirst, let him come to me and drink.* He who believes in me, as the scripture has said, *"Out of his heart shall flow rivers of living water."* Now this he said about *the Spirit, which those who believed in him were to receive;* for as yet the Spirit had not been given, because Jesus was not yet glorified.
>
> (John 7:37–39)

Once we know that in Jewish Scripture, God himself is identified as the "fountain of living waters" (Jeremiah 2:13), then Jesus' offer of "living water" to the Samaritan woman begins to make sense. In short, Jesus is inviting her to believe in him so that she can receive the gift of eternal life through the indwelling Spirit of God, who alone is able to satisfy the spiritual thirst of the human heart.[12] Later on, during the Last Supper, Jesus will explicitly reveal to his disciples that he is going to give them "the Spirit of truth," who not only will dwell "with" them but also will be "in" them (John 14:16–17). Although the Samaritan woman clearly does not yet fully understand what Jesus is offering her, his words nevertheless move her to ask him to give her this gift: "Sir, give me this water, that I may not thirst, nor come here to draw" (John 4:15).[13]

The Living Water and the Crucifixion

But when exactly does Jesus give the gift of living water? To be sure, it is only after the Resurrection that Jesus breathes on the disciples and explicitly says, "Receive the Holy Spirit" (John 20:22). However, if we look at the Crucifixion in the light of Jewish Scripture, we discover that the living water of salvation first begins to flow on the day of Jesus' death:

> Jesus, knowing that all was now finished, said (to fulfil the scripture), "I thirst." A bowl full of common wine stood there; so they put a sponge full of the wine on hyssop and held it to his mouth. *When Jesus had received the wine, he said, "It is finished"; and he bowed his head and gave up his spirit. . . . But one of the soldiers pierced his side with a spear, and at once there came out blood and water. . . .* These things took place that the scripture might be fulfilled, . . . "They shall look upon him whom they have pierced."
>
> (John 19:28–30, 34, 36–37)[14]

Just as Zechariah foretold that on the day that the Messiah was "pierced," a fountain of "living waters" would be opened up in Jerusalem to cleanse the world from "sin" (Zechariah 12:10–14:8), so now the cleansing blood and water flow from the pierced side of Jesus crucified. And just as the prophet Ezekiel foretold that one day a stream of life-giving water would flow from the side of the new Temple (Ezekiel 47:1–2), so now a stream of blood and water flows from the side of Jesus—whose "body" is God's "temple" (John 2:21). And just as Jesus had stood up in the Temple and declared that the "living water" would flow from his "heart," so now, in his dying breath, he bows his head and gives up "his spirit" (John 7:38; 19:30).[15]

In short, it is here, here on Calvary, that Jesus ultimately answers the request of the Samaritan woman: "Give me this water"

(John 4:15). In support of this point, notice three striking parallels between the two scenes:

Jesus beside the Well	The Crucifixion
"the sixth hour"	"the sixth hour"
"Give me a drink"	"I thirst"
"living water"	"water" flows from Jesus' heart
(John 4:6–7, 10)	(John 19:14, 28, 34)

Once we see these connections, we realize that when Jesus asks the Samaritan woman for a drink, he is not just thirsting for earthly water. *He is thirsting for her salvation*—and for the salvation of the whole world—which will begin when the living water starts to flow from the temple of his body and the altar of his sacred heart.[16] He is thirsting for the day when the Holy Spirit will begin to wash over the world in a flood of grace, to cleanse it from sin and make all things new through the gift of eternal life.

BESIDE THE WELL WITH JESUS

With all this in mind, we can bring our journey together to a close. Before doing so, however, I want to reiterate that in this book, we have focused only on the *beginning* of the spiritual path of Jesus—commonly known as the purgative way. There is much, much more that could be said about Jesus and the biblical roots of the illuminative and unitive ways. For now, we will end with a few final thoughts that flow from the encounter between Jesus and the woman at the well and shed light on the mystery of the gift of prayer.

The Spirit Poured into Our Hearts

First and foremost, through faith and baptism, followers of Jesus have been filled with the living water of the Holy Spirit. In the words of the apostle Paul:

> By *one Spirit* we were all baptized into one body—Jews or Greeks, slaves or free—and all were made *to drink of one Spirit.*
>
> (1 Corinthians 12:13)

> God's love has been *poured into our hearts* through *the Holy Spirit* who has been given to us.
>
> (Romans 5:5)

Notice here that in both sayings, Paul describes the Holy Spirit as living water that has the power to both quench our spiritual thirst and fill the wells of our hearts with the supernatural love of God.

The Spirit Helps Us in Our Weakness

Second, if the Holy Spirit has really been poured into our hearts, then whenever we pray *from the heart,* it is not just something we do on our own. Rather, the Holy Spirit who dwells with us prays with us and for us. The living water that has been given to us wells up inside our hearts and fills us with the love of God. In the unforgettable words of Paul:

> *The Spirit helps us in our weakness; for we do not know how to pray as we ought, but the Spirit himself intercedes for us with sighs too deep for words.* And he who searches the hearts of men

knows what is the mind of the Spirit, because the Spirit in-
tercedes for the saints according to the will of God.

(Romans 8:26–27)

If you have ever felt while trying to pray like you don't know what
you're doing, then take heart. You are not alone. As Paul says, because only God can ever really fathom the mystery of each human
heart, only the Holy Spirit can truly pray in us and for us in ways
that go infinitely beyond human words. This means humbly ad-
mitting that we need the Spirit of God to teach us, to guide us,
and to pray in us. We need the living water of the Holy Spirit to
well up within us and water the "tree" of our hearts so that we
might grow in virtue and bear fruit. For just as Jesus is the model
of Christian prayer, "the Holy Spirit is *the master of the interior
life*."[17]

Jesus Is Still Waiting at the Well

Finally, and most important of all, if we go to the wellspring of
prayer—every day, for the rest of our lives—we will discover something beautiful and mysterious. Like the Samaritan woman at the
well, we will discover that *Jesus is already there, waiting for us*. Consider these beautiful and unforgettable words:

> "If you knew the gift of God!" *The wonder of prayer is revealed
> beside the well where we come seeking water: there, Christ comes to
> meet every human being*. It is he who first seeks us and asks us
> for a drink. Jesus thirsts; his asking arises from the depths of
> God's desire for us. Whether we realize it or not, prayer is the
> encounter of God's thirst with ours. *God thirsts that we may
> thirst for him*.[18]

It's true: Jesus is still waiting at the well. Today, right now. At this
very moment, *Jesus is waiting beside the well of your heart*—and mine.

He is waiting for us to come to him, to sit with him, and to talk with him in prayer. He is waiting for us to bring our thirst to him, to bring our sorrows to him, to bring our hearts to him. He is waiting for us to simply *gaze* at him, in the silent mystery of love.

Above all, he is waiting for us to ask him, like the woman of Samaria once did, to give *us* the living water that will give us the strength to continue down the path that leads to eternal life. For, as Thérèse of Lisieux teaches us, Jesus *still thirsts:*

> The same God who declares He has no need to tell us when He is hungry did not fear to beg for a little water from the Samaritan woman. He was thirsty. But when He said: "Give me to drink," it was the *love* of His poor creature the Creator of the universe was seeking. *He was thirsty for love.*[19]

Thérèse is right. Jesus is still thirsty. He is thirsting for your love and for mine, for your salvation and for mine, and his thirst will not be quenched until the very last day, when the very last soul on earth says to him, "Lord, give me this water, that I may not thirst."

ACKNOWLEDGMENTS

I must begin by thanking Fr. Dennis Dinan for his extremely generous act of theological almsgiving to me when I was a young professor just getting started. This book would not exist if he had not been willing to donate so many volumes of spiritual theology to me at such a formative stage in my life. I am eternally grateful. I also could not have written it without the feedback of the students who participated in that first course I taught on the Bible and the spiritual life so many years ago at Our Lady of Holy Cross College (now University of Holy Cross), as well as later versions of the course at Notre Dame Seminary in New Orleans and the Augustine Institute Graduate School of Theology. Thank you all for helping me think through the biblical roots of Christian spirituality and for sharing insights from your own journeys.

I am also deeply grateful to my editors at Image Books, Keren Baltzer and Ashley Hong. Your excitement, encouragement, and support for this project from its inception gave me the courage to keep going and bring the book to a timely completion in the midst of the infamous year that was 2020! Likewise, I'm greatly indebted to my dear friend Gary Jansen, who was the first to think this book would be a good idea. Thank you, brother, for all you've done for me over these last ten years. I also want to offer a heartfelt thank-you to several friends and colleagues who read various drafts of the book and discussed the finer details of spiritual theology with me: Dr. Michael Barber, Fr. Michael Champagne,

C.J.C., Sr. Julia Darrenkamp, F.S.P., Dr. Scott Hefelfinger, Fr. Josh Johnson, Matthew Leonard, Fr. Jeffrey Montz, Dr. Tom Neal, Dr. Kevin Redmann, Todd Russell, Dr. Mario Sacasa, Jimmy Seghers, Fr. Mitch Semar, and Dr. John Sehorn. Your feedback was absolutely invaluable. A special word of gratitude goes to Archbishop Alfred C. Hughes for generously taking time to read the manuscript and share his wisdom gained from decades of teaching and living the Christian spiritual life. Thank you for being a good shepherd to me and my family. Once again, I am profoundly grateful to those friends—clergy, religious, and laity—who have supported me with their prayers. In particular, I want to thank the Discalced Carmelites of Lafayette, Louisiana, who promised to pray for me while I was writing this book. Thank you for your witness to Christ, for your joy, and for being my sisters. I do hope that I quoted enough Carmelites to make you happy!

I cannot end without expressing my gratitude and love for my wife, Elizabeth, and our children: Morgen, Aidan, Hannah, Marybeth, and Lillia. Elizabeth, who is a much better writer than I am, reads (and critiques!) everything I write and always helps me improve. But we have never had as many wonderful conversations about a manuscript as we did about this book. Thank you, Liz, for walking the path of Jesus with me all these many years. Finally, in a very special way, this book is dedicated to my daughter Hannah. In Hebrew, your name means "grace." May you be filled with God's grace all the days of your life so that you, too, can sing the ancient song of Hannah: "My heart exults in the LORD" (1 Samuel 2:1).

October 15, 2020
Memorial of St. Teresa of Avila,
Virgin and Doctor of the Church

NOTES

∽

Introduction

1. See Brant Pitre, *Spiritual Theology: Christian Prayer and the Three Stages of the Spiritual Life* (available at www.brantpitre.com) for an edited audio recording of the original lectures.

2. Unless otherwise noted, all translations of Luke 10:42 contained herein are the author's translation.

3. Regarding both these passages, Origen of Alexandria wrote, "I think no one can doubt that John here uses the terms 'children,' 'youths' or 'young men,' and 'fathers' according to *the age of the soul* and not of the body. . . . And [Paul] uses the expression 'babe in Christ' undoubtedly according to *the age of the soul* and not according to that of the flesh." Origen, *Commentary on the Song of Songs*, Prologue, in *An Exhortation to Martyrdom, Prayer and Selected Works*, trans. Rowan A. Greer, Classics of Western Spirituality (Mahwah, N.J.: Paulist, 1979), 221.

4. In ancient Eastern Christianity, see Origen of Alexandria, who links the books of Proverbs, Ecclesiastes, and the Song of Songs with spiritual "childhood," "youth," and "mature manhood" (Origen, *Commentary on the Song of Songs*, Prologue 2). Dionysius the Areopagite is the first to speak explicitly of three stages of "purification, illumination, and perfection" (Dionysius the Areopagite, *Celestial Hierarchy*, 3.2). John Climacus likewise describes the spiritual life in terms of three stages: "the beginning," "the middle stage," and "perfection" (John Climacus, *Ladder of Divine Ascent*, 28). In the Latin-speaking West, Augustine speaks of "charity" as being "nursed" in infancy, "fortified" in adolescence, and "perfected" in adulthood (Augustine, *Homilies on 1 John*, 5.4),

and Gregory the Great speaks of "three stages of conversion": "the beginning, the middle, and perfection" (Gregory the Great, *Morals in Job*, 24.11.28). In medieval Eastern Christianity, Niketas Stethatos speaks of "three stages": "the purgative, the illuminative, and finally the mystical, which is perfection itself" (Niketas Stethatos, *Gnostic Chapters*, 41). In medieval Western Christianity, Bonaventure of Bagnoregio writes an entire treatise book on the three stages of "purgation, illumination, and perfection" (Bonaventure, *The Threefold Way*, prologue 1), and Thomas Aquinas speaks of three "degrees of charity": that of "beginners," who are chiefly occupied with "avoiding sin," "the proficient," whose primary aim is to make "progress in good," and "the perfect," who desire "union with and the enjoyment of God" (Thomas Aquinas, *Summa Theologica*, II–II, q. 24, art. 9; cf. I–II, q. 102, art. 3). Catherine of Siena likewise speaks of the "three degrees" or "stages of the soul": the "imperfect," the "more perfect," and the "most perfect" (Catherine of Siena, *The Dialogue*, 56). In modern times, Ignatius of Loyola links the "First Week" and "Second Week" of his *Spiritual Exercises* with "the purgative way" and the "illuminative way" (Ignatius of Loyola, *Spiritual Exercises*, no. 10), and John of the Cross writes extensively about "the three states": "the purgative way," "the illuminative way," and "the unitive way" (John of the Cross, *The Spiritual Canticle*, theme 1–2). Most recently of all, John Paul II describes the Christian life as a path consisting of "three stages": "the purgative way, the illuminative way, and the unitive way" (John Paul II, *Memory and Identity*, 6.2–6). For the above quotations, see Origen, *Exhortation to Martyrdom*, 220; Pseudo-Dionysius, *The Complete Works*, trans. Colm Luibheid and Paul Rorem, Classics of Western Spirituality (Mahwah, N.J.: Paulist, 1987), 155; Saint John Climacus, *The Ladder of Divine Ascent*, rev. ed. (Boston: Holy Transfiguration Monastery, 2019), 235–36; Saint Augustine, *Homilies on the First Epistle of John*, trans. Boniface Ramsey, ed. Daniel E. Doyle, O.S.A., and Thomas Martin, O.S.A., vol. 1 (Hyde Park, N.Y.: New City Press, 2008), 79; Gregory the Great, *Moral Reflections on the Book of Job*, trans. Brian Kerns, O.C.S.O., vol. 5 (Collegeville, Minn.: Liturgical Press, 2019), 91 (unless otherwise noted, all translations from this edition); John Anthony McGuckin, trans., *The Book of Mystical Chapters: Meditations on the Soul's Ascent, from the Desert Fathers and Other Early Christian Contemplatives* (Boston: Shambhala,

2002), 117; Robert J. Karris, O.F.M., ed., *Works of St. Bonaventure*, vol. 10, *Writings on the Spiritual Life* (St. Bonaventure, N.Y.: Franciscan Institute, 2006), 90; St. Thomas Aquinas, *Summa Theologica: Complete English Edition in Five Volumes* (repr.; trans. Fathers of the English Dominican Province; Allen, Tex.: Christian Classics, 1981), 3.1275 (unless otherwise noted, all translations of the *Summa Theologica* contained herein are from this edition); Catherine of Siena, *The Dialogue*, trans. Suzanne Noffke, O.P. (Mahwah, N.J.: Paulist, 1980), 111 (unless otherwise noted, all translations of *The Dialogue* contained herein are from this edition); *The Spiritual Exercises of St. Ignatius*, Preface by Avery Dulles, S.J., trans. Louis J. Puhl, S.J. (New York: Vintage Books, 2000), 7 (unless otherwise noted, all translations of the *Spiritual Exercises* contained herein are from this edition); *The Collected Works of St. John of the Cross*, trans. Kieran Kavanaugh, O.C.D., and Otilio Rodriguez, O.C.D., 3rd ed. (Washington, D.C.: ICS Publications, 1991), 477; Pope John Paul II, *Memory and Identity: Conversations at the Dawn of a Millennium* (New York: Rizzoli, 2005), 28–29.

5. See, for example, Jordan Aumann, O.P., *Spiritual Theology* (London: Continuum, 1980), 116: "The three stages or degrees of charity are nothing more than divisions that characterize in a general way the infinite variety of aspects in the Christian life. The path of supernatural life is a winding path, and its stages offer a variety of transitions and levels that will differ with each individual. We must never think that the three basic stages are self-contained compartments, and that those who are at a given time in one stage will never participate in the activities of another stage."

6. See Frederick William Danker, ed., *A Greek-English Lexicon of the New Testament and Other Early Christian Literature*, 3rd ed. (Chicago: University of Chicago Press, 2000), 609–10. The Hebrew word for "disciple" (Hebrew *talmid*), also from the verb "to learn" (Hebrew *lamad*), occurs once in Jewish Scripture (see 1 Chronicles 25:8). See Richard N. Longenecker, ed., *Patterns of Discipleship in the New Testament* (Grand Rapids, Mich.: Eerdmans, 1996), 2.

7. For more on Jesus' messianic identity, see Brant Pitre, *The Case for Jesus: The Biblical and Historical Evidence for Christ* (New York: Image, 2016).

8. For example, among ancient Christians, John Climacus writes, "Someone caught up in the affairs of the world can make progress, if he is determined. But it is not easy" (*Ladder of Divine Ascent*, 1.20). In the Middle Ages, Thomas Aquinas argued that the essence of Christian holiness consists in keeping the two greatest commandments: love of God and neighbor, something which can be done by laity who have not taken vows of poverty, chastity, or obedience. See Thomas Aquinas, *Summa Theologica*, II–II, q. 184, art. 3-4. In the seventeenth century, Francis de Sales insisted that "It is an error, or rather a heresy, to wish to banish the devout life from the regiment of soldiers, the mechanic's shop, the court of princes, or the home of married people.... Wherever we may be, we can and should aspire to a perfect life" (*Introduction to the Devout Life*, 1.3). Finally, and perhaps most significant of all, in the twentieth century, the Second Vatican Ecumenical Council solemnly taught that "all the faithful, whatever their condition or state, are called by the Lord—each in his or her own way—to that perfect holiness by which the Father himself is perfect." Vatican II, Dogmatic Constitution on the Church, *Lumen Gentium* no. 11, as quoted by Pope Francis, Apostolic Exhortation on the Call to Holiness in Today's World, *Gaudete et Exsultate*, no. 10. Unless otherwise noted, all English translations of John Climacus contained herein are from John Climacus, *The Ladder of Divine Ascent*, trans. Colm Luibheid and Norman Russell, The Classics of Western Spirituality (Mahwah, N.J.: Paulist, 1982). For the sake of specificity, however, I will follow the paragraph numbering system found in Saint John Climacus, *The Ladder of Divine Ascent*, rev. ed. (Boston: Holy Transfiguration Monastery, 2019). Also, unless otherwise noted, all translations of Francis de Sales contained herein are from Francis de Sales, *Introduction to the Devout Life*, trans. J. K. Ryan (New York: Image, 2014).

9. See chapter 23 and Brant Pitre, *Jesus the Bridegroom: The Greatest Love Story Ever Told* (New York: Image, 2014), 55–81.

10. Thomas à Kempis, *The Imitation of Christ*, 1.1. Unless otherwise noted, all translations of the *Imitation* contained herein are from Thomas à Kempis, *The Imitation of Christ*, ed. Mary Lea Hill, F.S.P., trans. Mary Nazarene Prestofillipo, F.S.P. (Boston: Pauline Books, 2015).

11. Pope John Paul II, *Memory and Identity*, 30.

12. Here I am using the general terminology taken from the title of John of the Cross' classic work *Dark Night of the Soul*. In that book, John actually distinguishes between *two* "dark nights" of the soul: (1) the "night of the senses," which is the transition between the purgative and illuminative ways (*Dark Night of the Soul*, Book 1.1–14), and (2) the "night of the spirit," which is the transition between the illuminative and unitive ways (*Dark Night of the Soul*, Book 2.1–25). Because our study is focused on the purgative way, we will only treat the first of the two "nights." Unless otherwise noted, all translations of *Dark Night of the Soul* contained herein are from John of the Cross, *Dark Night of the Soul: A Masterpiece in the Literature of Mysticism*, trans. E. Allison Peers (New York: Image/Doubleday, 2005).

1: Vocal Prayer

1. For a discussion of vocal prayer, meditation, and the various degrees of contemplative prayer, see Aumann, *Spiritual Theology*, 316–57. For the use of a similar triad in Eastern Christian spirituality, see Tomas Spidlik, S.J., *The Spirituality of the Christian East: A Systematic Handbook*, trans. Anthony P. Gythiel (Collegeville, Minn.: Liturgical Press, 2008), 317: "In keeping with what has been said about prayer in general, there are three distinct degrees to this prayer [the Jesus prayer]: oral, mental, and of the heart" (cf. ibid., 311–12). See also the *Catechism of the Catholic Church* (2nd ed.; Vatican City: Libreria Editrice Vaticana, 1997) (hereafter cited as CCC) no. 2699: "Christian Tradition has retained three major expressions of prayer: vocal, meditative, and contemplative."

2. John Climacus, *Ladder of Divine Ascent*, 28.1.

3. John Damascene, *The Orthodox Faith*, 3.24. Cited in CCC no. 2559.

4. Teresa of Avila, *The Way of Perfection*, 21.10. In *The Collected Works of Saint Teresa of Avila*, trans. Kieran Kavanaugh, O.C.D., and Otilio Rodriguez, O.C.D., vol. 2 (Washington, D.C.: ICS Publications, 1980), 121.

5. Teresa of Avila, *Interior Castle*, 1.1.7. In Teresa of Avila, *Interior Castle*, trans. and ed. E. Allison Peers (New York: Image, 2004), 7.

6. See F. Brown, S. R. Driver, and C. A. Briggs, *A Hebrew and English Lexicon of the Old Testament* (2nd ed.; Oxford: Clarendon, 1977), 524–25.

7. It is worth noting here that vocal prayers can be *sung,* not just recited. The greatest example of this is the Psalter itself, which is a collection of 150 *prayer songs,* called "praises" (Hebrew *tehillim*) or "psalms" (Greek *psalmoi*). The very name of the Psalter is based directly on the word for a "harp" (Greek *psaltērion*) because the psalms were originally meant to be *sung* prayers, accompanied by stringed instruments.

8. See Judith H. Newman, "Psalms, Book of," in *The Eerdmans Dictionary of Early Judaism,* ed. John J. Collins and Daniel C. Harlow (Grand Rapids, Mich.: Eerdmans, 2010), 1105–7, who says the book of Psalms is sometimes described as "the 'Songbook of the Second Temple.'"

9. Thomas Aquinas, *Summa Theologica,* II–II, q. 83, art. 14. Aquinas goes on to draw an important distinction between *deliberate* lack of attention and the *unintentional* distraction that takes place when one's mind "wanders off through weakness."

10. Francis de Sales, *Introduction to the Devout Life,* 2.1.5 (emphasis added). Francis immediately goes on to give some specific ways of doing this (see ibid., 2.2).

11. Teresa of Avila, *The Way of Perfection,* 22.7, 8 (emphasis added). Unless otherwise noted, all translations of this work are from Teresa of Avila, *The Way of Perfection,* trans. and ed. E. Allison Peers (New York: Image, 2004).

12. Teresa of Avila, *The Way of Perfection* 30.7 (emphasis added). In *The Collected Works of Saint Teresa of Avila,* Volume 2, 152.

2: Meditation

1. John Cassian, *Conferences,* 11.15. Unless otherwise noted, all translations of Cassian's *Conferences* contained herein are from John Cassian, *The Conferences,* trans. Boniface Ramsey, O.P., Ancient Christian Writers 57 (Mahwah, N.J.: Paulist, 1997).

2. Thomas à Kempis, *The Imitation of Christ,* 1.1.

3. Teresa of Avila, *The Way of Perfection*, 16.3. In *The Collected Works of Saint Teresa of Avila*, trans. Kieran Kavanaugh, O.C.D., and Otilio Rodriguez, O.C.D., vol. 2 (Washington, D.C.: ICS Publications, 1980), 94.

4. See Kim Huat Tan, "Jesus and the Shema," in *Handbook for the Study of the Historical Jesus*, ed. Tom Holmén and Stanley E. Porter, 4 vols. (Leiden, The Netherlands: Brill, 2011), 3:2677–707; E. P. Sanders, *Judaism: Practice and Belief, 63 BCE–66 CE* (Minneapolis: Fortress, 2016), 321: "The mishnaic rabbis simply took it for granted, as something that did not require debate or proof, that every Jew said the Shema' (along with daily prayers) twice a day." For a first-century description of Jews praying "twice each day" that likely refers to the *Shema*, see Josephus, *Antiquities*, 4.212–13. In Josephus, *Jewish Antiquities, Books IV–VI*, trans. H. St. J. Thackeray and Ralph Marcus (Loeb Classical Library 490; Cambridge, Mass.: Harvard University Press, 1930), 103. In later centuries, the *Shema* expanded and developed to include Deuteronomy 6:8–9; 11:13–21; and Numbers 15:37–41. See Mishnah, *Berakoth* 2:2.

5. F. Brown, S. R. Driver, and C. A. Briggs, *A Hebrew and English Lexicon of the Old Testament* (Oxford: Clarendon, 1977), 211.

6. See Frederick William Danker, ed., *A Greek-English Lexicon of the New Testament and Other Early Christian Literature*, 3rd ed. (Chicago: University of Chicago Press, 2000), 627.

7. See Adela Yarbro Collins, *Mark: A Commentary*, Hermeneia (Minneapolis: Fortress, 2007), 574: "The phrase 'with your whole mind . . .' is added."

8. Danker, *Greek-English Lexicon*, 234.

9. See Joseph A. Fitzmyer, S.J., *The Gospel according to Luke*, 2 vols., Anchor Bible 28–28A (New York: Doubleday, 1983–85), 1:712–13.

10. See Danker, *Greek-English Lexicon*, 533. Cf. 1 Corinthians 15:2.

11. Fitzmyer, *Gospel according to Luke*, 1:714: the "heart" is "the OT term for the seat of human reaction to God and his promptings."

12. Ignatius of Loyola, *Spiritual Exercises*, no. 19.1–2. This is the famous "nineteenth annotation," in which Ignatius adapts the

thirty-day retreat version of his *Spiritual Exercises* for people who are only able to make the exercises in the midst of their daily lives. In George E. Ganss, S.J., *The Spiritual Exercises of Saint Ignatius* (Chicago: Loyola, 1992), 27–28.

13. Francis de Sales, *Introduction to the Devout Life,* 2.3.

14. Ignatius of Loyola, *Spiritual Exercises*, no. 1.

15. Thomas à Kempis, *The Imitation of Christ,* 1.20.1.

16. Francis de Sales, *Introduction to the Devout Life,* 2.1.9. In Francis de Sales, *Introduction to the Devout Life,* trans. Missionaries of St. Francis de Sales (Bangalore, India: SFS Publications, 2020), 57 (emphasis added).

17. Ignatius of Loyola, *Spiritual Exercises*, nos. 252–53 (emphasis added).

18. Thomas à Kempis, *The Imitation of Christ,* 1.1.

19. Thérèse of Lisieux, *Story of a Soul,* chapter 8, 83v. In *Story of a Soul: The Autobiography of St. Thérèse of Lisieux,* trans. John Clarke, O.C.D. (Washington, D.C.: ICS Publications, 1996), 258. Unless otherwise noted, all translations of the *Story of a Soul* contained herein are from this edition. See also Teresa of Avila, *The Way of Perfection,* 21.4: "I have always been fond of the words of the Gospels and have found more recollection in them than in the most carefully planned books."

20. Thomas à Kempis, *The Imitation of Christ,* 3.48.5: "I am wherever my thought is, and that so often is wherever what I love may be."

21. Ignatius of Loyola, *Spiritual Exercises*, no. 104 (emphasis added).

3: Contemplation

1. Charlton T. Lewis and Charles Short, *A Latin Dictionary* (1879; repr., Oxford: Oxford University Press, 1998), 445.

2. See, e.g., Gregory of Nyssa, *The Lord's Prayer,* 1.7: "Prayer is intimacy with God and contemplation of the invisible." In St. Gregory of Nyssa, *The Lord's Prayer, the Beatitudes,* trans. Hilda C. Graef, Ancient Christian Writers 18 (New York: Newman, 1954), 24.

Unless otherwise noted, all translations of Gregory of Nyssa contained herein are from this volume.

3. John Cassian, *The Conferences*, 1.8.1.

4. Thomas Aquinas, *Summa Theologica*, II–II, q. 180, art. 3.

5. Thomas à Kempis, *The Imitation of Christ*, 31.1.

6. Francis de Sales, *On the Love of God*, 6.6. Translation in St. Francis de Sales, *On the Love of God* (2 vols.; trans. John K. Ryan; New York: Image, 1963), 1.283–84.

7. *CCC* no. 2724 (emphasis added).

8. For Moses as a classic biblical model of contemplation, see Gregory of Nyssa, *The Life of Moses,* trans. Abraham J. Malherbe and Everett Ferguson (Mahwah, N.J.: Paulist, 1978).

9. See William H. C. Propp, *Exodus*, 2 vols., The Anchor Bible 2–2A (New York: Doubleday, 2006), 2:600: "Face to face" means a "direct encounter."

10. See, e.g., Augustine, *On the Psalms,* Second Discourse on Psalm 26.9: "Now you see, says the Psalmist, why I wish to dwell in the house of the Lord all the days of my life. I have told you the reason: *That I may contemplate the delight of the Lord.* . . . To contemplate him will be my happiness." In St. Augustine, *On the Psalms,* trans. Scholastica Hebgin and Felicitas Corrigan, Ancient Christian Writers 29 (Westminster, Md.: Newman, 1960), 269. See also Francis de Sales, *On the Love of God,* 6.1, who cites Psalm 27:7 as an example of contemplation or "mystical theology."

11. RSV, slightly altered.

12. See Artur Weiser, *The Psalms,* trans. Herbert Hartwell, The Old Testament Library (Philadelphia: Westminster, 1962), 248–49, who points out that the language of "beholding" describes a kind of "theophany"—an appearance of God—that takes the form of "the experience and assurance of the nearness and reality of the Living God." In the ancient Greek translation of the Psalms, this verse was translated as the desire to "behold [Greek *theōreō*] the pleasantness of the Lord" (Psalm 27:4 LXX), which comes from the same root word as that which was often used by ancient Christian writers for "contemplation" (Greek *theōria*).

13. See Jane Ackerman, *Elijah: Prophet of Carmel* (Washington, D.C.: Institute of Carmelite Studies, 2002).

14. See Mordechai Cogan, *1 Kings,* Anchor Bible 10 (New York: Doubleday, 2001), 453, who favors the translation "sound of sheer silence" (NRSV).

15. See Origen, *Fragments on Luke,* no. 171: "You might reasonably take Martha to stand for action and Mary for contemplation." In Origen, *Homilies on Luke,* trans. Joseph T. Lienhard, S.J., Fathers of the Church 94 (Washington, D.C.: Catholic University of America, 1996), 192.

16. RSV, slightly adapted.

17. RSV, slightly adapted.

18. Joseph A. Fitzmyer, S.J., *The Gospel according to Luke,* 2 vols., Anchor Bible 28–28A (New York: Doubleday, 1983–85), 2:893: "Her position is that of a listening disciple." Compare the apostle Paul, who is described as being brought up "at the feet" of Rabbi Gamaliel (Acts 22:3).

19. Herbert Danby, *The Mishnah* (Oxford: Oxford University Press, 1933), 446 (slightly adapted).

20. Compare, for example, the famous example of hospitality shown to the three guests by Abraham and Sarah (see Genesis 18:2–8; Josephus, *Antiquities,* 1.196).

21. François Bovon, *Luke 2,* trans. Donald S. Deer, Hermeneia (Minneapolis: Fortress, 2013), 71: "Whatever criticism of Martha there might have been was not directed at either her hospitality or her desire to serve but rather at her excess activity and the worries that occasioned it." See also Thérèse of Lisieux, *Story of a Soul* 11 [C 36r]: "It is not Martha's works that Jesus finds fault with. . . . It is only the *restlessness* of His ardent hostess that He willed to correct."

22. Frederick William Danker, ed., *A Greek-English Lexicon of the New Testament and Other Early Christian Literature,* 3rd ed. (Chicago: University of Chicago Press, 2000), 804.

23. See also Psalm 119:57: "The LORD is my portion; I promise to keep your words."

24. Gregory the Great, *Morals in Job*, 6.61. Translation in Gregory the Great, *Moral Reflections on the Book of Job, Volume 2: Books 6–10* (trans. Brian Kerns, O.C.S.O.; Cistercian Studies 257; Collegeville, Minn.: Liturgical Press, 2015), 87.

25. Teresa of Avila, *The Way of Perfection*, 26.3.

26. John of the Cross, *Dark Night of the Soul*, Book 2.18.5.

4: The First Step

1. John Climacus, *Ladder of Divine Ascent*, 26.65 (see also 5.1).

2. Thomas à Kempis, *The Imitation of Christ*, 1.21.1. In Thomas à Kempis, *The Imitation of Christ*, trans. Joseph N. Tylenda, S.J. (New York: Random House, 1998), 29.

3. Ignatius of Loyola, *Spiritual Exercises*, no. 82.10.

4. C. Soanes and A. Stevenson, eds., *Concise Oxford English Dictionary*, 11th ed. (Oxford: Oxford University Press, 2004), s.v. "repent."

5. See David Lambert, "Repentance," in *The Eerdmans Dictionary of Early Judaism*, ed. John J. Collins and Daniel C. Harlow (Grand Rapids, Mich.: Eerdmans, 2010), 1134–35, who defines repentance as "returning to a previous commitment, turning aside from a path of behavior, showing regret or remorse for misdeeds, and having a change of mind."

6. F. Brown, S. R. Driver, and C. A. Briggs, *A Hebrew and English Lexicon of the Old Testament* (Oxford: Clarendon, 1977), 996.

7. For a full discussion, see Robert L. Webb, *John the Baptizer and Prophet: A Socio-historical Study* (London: Sheffield Academic Press, 1991), 179–213.

8. Frederick William Danker, ed., *A Greek-English Lexicon of the New Testament and Other Early Christian Literature*, 3rd ed. (Chicago: University of Chicago Press, 2000), 640. In the Greek Septuagint, *metanoeō* can be used to speak of repentance from sin (e.g., Jeremiah 8:6 LXX), but it is more commonly used to refer to a "change of mind." See J. Lust, E. Eynikel, and K. Hauspie, *A*

Greek-English Lexicon of the Septuagint, 2 vols. (Stuttgart: Deutsche Bibelgesellschaft, 1992), 2:300.

9. Danker, *Greek-English Lexicon,* 351.

10. See Amy-Jill Levine and Marc Zvi Brettler, eds., *The Jewish Annotated New Testament,* 2nd ed. (Oxford: Oxford University Press, 2017), 147: God is depicted as a shepherd in Psalm 23; 78:52; 80:1; 100:3, and the people are depicted as lost sheep in Jeremiah 50:6; Ezekiel 34:15–16; Psalm 119:176.

11. See Joseph A. Fitzmyer, S.J., *The Gospel according to Luke,* 2 vols., Anchor Bible 28–28A (New York: Doubleday, 1983–85), 2:1077: it is "the initiative of divine love seeking out the lost sinner."

12. Intriguingly, Fitzmyer, *Gospel according to Luke,* 2:1081, notes that the word "coin" (Greek *drachma*) refers to a Greek silver coin of substantial value, just "enough to buy a sheep."

13. See Fitzmyer, *Gospel according to Luke,* 2:1081: when Jesus says "there is joy *before* the angels of God" (Luke 15:10), he most likely means "God himself in the presence of the angels," not the other way round.

14. Fitzmyer, *Gospel according to Luke,* 2:1088: "This detail suggested the degradation to which the young son has been brought." In support of this, he cites a later rabbinic saying that reads, "Cursed be the man who raises pigs" (Babylonian Talmud, *Baba Kamma* 82b).

15. Fitzmyer, *Gospel according to Luke,* 2:1088.

16. Francis de Sales, *Introduction to the Devout Life,* 5.4.

5: The Ten Commandments

1. Benedict of Nursia, *The Rule,* 7. In *The Rule of Saint Benedict,* trans. Anthony C. Meisel and M. L. del Mastro (New York: Image, 1975), 57. See also John Climacus, *Ladder of Divine Ascent,* 1.17: "All praise to those who from the beginning keep the commandments of God."

2. Thomas à Kempis, *The Imitation of Christ,* 4.18.2.

3. Francis de Sales, *Introduction to the Devout Life,* 1.1.

4. See Hindy Najman, "Decalogue," in *The Eerdmans Dictionary of Early Judaism,* ed. John J. Collins and Daniel C. Harlow (Grand Rapids, Mich.: Eerdmans, 2010), 526-28.

5. In what follows, I have adapted the RSVCE's "ten commandments" to the more literal "ten words." We get the English word "Decalogue" from the ancient Greek translation of "ten words" (Greek *deka logous*) (Exodus 34:28 LXX). See also Hosea 4:2; Jeremiah 7:9; Ezekiel 18:5-9.

6. See John Bergsma and Brant Pitre, *A Catholic Introduction to the Bible: The Old Testament* (San Francisco: Ignatius, 2018), 64: "A covenant may be defined as . . . a *sacred family bond:* (1) a bond, because it unites two parties in a permanent way; (2) family, because the united parties become *kin* to one another; (3) sacred, because the relationship is solemnized and enforced by oaths taken in the name of God."

7. F. Brown, S. R. Driver, and C. A. Briggs, *A Hebrew and English Lexicon of the Old Testament* (Oxford: Clarendon, 1977), 872. For a recent discussion that emphasizes the Hebrew meaning of holiness as "consecration" or "devotedness" to God, see Peter J. Gentry, "The Meaning of 'Holy' in the Old Testament," *Bibliotheca Sacra* 170 (2013): 400-417.

8. See James L. Kugel, *Traditions of the Bible: A Guide to the Bible as It Was at the Start of the Common Era* (Cambridge, Mass.: Harvard University Press, 1998), 638-45. On the one hand, the Jewish, Orthodox, and Protestant traditions follow Exodus 20:1-17 and separate the commandment against other gods (Exodus 20:3) and the prohibition of idols (Exodus 20:4) into two commandments, while combining the prohibition against coveting wives and property into one (Exodus 20:17). On the other hand, the Catholic and Lutheran traditions follow Deuteronomy 5:7-21 by treating the prohibition of worship of other gods and idolatry as one command (Deuteronomy 5:7-10) and distinguishing the commandment against coveting someone's wife (Deuteronomy 5:21a) from the commandment against coveting someone's property (Deuteronomy 5:21b). Here I follow the Catholic and Lutheran traditions, which go back to Augustine of Hippo, *Questions on Exodus* 71.1-6. See Saint Augustine, *Writings on the Old Testament,* ed. Boniface Ramsey (The Works of Saint Augustine I/14; Hyde Park, N.Y.: New City Press, 2016), 121-24.

9. Brown, Driver, and Briggs, *Hebrew and English Lexicon*, 202. See also Moshe Weinfeld, *Deuteronomy 1–11*, Anchor Bible 5 (New York: Doubleday, 1991), 327: "'The way' as a metaphor for right behavior is very common in biblical . . . literature." See, e.g., Genesis 18:19; Deuteronomy 10:12; 1 Kings 8:58; Jeremiah 7:23.

10. Brown, Driver, and Briggs, *Hebrew and English Lexicon*, 306. See also Hannah K. Harrington, "Sin," in *Eerdmans Dictionary*, 1230–31: "The root means 'to be mistaken, found deficient, or lacking; to be at fault; or to miss a specified goal or mark.'" For a full study, see Gary A. Anderson, *Sin: A History* (New Haven: Yale University Press, 2009).

11. See, for example, Exodus 21:15–16; 22:20; 31:15; Deuteronomy 19:18–19; 22:22.

12. Paula Fredriksen, *Sin: The Early History of an Idea* (Princeton, N.J.: Princeton University Press, 2012), 16: "Jesus defined living rightly as living according to the Torah, as summed up in and by the Ten Commandments; . . . he defined sin as breaking God's commandments; . . . he defined 'repentance' as (re)turning to this covenant."

13. Adela Yarbro Collins, *Mark: A Commentary*, Hermeneia (Minneapolis: Fortress, 2007), 577: "Jesus' *double love-command* expresses a genuinely Jewish understanding of the Law" (emphasis added).

14. See J. Lust, E. Eynikel, and K. Hauspie, *A Greek-English Lexicon of the Septuagint*, 2 vols. (Stuttgart: Deutsche Bibelgesellschaft, 1992), 2.471, and Frederick William Danker, ed., *A Greek-English Lexicon of the New Testament and Other Early Christian Literature*, 3rd ed. (Chicago: University of Chicago Press, 2000), 995.

15. W. D. Davies and D. C. Allison, Jr., *The Gospel according to Saint Matthew*, 3 vols., International Critical Commentary (London: T&T Clark, 1988–97), 1:561–63: "Without doubt, 'moral perfection' is the meaning in [Matthew] 5.48a. . . . To obey Jesus' words, his law, is, therefore, to love utterly. . . . And in this lies perfection: love of unrestrained compass lacks for nothing. It is catholic, all-inclusive. It is perfect."

16. Ignatius of Loyola, *Spiritual Exercises*, nos. 240–41.

6: The Three Temptations

1. John Cassian, *Conferences*, 5.6.1.

2. Gregory the Great, *Homilies on the Gospels*, 14. Unless otherwise noted, all translations of Gregory's homilies on the Gospels are from Gregory the Great, *Forty Gospel Homilies*, trans. Dom David Hurst, Cistercian Studies 123 (Kalamazoo, Mich.: Cistercian, 1990).

3. Cf. CCC no. 377.

4. Slightly adapted. (I have added "who was with her" since it is present in the Hebrew but for some reason is missing in the English translation.)

5. Thomas Aquinas, *Summa Theologica*, I–II, q. 84, art. 4: "Man's good is *threefold*. For, in the first place, there is a certain good of the soul, which derives its aspect of appetibility, merely through being apprehended, viz. the excellence of honour and praise, and this good is sought inordinately by *vainglory*.—Secondly, there is the good of the body, and this regards either the preservation of the individual, e.g. meat and drink, which good is pursued inordinately by *gluttony*,—or the preservation of the species, e.g. sexual intercourse, which good is sought inordinately by *lust*.— Thirdly, there is external good, viz. riches, to which *covetousness* is referred."

6. E.g., Gregory the Great, *Homilies on the Gospels*, 14: "He [the devil] tempted him [Jesus] by *gluttony* when he said, '*Tell these stones to become bread.*' He tempted him by *vain glory* when he said, '*If you are the son of God, cast yourself down.*' He tempted him by an *avaricious desire* for high position when *he showed him all the kingdoms of the world, saying, 'I will give you all these if you will fall down and worship me*'" (emphasis added).

7. See Frederick William Danker, ed., *A Greek-English Lexicon of the New Testament and Other Early Christian Literature*, 3rd ed. (Chicago: University of Chicago Press, 2000), 372: when used negatively, "lust" (Greek *epithymia*) means "a desire for something forbidden or simply inordinate, *craving, lust*." That is why the ancient Latin Bible of Jerome translated the Greek as "longing" or "concupiscence" (Latin *concupiscentia*) (1 John 2:16–17 Vulgate).

This is the biblical origin of the later phrase, the "triple concupiscence."

8. Danker, *Greek-English Lexicon*, 40. Once again, the Latin translation "vainglory" (Latin *superbia*) captures the meaning well (1 John 2:17 Vulgate).

9. Augustine, *Homilies on 1 John*, 2.14 (emphasis added and slightly adapted).

10. John of the Cross, *The Ascent of Mount Carmel*, 1.13.8. In *The Collected Works of St. John of the Cross*, trans. Kieran Kavanaugh, O.C.D., and Otilio Rodriguez, O.C.D., 3rd ed. (Washington, D.C.: ICS Publications, 1991), 149.

7: Fasting

1. Basil the Great, *First Homily on Fasting*, 6. In Saint Basil the Great, *On Fasting and Feasts*, trans. Susan R. Holman and Mark DelCogliano, Popular Patristics 50 (Yonkers, N.Y.: St Vladimir's Seminary Press, 2013), 62.

2. Gregory the Great, *Homilies on the Gospels*, 14.

3. Francis de Sales, *Introduction to the Devout Life*, 3.23.

4. See Noah Hacham, "Fasting," in *The Eerdmans Dictionary of Early Judaism*, ed. John J. Collins and Daniel C. Harlow (Grand Rapids, Mich.: Eerdmans, 2010), 634–36.

5. Centuries ago, Basil the Great pointed this out: "Fasting is as old as humanity: it was legislated in paradise. It was the first command that Adam received: 'You shall not eat from the tree of the knowledge of good and evil' (Gen 2:17). 'You shall not eat' legislates fasting and self-control. If Eve had fasted from the tree, we would not need this fasting now. . . . It is because we did not fast that we were banished from paradise. So let us fast that we may return to it" (Basil the Great, *First Homily on Fasting*, 3).

6. See Jacob Milgrom, *Leviticus 1–16*, Anchor Bible 3 (New Haven: Yale University Press, 1998), 1054.

7. Basil the Great, *First Homily on Fasting*, 10: "True fasting is being a stranger to vice."

8. Basil the Great, *First Homily on Fasting*, 9: "Our Lord is the princi-pal example . . . [of fasting]. Only after he fasted to fortify the flesh that he assumed for our sake did he receive it in the devil's assaults. In this, he . . . instructed us to fast in order to prepare and train ourselves for struggles with temptation."

9. RSV, slightly adapted (see RSV note on Mark 9:29). It is impor-tant to note that while most ancient Greek manuscripts contain the words "and fasting," they are missing from some of the most ancient copies. For a discussion of the textual-critical issues in-volved, see Adela Yarbro Collins, *Mark: A Commentary*, Herme-neia (Minneapolis: Fortress, 2007), 434, and Bruce M. Metzger, *A Textual Commentary on the Greek New Testament*, 2nd ed. (Stutt-gart: Deutsche Bibelgesellschaft, 1994), 85. For our purposes here, we include them because of the enormous impact this verse had on the practice of fasting in ancient Christianity.

10. See Noah Hacham, "Fasting," in *Eerdmans Dictionary*, 635, who points out that in ancient Judaism, "Together with prayer, fast-ing serves as a means of convincing God to answer requests and to effect release from difficulty," citing Jeremiah 14:12; Mishnah, *Ta'anith* 4:3; Jerusalem Talmud, *Ta'anith* 65a. In later Christian tradition, see Basil the Great, *First Homily on Fasting*, 7, 9: "Fasting sends prayer up to heaven. . . . Fasting is a weapon used in the fight against demons."

11. W. D. Davies and D. C. Allison, Jr., *The Gospel according to Saint Matthew*, 3 vols., International Critical Commentary (London: T&T Clark, 1988–97), 1:617: "What counts is not external show but humility."

12. See Craig S. Keener, *Acts: An Exegetical Commentary*, 4 vols. (Grand Rapids, Mich.: Baker Academic, 2012–15), 2:1991, who points out that the word for "worship" (Greek *leitourgeō*) used in Acts 13:2 is used in Scripture to refer to "priestly, cultic worship" such as that which takes place in the Jewish Temple (e.g., 1 Chronicles 6:32; 16:4; 2 Chronicles 31:2 LXX). Regarding Jewish fasting and Passover, see Mishnah, *Pesahim* 10:1: "On the eve of Passover, from about the time of the Evening Offering, a man must eat naught until nightfall." In Danby, *Mishnah*, 150.

13. "You must fast on Wednesday and Friday" (*Didache* 8:1). In Mi-chael W. Holmes, trans., *The Apostolic Fathers: Greek Texts and En-*

glish Translations, 3rd ed. (Grand Rapids, Mich.: Baker Academic, 2007), 355. "'The canonical fasts,' [Abba Apollo] said, 'must not be broken except under extreme necessary. For the Saviour was betrayed on a Wednesday and crucified on a Friday.'" In *The Lives of the Desert Fathers,* trans. Norman Russell (Kalamazoo, Mich.: Cistercian Publications, 1981), 78. "He [Jesus] commanded us to fast on the fourth and sixth days of the week; the former on account of His being betrayed, and the latter on account of his passion" (*Apostolic Constitutions* 5.15; cf. also 5.18). In Alexander Roberts and James Donaldson, eds., *Ante-Nicene Fathers,* 12 vols. (Peabody, Mass.: Hendrickson, 1994), 7:445.

14. Thomas à Kempis, *The Imitation of Christ,* 2.11.1.

15. CCC no. 540.

16. Basil the Great, *Second Homily on Fasting,* 5.

8: Almsgiving

1. John Chrysostom, *Homilies on the Gospel of John* #23. In Gary A. Anderson, *Charity: The Place of the Poor in the Biblical Tradition* (New Haven: Yale University Press, 2013), frontispiece.

2. Thomas Aquinas, *Summa Theologica,* II–II, q. 32, art. 5.

3. Francis de Sales, *Introduction to the Devout Life,* 3.15.

4. See Kyong-Jin Lee, "Almsgiving," in *The Eerdmans Dictionary of Early Judaism,* ed. John J. Collins and Daniel C. Harlow (Grand Rapids, Mich.: Eerdmans, 2010), 324–25.

5. For a full discussion of Proverbs 19:17, see especially Anderson, *Charity,* 35–52.

6. Translation in Anderson, *Charity,* front matter.

7. F. Brown, S. R. Driver, and C. A. Briggs, *A Hebrew and English Lexicon of the Old Testament* (Oxford: Clarendon, 1977), 531. Compare Proverbs 22:7.

8. See also John Chrysostom, *Homilies on Repentance and Almsgiving,* 7.6.23: "Whoever has mercy upon the poor lends to God. Let us lend to God almsgiving so we may receive from Him clemency in exchange." Unless otherwise noted, all translations of Chrysos-

tom's homilies on repentance and almsgiving are from St. John Chrysostom, *On Repentance and Almsgiving*, trans. Gus George Christo, Fathers of the Church 96 (Washington, D.C.: Catholic University of America Press, 1997).

9. Compare Tobit 4:7-11; Sirach 29:9-12.

10. John Chrysostom, *Homilies on Repentance and Almsgiving*, 10.4.15.

11. John Chrysostom, *Homilies on Ephesians* 20: "If we thus regulate our own houses, we shall be also fit for the management of the Church. For indeed a house is a little church." In Philip Schaff, ed., *Nicene and Post-Nicene Fathers, First Series*, 14 vols. (Peabody, Mass.: Hendrickson, 1994), 13:148. Augustine of Hippo, *Letter* 14*.1: "I know how much you love Christ and that your whole household is his family, just as the Apostle speaks of a 'household church.'" In St. Augustine, *Letters, Volume VI (1*–29*)*, trans. Robert B. Eno, S.S.; Fathers of the Church 81 (Washington, D.C.: Catholic University of America Press, 1989), 112. Augustine's expression appears to be derived from the Latin translation of Paul's reference to "churches" in people's "houses" (cf. Romans 16:5; 1 Corinthians 16:19).

12. Francis de Sales, *Introduction to the Devout Life*, 3.15.

9: The Lord's Prayer

1. Tertullian, *On Prayer*, 1. In Tertullian, Cyprian, and Origen, *On the Lord's Prayer*, trans. Alistair Stewart-Sykes, Popular Patristics 29 (Yonkers, N.Y.: St Vladimir's Seminary Press, 2004), 42.

2. Thomas Aquinas, *Summa Theologica*, II–II, q. 83, art. 9. Cited in *CCC* no. 2763.

3. Teresa of Avila, *The Way of Perfection*, 37.1. For the sake of clarity, I have reversed the order of the two sentences.

4. For an in-depth exegetical study of the Lord's Prayer, see Brant Pitre, *Jesus and the Last Supper* (Grand Rapids, Mich.: Eerdmans, 2015), 159-93.

5. See, e.g., Psalm 5:1-3; 6:1; 7:1; 8:1, etc.

6. See Psalm 68:5; 89:26; 103:13.

7. Matthew 5:16, 45, 48; 6:1, 4, 6 (2x), 8, 9, 14, 15, 18 (2x), 26, 32; 7:11, 21.

8. For the use of the term "inner room" (Greek *tameion*) as the innermost room of a house or "bedchamber," see Genesis 43:30; Exodus 8:3; Judges 15:1; Isaiah 26:20.

9. See, e.g., Mark 1:35; 6:46; 14:32–42; Luke 5:16; 6:12; 9:18, 28–29.

10. Think here of the prophets of the Canaanite god Baal, who "raved on" for hours, cutting themselves with swords, trying to get Baal to respond (1 Kings 18:20–29). Contrast this with the prophet Elijah's simple and straightforward act of prayer and sacrifice, to which God responds immediately (1 Kings 18:36–40).

11. See Pitre, *Jesus and the Last Supper,* 171–75, for a full discussion.

12. See Brant Pitre, *Jesus and the Jewish Roots of the Eucharist: Unlocking the Secrets of the Last Supper* (New York: Image, 2011), 77–115.

13. See Gary A. Anderson, *Sin: A History* (New Haven: Yale University Press, 2009), 27–39.

14. According to the fourth-century writer John Cassian, some ancient Christians actually refused to say aloud the petition in the Lord's Prayer about forgiveness during the Eucharistic liturgy! "Some people fear this, and when this prayer is recited together in church by the whole congregation they pass over this line in silence, lest by their own words they obligate rather than excuse themselves." John Cassian, *Conferences,* 9.17.4.

15. See W. D. Davies and D. C. Allison, Jr., *The Gospel according to Saint Matthew,* 3 vols., International Critical Commentary (London: T&T Clark, 1988–97), 1:613: "Rather does *mē eisenengkēs* ["lead us not"], reflecting perhaps a Semitic causative, have permissive force: 'Do not let us fall victim.'" In support of this permissive use of a causative verb, Davies and Allison cite the strikingly similar line from a later rabbinic prayer: "Bring me not . . . into the power of temptation" (Babylonian Talmud, *Berakoth* 60b). See also Pope Francis, *Our Father: Reflections on the Lord's Prayer,* trans. Matthew Sherry (New York: Image, 2018), 94, who emphasizes that this line of the prayer means "Do not let me fall into temptation."

16. CCC no. 2775.

17. Michael W. Holmes, trans., *The Apostolic Fathers: Greek Texts and English Translations*, 3rd ed. (Grand Rapids, Mich.: Baker Academic, 2007), 355, 357.

18. Teresa of Avila, *The Way of Perfection*, 24.4: "Now, in the first place, you know that His Majesty teaches that this prayer must be made when we are alone, just as He was often alone when he prayed."

19. Gregory of Nyssa, *The Lord's Prayer*, Sermon 1.

20. Teresa of Avila, *The Way of Perfection*, 26.9. For the sake of clarity, I have updated E. Allison Peers' archaic use of the word "intercourse" with "communicate," following the translation of Kieran Kavanaugh, O.C.D., and Otilio Rodriguez, O.C.D., in *The Collected Works of Saint Teresa of Avila*, vol. 2 (Washington, D.C.: ICS Publications, 1980), 136.

21. Francis de Sales, *Introduction to the Devout Life*, 2.1.6 (emphasis added).

22. Teresa of Avila, *The Way of Perfection*, 24.6, 7 (emphasis added).

23. CCC no. 2559, quoting Romans 8:26 and Augustine, *Sermon* 56.6, 9 (emphasis added).

24. Cyprian of Carthage, *On the Lord's Prayer*, no. 3. In Tertullian, Cyprian, and Origen, *On the Lord's Prayer*, 66. My thanks to John Sehorn for bringing this passage to my attention.

10: The Seven Sins

1. See Jeffrey P. Greenman, "Seven Deadly Sins," in *Dictionary of Scripture and Ethics*, ed. Joel B. Green et al. (Grand Rapids, Mich.: Baker Academic, 2011), 717–18. Despite the centrality of the seven capital sins in Catholic and Orthodox Christianity, Greenman points out that "their importance diminished dramatically for Protestants after the Reformation, partly owing to their lack of biblical foundation" (ibid., 718). Hopefully, this chapter (and the ones to follow) will show that their "biblical foundation" is hardly lacking.

2. Gregory the Great, *Morals in Job*, 31.87. See Saint Gregory the Great, *Moralia in Job*, trans. James Bliss and Charles Marriott,

3 vols. (London: J. G. F. and J. Rivington, 1850; repr., Ex Fontibus, 2012), 3:453.

3. Thomas Aquinas, *Summa Theologica,* I–II, q. 84, art. 3, 4: "A capital vice is one from which other vices arise. . . . [There are] seven capital vices, viz., vainglory, envy, anger, avarice, sorrow, gluttony, lust" (Latin *inanis gloria, invidia, ira, avaritia, tristitia, gula, luxuria*).

4. Ignatius of Loyola, *Spiritual Exercises,* no. 18: "Let him be given for half an hour each morning the method of prayer on the Commandments and on the Capital Sins." Cf. ibid., no. 245: "In order to understand better the faults committed that come under the Seven Capital Sins, let the contrary virtues be considered."

5. John Climacus, *Ladder of Divine Ascent,* 22.1: "[Some] claim there are eight deadly sins. But against this is the view of Gregory the Theologian and other teachers that in fact *the number is seven.* I also hold this view" (emphasis added).

6. See, e.g., *CCC* no. 1866.

7. Ken M. Penner, ed., *The Lexham English Septuagint* (Bellingham, Wash.: Lexham Press, 2019), 763.

8. F. Brown, S. R. Driver, and C. A. Briggs, *A Hebrew and English Lexicon of the Old Testament* (Oxford: Clarendon, 1977), 1073. Cf. Leviticus 18:22, 26–29; Proverbs 3:32; 8:7; 13:19; 16:12; 21:27; 28:9; 29:27; Isaiah 1:13.

9. See Albert Pietersma and Benjamin G. Wright, eds., *A New English Translation of the Septuagint* (New York: Oxford University Press, 2007), 644: "There are seven iniquities in his soul" (Proverbs 26:25 LXX).

10. John Cassian, *Conferences,* 25.2: "In the Book of Proverbs Solomon also speaks of this sevenfold source of vice in this way: 'If your enemy asks you in a loud voice, do not give in to him, for there are *seven evils* in his soul.'"

11. Although English translations of Proverbs use different words for mercy or compassion, in the ancient Greek translation known as the Septuagint, all three of these verses render the Hebrew verb meaning to "be merciful" or "compassionate" (Hebrew

chanan) as "have mercy" (Greek *eleeō*) (Proverbs 14:31; 19:17). See Brown, Driver, and Briggs, *Hebrew and English Lexicon,* 335–36; Frederick William Danker, ed., *A Greek-English Lexicon of the New Testament and Other Early Christian Literature,* 3rd ed. (Chicago: University of Chicago Press, 2000), 315.

12. Augustine, *Questions on the Gospels,* 1.8: "The man will have not only those seven vices that are contrary to the seven spiritual virtues themselves." In Saint Augustine, *The New Testament I and II,* ed. Boniface Ramsey, O.P. (Hyde Park, N.Y.: New City Press, 2014), 365.

13. See John Cassian, *Conferences,* 5.25.1–2, where Cassian oscillates between speaking of the "eight vices" (5.25.1) and the "sevenfold source of vice" (5.25.2), depending on whether he is emphasizing Matthew 12:45 or Proverbs 26:25.

14. John Cassian, *Conferences,* 5.25.1: "These eight vices are alluded to in the Gospel in this way: 'When an unclean spirit has gone out of a person . . .'"

15. John Cassian, *Conferences,* 5.16.2, 5: "[Numerous] carnal passions [proceed] from *this sevenfold stock and root of the vices.*"

16. Gregory the Great, *Morals in Job,* 31.88. In Saint Gregory the Great, *Moralia in Job,* 3:454.

17. See the famous passage in Gregory the Great, *Morals in Job,* 31.88: "But these several sins have each their army against us. [1] For from vain glory there arise disobedience, boasting, hypocrisy, contentions, obstinacies, discords, and the presumption of novelties. [2] From envy there spring hatred, whispering, detraction, exultation at the misfortunes of a neighbor, and affliction at his prosperity. [3] From anger are produced strifes, swelling of mind, insults, clamour, indignation, blasphemies. [4] From melancholy there arise malice, rancor, cowardice, despair, slothfulness in fulfilling the commands, and a wandering of the mind on unlawful objects. [5] From avarice there spring treachery, fraud, deceit, perjury, restlessness, violence, and hardness of heart against compassion. [6] From gluttony are propagated foolish mirth, scurrility, uncleanness, babbling, dullness of sense in understanding. [7] From lust are generated blindness of mind, inconsiderateness, inconstancy, precipitation, self-love, hatred of God,

affection for this present world, but dread or despair of that which is to come. Because, therefore, seven principal vices produce from themselves so great a multitude of vices, when they reach the heart, they bring, as it were, the bands of an army after them. But of these seven, five namely are spiritual, and two are carnal." In Gregory the Great, *Moralia in Job,* 3:454.

18. John Cassian, *Conferences,* 5.13.

19. John Climacus, *Ladder of Divine Ascent,* 27.72.

20. Ignatius of Loyola, *Spiritual Exercises,* no. 245 (emphasis added).

21. Francis de Sales, *Introduction to the Devout Life,* 3.1 (emphasis added).

11: Pride vs. Humility

1. See Frederick William Danker, ed., *A Greek-English Lexicon of the New Testament and Other Early Christian Literature,* 3rd ed. (Chicago: University of Chicago Press, 2000), 1033.

2. Charlton T. Lewis and Charles Short, *A Latin Dictionary* (1879; repr., Oxford: Oxford University Press, 1998), 1804: "loftiness, haughtiness, pride, arrogance."

3. John Cassian, *Institutes,* 12.3.1. All translations of Cassian's *Institutes* contained herein are from John Cassian, *The Institutes,* ed. Dennis D. McManus, trans. Boniface Ramsey, O.P., Ancient Christian Writers 58 (New York: Newman, 2000).

4. Gregory the Great, *Morals in Job,* 31.87. In Gregory the Great, *Moralia in Job,* 3:453.

5. John Climacus, *Ladder of Divine Ascent,* 22.45.

6. Catherine of Siena, *The Dialogue,* 56.

7. Victor P. Hamilton, *The Book of Genesis,* 2 vols., The New International Commentary on the Old Testament (Grand Rapids, Mich.: Eerdmans, 1990, 1995), 1:189: "Disobedience will bring positive blessings. Consumption of the forbidden fruit will make the woman *godlike.* . . . [The serpent's statement] is to be understood as predicative—'you shall be as God.'"

8. See John Cassian, *Institutes,* 12.5: "This [pride] is the cause of the first downfall and the ultimate origin of the disease that . . . crept into the first man and produced the weaknesses and the wherewithal of all the vices. For in his belief that he could attain to the glory of the Godhead by his own free will and effort, he lost even that which was his by the grace of the Creator."

9. See Joseph Blenkinsopp, *Isaiah 1–39,* Anchor Bible 19 (New York: Doubleday, 2000), 288, who links this passage with other prophetic descriptions of "the fall from grace of rebellious deities (cf. Ezek 28:11-19; Ps 82:6-7)" and points to it as the origin of the later "doctrine of the fall of Lucifer (the Vulgate translation of *Hêlēl*)."

10. See Isaiah 36:18-20; Daniel 10:13-14.

11. See John Cassian, *Institutes,* 12.4.1: "We see that that angel who, on account of his great splendor and beauty, was called Lucifer was cast out of heaven for no other vice than this one, and that, having been wounded by the dart of pride, he fell from the blessed and sublime post of the angels into hell."

12. In this proverb, the word "arrogant" literally means "high" or "exalted" (Hebrew *gaboah*). Eventually, it gets translated into Greek as "high hearted" (Greek *hypsēlokardios*) and Latin as "arrogant" (Latin *arrogans*) (Proverbs 16:5 LXX and Vulgate).

13. F. Brown, S. R. Driver, and C. A. Briggs, *A Hebrew and English Lexicon of the Old Testament* (Oxford: Clarendon, 1977), 1073.

14. In the original Greek, the word for "pride" is *hyperēphania*. It is later translated into Latin as *superbia* (see Mark 7:22 Vulgate).

15. See Josephus, *Antiquities,* 18.12, 15: "The Pharisees . . . are . . . extremely influential among the townsfolk; and all prayers and sacred rites of divine worship are performed according to their exposition. This is the great tribute that the inhabitants of the cities, by practising the highest ideals both in their way of living and in their discourse, have paid to the excellence of the Pharisees." In Josephus, *Jewish Antiquities, Books 18–19,* trans. Louis H. Feldman, Loeb Classical Library 433 (Cambridge, Mass.: Harvard University Press, 1965), 11, 13. For a helpful corrective to the tendency to negatively stereotype the Pharisees and ignore

their popularity, see especially Lawrence H. Schiffman, "Pharisees," in Amy-Jill Levine and Marc Zvi Brettler, eds., *The Jewish Annotated New Testament*, 2nd ed. (Oxford: Oxford University Press, 2017), 619–22.

16. François Bovon, *Luke 2*, trans. Donald S. Deer, Hermeneia (Minneapolis: Fortress, 2002), 546: "He prayed to himself."

17. In the Bible, the word "sin" literally means "miss the mark" (Greek *hamartia*). When a person aims the arrow of love at themselves instead of their Creator, they infinitely miss the mark. That is why pride—to put oneself in the place of God—is actually the worst sin.

18. Ignatius of Loyola, *Spiritual Exercises*, no. 165 (emphasis altered).

19. See Michael V. Fox, *Proverbs*, 2 vols., Anchor Bible 18–18A (New Haven: Yale University Press, 2000–2009), 1:69: "The noun *yir'ah* (fear) and the verb *yare'* [to fear] may refer to everything from dread of danger (1 Sam 12:18) to gentle awe and respect, such as one feels toward the merciful God (Ps 130:4) or for one's parents (Lev 19:3)."

20. Thomas à Kempis, *The Imitation of Christ*, 1.7.3.

21. Danker, *Greek-English Lexicon*, 610. In fact, the word "beatitude" comes from the ancient Latin translation of this verse: "Happy (Latin *beati*) are the poor in spirit" (Matthew 5:3 Vulgate). With that said, the kind of happiness implied here is not a transient *feeling* of euphoria but the supernatural *joy* of a life lived according to the will of God. For a discussion of the difficulty in translating *makarios* into English, see Jonathan T. Pennington, *The Sermon on the Mount and Human Flourishing: A Theological Commentary* (Grand Rapids, Mich.: Baker Academic, 2017), 41–67.

22. See W. D. Davies and D. C. Allison, Jr., *The Gospel According to Saint Matthew*, 3 vols., International Critical Commentary (London: T&T Clark, 1988–97), 1:443: "The primary reference [of *ptōchos*] is to economic poverty. . . . But already in the OT, especially in the Psalms, the Greek word and its Hebrew equivalents refer to those who are in special need of God's help." See Psalm 12:5; 37:14; 70:5; 86:1.

23. See Gregory of Nyssa, *The Beatitudes*, Sermon 1: "It seems to me that by poverty of spirit the Word [Jesus] understands *voluntary*

humility. . . . Since, therefore, the vice of arrogance is ingrained in almost everyone who shares the human nature, the Lord begins the Beatitudes with this. He removes pride, the root evil, from our character by counselling us to imitate Him who became poor of His own will" (emphasis added).

24. Consider John Cassian's fourth-century profile of an arrogant person: "He will be devoid of patience, without love, quick to inflict abuse, slow to accept it, reluctant to obey except when his desire and will anticipate the matter, implacable in receiving exhortations, weak in restraining in his own will, very unyielding when submitting to others, constantly fighting on behalf of his own opinions but never acquiescing or giving in to those of others" (John Cassian, *Institutes*, 12.29.2–3).

12: Envy vs. Mercy

1. Basil the Great, *Concerning Envy*, Homily 11. In St. Basil, *Ascetical Works*, trans. M. Monica Wagner, C.S.C., Fathers of the Church 9 (Washington, D.C.: Catholic University of America Press, 1950), 463.

2. Gregory the Great, *Morals in Job*, 5.85. In Gregory the Great, *Moral Reflections on the Book of Job, Volume 1: Preface and Books 1–5* (trans. Brian Kerns, O.C.S.O.; Cistercian Studies 249; Collegeville, Minn.: Liturgical Press, 2014), 385–86.

3. John Damascene, *On the Orthodox Faith*, 2.14. In Philip Schaff and Henry Wace, eds., *Nicene and Post-Nicene Fathers*, Second Series, 14 vols. (Peabody, Mass.: Hendrickson, 1994), 9:33.

4. John of the Cross, *Dark Night of the Soul*, Book 1.7.1.

5. RSV, slightly adapted.

6. Victor P. Hamilton, *The Book of Genesis*, 2 vols., The New International Commentary on the Old Testament (Grand Rapids, Mich.: Eerdmans, 1990, 1995), 1:223.

7. CCC no. 2553.

8. Gregory the Great, *Morals in Job*, 5.46, 84: "It was envy that corrupted Cain to the point of committing fratricide; when his own sacrifice was disregarded, he was maddened against the one who

was preferred to him, whose offering God accepted, and him whom he hated for being better than himself he cut down, to put a final end to his existence." In Gregory the Great, *Moral Reflections on the Book of Job, Volume 1,* 384.

9. F. Brown, S. R. Driver, and C. A. Briggs, *A Hebrew and English Lexicon of the Old Testament* (Oxford: Clarendon, 1977), 326.

10. RSV, slightly adapted.

11. Gregory the Great, *Morals in Job,* 5.46.85. In Gregory the Great, *Moral Reflections on the Book of Job, Volume 1,* 386. See also Michael V. Fox, *Proverbs,* 2 vols., Anchor Bible 18–18A (New Haven: Yale University Press, 2000–2009), 2:584, who points out that Proverbs emphasizes "the psychosomatic benefits of a gentle and cheerful heart and spirit" elsewhere. See Proverbs 17:22; 18:14.

12. See David Winston, *The Wisdom of Solomon,* The Anchor Bible 43 (New York: Doubleday, 1979), 121–22, citing Josephus, *Jewish Antiquities,* 1.41: "The serpent, living in the company of Adam and his wife, grew *envious* (Greek *pthonerōs*) of the blessings which he supposed were destined for them if they obeyed God's behests." In Josephus, *Jewish Antiquities, Books 1–3,* trans. H. St. J. Thackeray, Loeb Classical Library 242 (Cambridge, Mass.: Harvard University Press, 1930), 21 (slightly adapted). For later Christian tradition on the role of envy in Satan's fall, see Gregory the Great, *Morals in Job,* 5.46.84: "We can envy only those, you see, whom we think to be better than ourselves in some respect. . . . That is why the cunning foe robbed the first couple in his envy, *because he had lost the blessed state and he was inferior to their immortality.*" In Gregory the Great, *Moral Reflections on the Book of Job, Volume 1,* 384. See also Thomas Aquinas, *Summa Theologica,* II–II, q. 36, art. 4: "When the devil tempts us to envy, he is enticing us to that which has its chief place in his heart."

13. Frederick William Danker, ed., *A Greek-English Lexicon of the New Testament and Other Early Christian Literature,* 3rd ed. (Chicago: University of Chicago Press, 2000), 824.

14. Adela Yarbro Collins, *Mark: A Commentary,* Hermeneia (Minneapolis: Fortress, 2007), 360. See, e.g., Sirach 14:8–10.

15. François Bovon, *Luke 2,* trans. Donald S. Deer, Hermeneia (Minneapolis: Fortress, 2002), 422.

16. See Gregory the Great, *Morals in Job,* 31.45: "From envy there spring hatred, whispering, detraction, exultation at the misfortunes of a neighbor, and affliction at his prosperity." In Gregory the Great, *Moralia in Job,* 3:453. See also Thomas Aquinas, *Summa Theologica,* II–II, q. 36, art. 4.

17. Thomas Aquinas, *Summa Theologica,* II–II, q. 36, art. 3: "Envy . . . is contrary to charity. . . . Now the object both of charity and of envy is our neighbor's good, but by contrary movements, since charity rejoices in our neighbor's good, while envy grieves over it." See also John of the Cross, *Dark Night of the Soul,* Book 1.7.1: "With respect to envy, many [beginners] are wont to experience movements of displeasure at the spiritual good of others. . . . All this is clean contrary to charity, which, as Saint Paul says, 'rejoices in goodness' (1 Cor 13:6)."

18. See especially Thomas Aquinas, *Summa Theologica,* II–II, q. 36, art. 3: "Envy [Latin *invidia*] . . . is directly contrary to mercy [Latin *misericordiae*], their principal objects being contrary to one another, since the envious man grieves over his neighbour's good, whereas the pitiful man grieves over his neighbour's evil, so that the envious have no pity, as he states in the same passage, nor is the merciful man envious" (translation slightly adapted). See also Gregory of Nyssa, *The Beatitudes,* Sermon 5, who says that if "mercy" reigned in human society, "envy would be futile" and all the vices that are "the offspring of covetousness" would disappear.

19. Thomas Aquinas, *Summa Theologica,* II–II, q. 36, art. 3. For the sake of clarity, I have translated the Latin *misericordes* as "merciful" rather than "pitiful."

20. The Greek verb for "put away" is *apotithēmi.* See Danker, *Greek-English Lexicon,* 123.

21. Danker, *Greek-English Lexicon,* 316.

13: Anger vs. Meekness

1. See CCC nos. 1767, 1772: "In themselves passions are neither good nor evil. They are morally qualified only to the extent that they effectively engage reason and will. . . . The principal passions are love and hatred, desire and fear, joy, sadness, and anger."

2. See Thomas Aquinas, *Summa Theologica*, II–II, q. 158, arts. 1–2: "To be angry is not always an evil. . . . If one desire revenge to be taken *in accordance with the order of reason*, the desire of anger is praiseworthy, and is called *'zealous anger.'* . . . On the other hand, if one desire the taking of vengeance in any way whatever contrary to the order of reason, for instance if he desire the punishment of one who has not deserved it, or beyond his deserts, or again contrary to the order prescribed by law, or not for the due end, namely the maintaining of justice and the correction of defaults, then the desire of anger will be sinful, and this is called *sinful anger.*"

3. Gregory the Great, *Morals in Job*, 5.82. In Gregory the Great, *Moral Reflections on the Book of Job, Volume 1*, 382.

4. John Cassian, *Institutes*, 8.1.1.

5. John Climacus, *Ladder of Divine Ascent*, 8.14.

6. Francis de Sales, *Introduction to the Devout Life*, 3.8.

7. The same expression is used to describe Potiphar's response when Joseph is (falsely) accused of having propositioned his wife: "his anger was kindled" (Hebrew *charah*) (Genesis 39:19). See also Wisdom of Solomon 10:3, which states that Cain abandoned wisdom "in his anger" and "in rage he slew his brother."

8. See also Michael V. Fox, *Proverbs*, 2 vols., The Anchor Bible 18–18A (New Haven: Yale University Press, 2000–2009), 2:584, who points out that the Hebrew word translated as "patient" literally means "long of nostrils"! Eventually, the Hebrew word in this proverb gets translated as "wrath" (Greek *orgē*) or "anger" (Latin *ira*) (Proverbs 14:29 LXX and Vulgate), which are the classic Greek and Latin names for the capital sin.

9. Notice that this is the exact same word used by later Christian writers to describe the capital sin of "anger" (Greek *orgē*; Latin *ira*) (Mark 3:5 Vulgate).

10. RSV, slightly adapted. It is worth noting here that many ancient manuscripts read "everyone who is angry with his brother *without cause* (Greek *eikē*)" (Matthew 5:22), thus leaving room for "righteous indignation." See W. D. Davies and D. C. Allison, Jr., *The Gospel according to Saint Matthew*, 3 vols., International Critical Commentary (London: T&T Clark, 1988–97), 1:512; Bruce M.

Metzger, *A Textual Commentary on the Greek New Testament*, 2nd ed. (Stuttgart: Deutsche Bibelgesellschaft, 1994), 11.

11. Frederick William Danker, ed., *A Greek-English Lexicon of the New Testament and Other Early Christian Literature*, 3rd ed. (Chicago: University of Chicago Press, 2000), 903.

12. Consider, for example, the following rabbinic traditions: "The judgment of the unrighteous in Gehenna shall endure twelve months" (Mishnah, *Eduyoth* 2:10). Likewise, "The House of [Rabbi] Shammai says, 'There are three groups, one for eternal life, one for "shame and everlasting contempt" (Dan. 12:2)— these are those who are completely evil. An intermediate group go down to Gehenna and scream and come up again and are healed'" (Tosefta, *Sanhedrin* 13:3). In Danby, *Mishnah*, 426; Jacob Neusner, *The Tosefta*, 2 vols. (Peabody, Mass.: Hendrickson, 2002), 2:1188-89. See also Joachim Jeremias, *"géenna,"* in *Theological Dictionary of the New Testament*, ed. Gerhard Kittel, trans. Geoffrey W. Bromily, 10 vols. (Grand Rapids, Mich.: Eerdmans, 1964), 1:657-58, who recognizes that Gehenna has "a purgatorial as well as a penal character."

13. See Gregory the Great, *Morals in Job*, 5.81: "[One] way to retain an even temper is that when we notice the transgressions of others, we may recall our own sins and transgressions against them. . . . Just as fire is extinguished by water, when anger rises in the mind, all should remember their own guilt, because we should be ashamed not to forgive sins when we remember that we have often sinned against God or neighbor and needed forgiveness." In Gregory the Great, *Moral Reflections on the Book of Job, Volume 1*, 381-82.

14. RSV, slightly adapted.

15. Gregory the Great, *Morals in Job*, 31.88: "From anger are produced *quarreling, commotion, abuse, shouting, insults, blasphemy*" (author's translation).

16. Gregory of Nyssa, *The Beatitudes*, Sermon 2: "Wrath is opposed to gentleness." For a similar view in the Middle Ages, see Thomas Aquinas, *Summa Theologica*, I-II, q. 46, art. 5: "Gentleness (Latin *mansuētūdo*) is contrary to anger."

17. Danker, *Greek-English Lexicon*, 861.

14: Avarice vs. Generosity

1. See John Climacus, *Ladder of Divine Ascent*, 16 (On Avarice); Thomas Aquinas, *Summa Theologica*, II–II, q. 118, arts. 1–8.

2. John Cassian, *Institutes*, 7.1–2.

3. John Climacus, *Ladder of Divine Ascent*, 16.

4. Thomas Aquinas, *Summa Theologica*, II–II, q. 118, art. 2.

5. Francis de Sales, *Introduction to the Devout Life*, 3.14.

6. F. Brown, S. R. Driver, and C. A. Briggs, *A Hebrew and English Lexicon of the Old Testament* (Oxford: Clarendon, 1977), 326.

7. RSV, adapted.

8. Michael V. Fox, *Proverbs*, 2 vols., Anchor Bible 18–18A (New Haven: Yale University Press, 2000–2009), 2:831, who translates "greedy" (Hebrew *rechab nephesh*) as "wide of appetite" or "voracious maw," also states, "Greed is a repudiation of trust in God, for he who trusts in God accepts what God gives and does not crave more."

9. RSV, slightly adapted.

10. See W. D. Davies and D. C. Allison, Jr., *The Gospel according to Saint Matthew*, 3 vols., International Critical Commentary (London: T&T Clark, 1988–97), 1:640: "Ancient Jewish texts often mention the 'impudent eye,' the 'beguiling eye,' and the 'evil eye.' . . . In all these places 'eye' seems to signify 'intent.' . . . What is involved is the antithesis of generosity." See, e.g., Tobit 4:7; Sirach 14:8; Mishnah, *Aboth* 2:9, 11; 5:19.

11. Frederick William Danker, ed., *A Greek-English Lexicon of the New Testament and Other Early Christian Literature*, 3rd ed. (Chicago: University of Chicago Press, 2000), 824.

12. Joseph A. Fitzmyer, S.J., *The Gospel according to Luke*, 2 vols., Anchor Bible 28–28A (New York: Doubleday, 1983–85), 2:974, rightly notes that being "rich" toward God involves "the proper use of material possessions for others"—i.e., almsgiving.

13. The Greek word used here is *pleonexia;* it is later translated into Latin as "avarice" (Latin *avaritia*) (Colossians 3:5 Vulgate).

14. Gregory the Great, *Morals in Job*, 31.88: "From avarice there spring treachery, fraud, deceit, perjury, restlessness, violence, and hardness of heart against compassion." In Gregory the Great, *Moralia in Job*, 3:453.

15. Francis de Sales, *Introduction to the Devout Life*, 3.14 (emphasis added).

15: Lust vs. Chastity

1. See, e.g., John Cassian, *Institutes*, 6.1–23; John Climacus, *Ladder of Divine Ascent*, 15; Thomas Aquinas, *Summa Theologica*, II–II, q. 153, art. 1: "Lust [Latin *luxuria*] is defined 'as the desire of wanton pleasure'"; and ibid., II–II, q. 154, art. 1: "The sin of lust consists in seeking venereal pleasure not in accordance with right reason." See also *CCC* no. 2351: "*Lust* is disordered desire for or inordinate enjoyment of sexual pleasure. Sexual pleasure is morally disordered when sought for itself, isolated from its procreative and unitive purposes."

2. John Cassian, *Institutes*, 6.1.

3. John Climacus, *Ladder of Divine Ascent*, 15.83.

4. Thomas à Kempis, *The Imitation of Christ*, 1.4.

5. William H. C. Propp, *Exodus*, 2 vols., Anchor Bible 2–2A (New York: Doubleday, 2006), 2.180: "The tenth command addresses *desire* as the emotional root of crime, most obviously of adultery."

6. Thomas Aquinas, *Summa Theologica*, II–II, q. 154, art. 2: "Fornication is contrary to the love of our neighbor."

7. Compare King Saul's military leadership in 1 Samuel 14–15. On warfare in ancient Israel, see Roland de Vaux, *Ancient Israel: Its Life and Institutions* (Grand Rapids, Mich.: Eerdmans, 1997), 250–54.

8. See Proverbs 2:16–19; 5:1–23; 6:23–35; 7:1–5.

9. Michael V. Fox, *Proverbs*, 2 vols., Anchor Bible 18–18A (New Haven: Yale University Press, 2000–2009), 1:227.

10. RSV, slightly adapted.

11. See Aline Rousselle, *Porneia: On Desire and the Body in Antiquity*, trans. Felicia Pheasant (London: Basil Blackwell, 1988).

12. See Adela Yarbro Collins, *Mark: A Commentary*, Hermeneia (Minneapolis: Fortress, 2007), 358: *porneiai* refers to "acts of unlawful intercourse" or "sexual immorality." For examples of prohibited forms of sexual activity, see the first-century Jewish writing *Pseudo-Phocylides* 175–206. In James H. Charlesworth, ed., *The Old Testament Pseudepigrapha*, 2 vols., Anchor Bible Reference Library (New York: Doubleday, 1983, 1985), 2.580–81.

13. RSV, slightly adapted.

14. For similar ancient Jewish prohibitions of lust, see W. D. Davies and D. C. Allison, Jr., *The Gospel according to Saint Matthew*, 3 vols., International Critical Commentary (London: T&T Clark, 1988–97), 1:522, citing the *Testament of Isaac* 4:53: "Do not look at a woman with a lustful eye," and *Pesiqta Rabbati* 24:2: "Even he who visualizes himself in the act of adultery is called an adulterer."

15. See Jonathan T. Pennington, *The Sermon on the Mount and Human Flourishing: A Theological Commentary* (Grand Rapids, Mich.: Baker Academic, 2017), 187.

16. Author's translation.

17. Frederick William Danker, ed., *A Greek-English Lexicon of the New Testament and Other Early Christian Literature*, 3rd ed. (Chicago: University of Chicago Press, 2000), 508: the "heart" (Greek *kardia*) is the "center and source of the whole inner life, w. its thinking, feeling, and *volition*" (emphasis added). See also Pennington, *Sermon on the Mount*, 93: "It is what comes out of the heart that reveals the quality of *the whole inner person*. . . . Biblical *kardia* has overlap with 'soul,' 'reasoning,' and 'mind' and is definitely closely associated with the seat of mental faculties, much broader and deeper than mere emotions" (emphasis added).

18. See John Cassian, *Institutes*, 6.3: A person with a "sickly mind" should avoid lustful "images."

19. Augustine, *Confessions*, 8.7.17. In *The Confessions of Saint Augustine*, trans. John K. Ryan (New York: Image, 2014), 156.

20. See, e.g., *CCC* no. 2390: "The sexual act must take place exclusively within marriage. Outside of marriage it always constitutes a grave sin and excludes one from sacramental communion."

21. RSV, slightly adapted.

22. In a Jewish context, when Paul mentions "impurity" (Greek *akatharsia*), he is probably referring to especially "dirty" lustful acts (cf. Galatians 5:19). See Danker, *Greek-English Lexicon*, 34.

23. Ignatius of Loyola distinguishes between delight and consent when he writes, "It is a venial sin if the same thought of sinning mortally comes to mind and for a short time one pays heed to it, or receives some sense pleasure, or is somewhat negligent in rejecting it. There are two ways of sinning mortally: (1) The first is to consent to the evil thought with the intention of carrying it out, or of doing so if one can. (2) The second . . . is actually carrying out the sin to which consent was given" (Ignatius, *Spiritual Exercises*, nos. 35–37).

24. Augustine, *The Lord's Sermon on the Mount*, 1.12.33. Augustine makes clear that Jesus' words do not refer simply to being "tickled by the pleasure of the flesh" but rather refer to "the full consent to the pleasure: the forbidden craving is not checked, but, given the opportunity, it would gratify its desire." In St. Augustine, *The Lord's Sermon on the Mount*, ed. Johannes Quasten, S.T.D., and Joseph C. Plumpe, trans. John J. Jepson, S.S., Ancient Christian Writers (New York: Paulist, 1948), 43. See also John Climacus, *Ladder of Divine Ascent*, 15.74: "The discerning Fathers have defined that assault is one thing, converse another, consent another. . . . Assault [is] a simple conception, or an image of something encountered for the first time, which has entered the heart. Converse is conversation with what has presented itself, accompanied by passion or dispassion. And consent is the bending of the soul to what has been presented to it, accompanied by delight." In Saint John Climacus, *The Ladder of Divine Ascent*, rev. ed. (Boston: Holy Transfiguration Monastery, 2019), 150–51.

25. Francis de Sales, *Introduction to the Devout Life*, 4.3.

26. Francis de Sales, *Introduction to the Devout Life*, 4.3.

27. Gregory the Great, *Homilies on the Gospels*, 14: "We should be aware that temptation is carried out in three ways: by suggestion, by delight, and by consent. . . . [Jesus] could therefore be tempted by suggestion, but no delight in sin took hold in his heart."

28. Francis de Sales, *Introduction to the Devout Life*, 4.3.

29. RSV, slightly adapted.

30. John Cassian, *Institutes*, 6.1.

31. Gregory the Great, *Morals in Job*, 31.89: "It is plain to all that lust springs from gluttony." In Gregory the Great, *Moralia in Job*, 3:454.

32. Experience shows that it is almost impossible to fill our imagination with lustful thoughts and regularly meditate on Scripture at the same time. One of the two is going to go.

16: Gluttony vs. Temperance

1. Author's translation.

2. On gluttony, see John Climacus, *Ladder of Divine Ascent*, 14 (On Gluttony); Thomas Aquinas, *Summa Theologica*, II–II, q. 148, arts. 1–6.

3. Gregory the Great, *Morals in Job*, 30.18.58. Cited in Thomas Aquinas, *Summa Theologica*, II–II, q. 148, art. 1. See also John Cassian, *Institutes*, 5.3: "The first contest upon which we must enter is against gluttony."

4. John Climacus, *Ladder of Divine Ascent*, 18.

5. Thomas Aquinas, *Summa Theologica*, II–II, q. 148, art. 1. See also ibid., II–II, q. 148, art. 6.

6. On the Hebrew terminology of "glutton" and "drunkard," see F. Brown, S. R. Driver, and C. A. Briggs, *A Hebrew and English Lexicon of the Old Testament* (Oxford: Clarendon, 1977), 272–73, 684–85.

7. RSV, slightly adapted.

8. Michael V. Fox, *Proverbs*, 2 vols., Anchor Bible 18–18A (New Haven: Yale University Press, 2000–2009), 2:735–36: "These vices

reinforce each other . . . [and] characterize the rebellious son in Deut 21:20 (which uses the same words as here) and seem to stand for dissolute behavior in general."

9. With regard to the wedding at Cana, it is important to emphasize that the quantity of wine Jesus produces—about 180 gallons (see John 2:6)—is not intended to promote drunkenness but to be a sign of the superabundant wine of the messianic banquet (see Amos 9:11-13; Joel 3:18; cf. 2 Baruch 29:1-5). For discussion, see Brant Pitre, *Jesus the Bridegroom: The Greatest Love Story Ever Told* (New York: Image, 2014), 42-43. At the same time, Jewish Scripture is also clear that God gives "wine" to "gladden the heart" of human beings (Psalm 104:15).

10. RSV, slightly adapted.

11. The word "dissipation" (Greek *kraipalē*) can be defined as "unbridled indulgence in a drinking party." Frederick William Danker, ed., *A Greek-English Lexicon of the New Testament and Other Early Christian Literature*, 3rd ed. (Chicago: University of Chicago Press, 2000), 564. Fitzmyer likewise defines it as "intoxication." Joseph A. Fitzmyer, S.J., *The Gospel according to Luke*, 2 vols., Anchor Bible 28-28A (New York: Doubleday, 1983-85), 2:1355.

12. See, e.g., John of the Cross, *The Ascent of Mount Carmel*, 3.25.5: "Joy in the delights of food directly engenders gluttony and drunkenness . . . and lack of charity toward one's neighbor and the poor, as toward Lazarus on the part of the rich man who ate sumptuously each day."

13. RSV, slightly adapted.

14. Fitzmyer, *Gospel according to Luke*, 2:1132, citing 1 Kings 1:21; 20:10; 11:21.

15. Fitzmyer, *Gospel according to Luke*, 2:1131, points out that when Luke says that Lazarus "longed to be fed" (Greek *epithymōn chortasthēnai*) (Luke 16:21), it is the same expression used to describe how the prodigal son "longed to be fed" (Greek *epethymei chortasthēnai*) (Luke 15:16).

16. RSV, slightly adapted.

17. See Walter Burkert, *Greek Religion*, trans. John Raffan (Cambridge, Mass.: Harvard University Press, 1985), 99-107, 161-67.

18. It is no coincidence that the word "revelry" (Greek *kōmos*) used by Peter and Paul is the actual *name* of Komos, the Greek god of partying. See Danker, *Greek-English Lexicon,* 580: "Orig. a festal procession in honor of Dionysus (cp. our festival of Mardi Gras) . . . in a bad sense *excessive feasting* . . . *carousing, revelry* Ro 13:13; Gal 5:21."

19. John Climacus, *Ladder of Divine Ascent,* 14: "We should everywhere and at all times cultivate temperance." See also Thomas Aquinas, *Summa Theologica,* II–II, q. 141, art. 2.

20. John Cassian, *Institutes,* 14.3.

17: Sloth vs. Diligence

1. J. Lust, E. Eynikel, and K. Hauspie, *A Greek-English Lexicon of the Septuagint,* 2 vols. (Stuttgart: Deutsche Bibelgesellschaft, 1992), 1:15. E.g., CCC no. 1866 speaks of "sloth" (Latin *pigritia*), instead of "acedia."

2. See John Cassian, *Institutes,* 10.1–25; John Climacus, *Ladder of Divine Ascent,* 13; Thomas Aquinas, *Summa Theologica,* II–II, q. 35, arts. 1–4; John of the Cross, *Dark Night of the Soul,* Book 1.7.2–5.

3. John Cassian, *Institutes,* 10.7.8: "the disease of sloth." Cassian goes on to speak in the strongest possible terms about "the gangrene of idleness" (10.7.8), "the vice of idleness" (10.8.1).

4. John Climacus, *Ladder of Divine Ascent,* 13.1–2.

5. Thomas Aquinas, *Summa Theologica,* II–II, q. 35, art. 1.

6. John of the Cross, *Dark Night of the Soul,* Book 1.7.2, 4.

7. John Cassian, *Institutes,* 10.5: "The true athlete of Christ, who wishes to engage lawfully in the struggle for perfection, must strive to cast out this disease as well from the depths of his soul."

8. See Proverbs 6:6, 9; 10:26; 13:4; 15:19; 19:24; 20:4; 21:25; 22:13; 24:30; 26:13–16. For related terms, see Proverbs 19:15; 31:27; Ecclesiastes 10:18.

9. Michael V. Fox, *Proverbs,* 2 vols., Anchor Bible 18–18A (New Haven: Yale University Press, 2000–2009), 2:798: "Like a door swinging back and forth, the sluggard turns over in his bed without going anywhere."

10. Fox, *Proverbs*, 2:798: "The lazy man is not merely devoid of energy and motivation, he is also smug and conceited."

11. RSV, slightly adapted.

12. See Klyne R. Snodgrass, *Stories with Intent: A Comprehensive Guide to the Parables of Jesus*, 2nd ed. (Grand Rapids, Mich.: Eerdmans, 2018), 528; Frederick William Danker, ed., *A Greek-English Lexicon of the New Testament and Other Early Christian Literature*, 3rd ed. (Chicago: University of Chicago Press, 2000), 988.

13. Snodgrass, *Stories with Intent*, 525: "The responsibility assigned the servants gives them an *obligation*" (emphasis added). For a full-scale study of how gifts in the ancient world implied obligations, see John M. G. Barclay, *Paul and the Gift* (Grand Rapids, Mich.: Eerdmans, 2015).

14. In this verse, the word "lazy" or "slothful" (Greek *oknēros*) (Matthew 25:26) is the very same word used to translate the Hebrew "sluggard" (Hebrew *'atzel*) (see Proverbs 6:9 LXX).

15. See Joel Marcus, *Mark*, 2 vols., Anchor Bible 27–27A (New Haven: Yale University Press, 2009), 2:920: "Since the Passover is called a night of vigil (lit. 'night of watching') in Exod 12:42, . . . at least by the time of the Tannaim some Jews were in the habit of staying up all night to celebrate it." See, e.g., Tosefta, *Pesahim* 10:12. Compare also the Vulgate's translation of "keep awake" (Latin *vigilate*) (Mark 14:34).

16. RSV, adapted.

17. See John Climacus, *Ladder of Divine Ascent*, 13.11, who describes acedia as "the gravest" of all the "capital vices." In Saint John Climacus, *The Ladder of Divine Ascent*, rev. ed. (Boston: Holy Transfiguration Monastery, 2019), 133.

18. See John Cassian, *Institutes*, 10.7.1: "The blessed Apostle, like a true and spiritual physician, long ago saw this malady, which springs from the spirit of acedia, creeping in." The bulk of John Cassian's famous treatise on acedia is devoted to a line-by-line exposition of Paul's words in 2 Thessalonians 3. See ibid., 10.7–19.

19. RSV, slightly adapted.

20. See Nathan Eubank, *First and Second Thessalonians* (Grand Rapids, Mich.: Baker Academic, 2019), 186: "Paul's command is not ad-

dressed to the 'unemployed,' those willing to work but unable to find it. . . . It is addressed to those who could be gainfully employed but choose not to be, those who are 'unwilling' to work. . . . [T]he commandment to feed the hungry is a grave obligation to which Jesus makes no exceptions" (see Matthew 5:42).

21. Cf. Danker, *Greek-English Lexicon*, 148: "The specific manner in which the irresponsible behavior manifests itself is described in the context: freeloading, sponging."

22. Benedict of Nursia, *The Rule*, 48.1. In *The Rule of Saint Benedict*, trans. Leonard J. Doyle, O.S.B. (Collegeville, Minn.: Liturgical Press, 2001), 109 (emphasis added).

23. CCC no. 2697.

24. For the original Latin, see Georg Holzherr, O.S.B., *The Rule of Benedict: An Invitation to the Christian Life*, trans. Mark Thamert, O.S.B. (Collegeville, Minn.: Liturgical Press, 2016), 363.

18: Sorrow vs. Patience

1. See, e.g., CCC no. 1866. For a classic medieval example of the seven capital sins, see Dante's *Divine Comedy*, Purgatorio, Cantos I–XXXIII, which describe the "Mountain" of Purgatory as consisting of seven levels corresponding to pride, envy, anger, sloth, avarice, gluttony, and lust. For a diagram, see Dante, *The Divine Comedy*, trans. C. H. Sisson (Oxford: Oxford University Press, 2008), 198. It is not a coincidence that these seven sins are linked with the sufferings of the purgative way (in this life) and Purgatory (after death).

2. See John Climacus, *Ladder of Divine Ascent*, 22.1, who notes that, already in the sixth century A.D., some Christian writers "claim that there are eight deadly sins. But against this is the view of Gregory the Theologian [= Gregory the Great] and other teachers that in fact the number is seven. I also hold this view." Here, Climacus is probably referring to the fourth-century writers John Cassian and Evagrius of Pontus, both of whom identify eight capital sins (or eight "evil thoughts"), both of whom include "sorrow" or "sadness" (Greek *lypē*; Latin *tristitia*) in their respective lists. See John Cassian, *Conferences*, 5.1–27 (On the

Eight Principal Vices), and Evagrius of Pontus, *On the Vices Opposed to the Virtues*, 1–10, and *On the Eight Thoughts*, 1–8. For the latter, see Evagrius of Pontus, *The Greek Ascetic Corpus*, trans. Robert E. Sinkewicz (Oxford: Oxford University Press, 2003), 60–90. Significantly, although Gregory the Great spoke of only seven capital sins, unlike later medieval Christian writers, Gregory included "sorrow" or "melancholy" (Latin *tristitia*) in his list of the "seven principal vices." See Gregory the Great, *Morals in Job*, 31.87. In Gregory the Great, *Moralia in Job*, 3:453.

3. Author's translation.

4. Augustine, *City of God*, 14.6: "When we turn away from that which has happened against our will, this act of will is called sorrow." In Schaff, *Nicene and Post-Nicene Fathers, First Series*, 2:266.

5. For discussions of both kinds of sorrow, see John Cassian, *Institutes*, 9.1–13; John Climacus, *Ladder of Divine Ascent*, 7 (On Mourning); Thomas Aquinas, *Summa Theologica*, I–II, qq. 35–39; Thomas à Kempis, *The Imitation of Christ*, 1.21.1–6; Francis de Sales, *Introduction to the Devout Life*, 4.12.

6. John Cassian, *Institutes*, 5.12.

7. Thomas Aquinas, *Summa Theologica*, I–II, q. 35, art. 7; q. 37, art. 4. For the sake of clarity, I have translated the Latin *tristitia* as "sorrow" rather than "sadness."

8. Francis de Sales, *Introduction to the Devout Life*, 4.12.

9. See Genesis 37:34; Isaiah 22:12; Jeremiah 7:29.

10. Although the original Hebrew here literally reads "Bless God and die" (Job 2:9), the Hebrew word "bless" (Hebrew *barak*) is used as a euphemism for "curse," just as it is earlier in the book, when Job worries that his children may have "sinned, and cursed [Hebrew *barak*] God in their hearts" (Job 1:5). See Marvin H. Pope, *Job*, Anchor Bible 15 (New York: Doubleday, 1965), 22.

11. Author's translation. Although this verse is missing from the ancient Hebrew copies of Proverbs, I include it here because it is present in the ancient Greek Septuagint and had a direct impact on Eastern Christian spiritual writers on sadness. See Albert Pietersma and Benjamin G. Wright, eds., *A New English Translation of the Septuagint* (New York: Oxford University Press, 2007), 644.

12. Bovon points to an expression in the Greek Septuagint, "You will fall asleep in sadness" (Isaiah 50:11 LXX), as possible background. François Bovon, *Luke 3*, trans. James Crouch, Hermeneia (Minneapolis: Fortress, 2012), 203. He also rightly points out that while sadness can sometimes lead to insomnia, sleep can also become "a refuge and a last protection" from profound "grief" or extreme "misfortune."

13. RSV, slightly adapted.

14. Adela Yarbro Collins, *Mark: A Commentary*, Hermeneia (Minneapolis: Fortress, 2007), 480: "He lacked . . . the self-mastery to let go of his wealth and to choose a higher good."

15. Francis de Sales, *Introduction to the Devout Life*, 4.12. A bit further in the same section, Francis writes, "Last of all, *resign yourself into God's hands* and be ready to suffer patiently this distressing sadness. . . . Do not doubt that after God has put you on trial he will deliver you from this evil."

16. Thomas Aquinas, *Summa Theologica*, II–II, q. 136, art. 1: "'A man's patience it is whereby he bears evil with an equal mind,' i.e., without being disturbed by sorrow"; and II–II, q. 136, art. 4: "It belongs to patience 'to suffer with an equal mind the evils inflicted by others.'" In the first passage, Aquinas is quoting Augustine, *On Patience*, 2; in the second, he is quoting Gregory the Great, *Homilies on the Gospels*, 35.

17. See, e.g., John Cassian, *Institutes*, 9.7: "Perfection of heart is attained not by separation from human beings but by the virtue of patience." See also Thomas Aquinas, *Summa Theologica*, II–II, q. 136, arts. 1–5.

18. Augustine, *On Patience*, 1: "Patience surely has its name from suffering (*patiendo*)." All translations of this treatise of Augustine are from St. Augustine, *Treatises on Various Subjects*, ed. Roy J. Deferrari, trans. Mary Sarah Muldowney, R.S.M. et al., Fathers of the Church 16 (Washington, D.C.: Catholic University of America Press, 1952).

19. Gregory the Great, *Homilies on the Gospels*, 35.

20. Augustine, *On Patience*, 15: "There are those who attribute it [patience] to the powers of man's will. . . . But, that is an arrogant error." Gregory the Great, *Homilies on the Gospels*, 35: "None of

you should count on being able to carry this [patience] out by his own strength: procure it by your prayers, so that he who commands it may provide it."

21. Augustine, *On Patience*, 17.

22. John Cassian, *Institutes*, 9.13.

23. Teresa of Avila, *Poems*, 30. Quoted in *CCC* no. 227.

19: Examination of Heart

1. John Cassian, *Conferences*, 5.10.1–2.

2. Catherine of Siena, *The Dialogue*, 10. See also ibid., 31–32, in which Jesus says to Catherine, "I made them *trees of love* through the life of grace, which they received in holy baptism. But they have become *trees of death*, because they *are* dead . . . The *fruits* of such trees are full of death, for their juice comes from *the root of pride*. . . . There are as many different *death-dealing fruits* on these trees of death as there are *sins*" (emphasis added).

3. Francis de Sales, *Introduction to the Devout Life*, 4.13.3.

4. See James L. Kugel, *Traditions of the Bible: A Guide to the Bible as It Was at the Start of the Common Era* (Cambridge, Mass.: Harvard University Press, 1998), 96–97, 136–39.

5. See Victor P. Hamilton, *The Book of Genesis*, 2 vols., New International Commentary on the Old Testament (Grand Rapids, Mich.: Eerdmans, 1990), 1:166: "What is forbidden to man is the power to decide for himself what is in his best interests and what is not. This is a decision God has not delegated to the earthling. This interpretation also has the benefit of according well with [Genesis] 3:22, 'the man has become like one of us, knowing good and evil.' Man has indeed become a god whenever he makes his own self the center, the springboard, and the only frame of reference for moral guidelines."

6. See Roland E. Murphy, O. Carm., *The Tree of Life: An Exploration of Biblical Wisdom Literature*, 3rd ed. (Grand Rapids, Mich.: Eerdmans, 2002), ix–x.

7. RSV, slightly adapted.

8. François Bovon, *Luke 1*, trans. Christine M. Thomas, Hermeneia (Minneapolis: Fortress, 2002), 252: "Those who believe are called to bring forth goodness continually out of the treasure of their hearts."

9. For more on the oracle in Genesis 3:15, see Brant Pitre, *Jesus and the Jewish Roots of Mary: Unveiling the Mother of the Messiah* (New York: Image, 2018), 14–40.

10. See W. D. Davies and D. C. Allison, Jr., *The Gospel according to Saint Matthew*, 3 vols., International Critical Commentary (London: T&T Clark, 1988–97), 1:668–69: "The imperative *mē krinete* ['judge not'], cannot refer to simple ethical judgements, and believers are not being instructed to refrain from critical thinking. . . . *Mē krinete* implies that the individual . . . is taking up a role he should not be playing because it is reserved for the only capable judge, God. . . . Thus *krinō* ['to judge'] is almost synonymous with *katakrinō* = 'condemn' (cf. [Matthew] 12.41-2; 20:18; Rom 2.1, 3). . . . 'Do not judge, *lest ye be judged*,' means, 'Do not judge, lest ye be condemned [by God at the final judgement].'"

11. For a classic description of the examination of conscience, see Ignatius of Loyola, *Spiritual Exercises*, nos. 24–43.

12. Joseph A. Fitzmyer, S.J., *First Corinthians*, Anchor Bible 32 (New Haven: Yale University Press, 2008), 446: "Self-examination and acknowledgement of one's status are to precede participation in the Supper."

13. See John Climacus, *Ladder of Divine Ascent*, 4.39: "I noticed that he [one of the monks] had a small book hanging in his belt, and I learned that every day he noted down his thoughts [Greek *logismoi*] in it and showed them to the shepherd. I found out that many of his brothers did this also as well as he."

14. John Chrysostom, *Homilies on Genesis*, 11.7. In St. John Chrysostom, *Homilies on Genesis 1–17*, trans. Robert C. Hill, Fathers of the Church 74 (Washington, D.C.: Catholic University of America Press, 1986), 146 (emphasis added).

15. Thomas à Kempis, *The Imitation of Christ*, 4.7.1.

16. Francis de Sales, *Introduction to the Devout Life*, 5.3; 7.1. The entire section on this method of examination (ibid., 5.3–9) is extremely helpful.

17. Perhaps the most famous method is that of Ignatius of Loyola, *Spiritual Exercises,* nos. 24–43.

18. Ignatius of Loyola, *Spiritual Exercises,* no. 244-25 (emphasis added); cf. no. 18.

19. For a somewhat different diagram of the two trees of vices and virtues, see Reginald Garrigou-Lagrange, O.P., *The Three Ages of the Interior Life: Prelude of Eternal Life,* Volume 2, trans. Sr. M. Timothea Doyle, O.P. (London: B. Herder, 1948), 365–66.

20. Francis de Sales, *Introduction to the Devout Life,* 4.10.

21. John of the Cross, *The Ascent of Mount Carmel* Book 1.12.5. Translation in *The Collected Works of St. John of the Cross,* 147 (emphasis added).

20: *Lectio Divina* and Jacob's Ladder

1. See Duncan Robertson, *Lectio Divina: The Medieval Experience of Reading,* Cistercian Studies 238 (Collegeville, Minn.: Liturgical Press, 2011).

2. John Cassian, *Conferences,* 14.10.2. Cassian goes on to say, "But as our mind is increasingly renewed by this study, the face of Scripture will also begin to be renewed, and the beauty of a more sacred understanding will somehow grow with the person who is making progress" (ibid., 14.11.1).

3. Guigo II, *The Ladder of Paradise,* 13. In Guigo II, "The Ladder from Earth to Heaven," trans. Jeremy Holmes, in *Letter and Spirit* 2 (2006): 175–88 (here 186).

4. Teresa of Avila, *The Way of Perfection,* 16.3. In *The Collected Works of Saint Teresa of Avila,* trans. Kieran Kavanaugh, O.C.D., and Otilio Rodriguez, O.C.D., vol. 2 (Washington, D.C.: ICS Publications, 1980), 94.

5. See, e.g., John Cassian, *Conferences,* Preface 5; 5.23.1; 12.11.2. The imagery goes back to Origen, *Homilies on Genesis,* 15.3; *Homilies on Numbers,* 11.4; *Commentary on the Song of Songs,* Prologue.

6. John Chrysostom, *Homilies on the Gospel of John,* 83.5. In Saint John Chrysostom, *Commentary on Saint John the Apostle and Evan-*

gelist: Homilies 48–88, trans. Thomas Aquinas Goggin, S.C.H., Fathers of the Church 41 (Washington, D.C.: Catholic University of America Press, 1959), 416.

7. Guig II, *The Ladder of Monks,* 2.1. Unless otherwise noted, all translations of this work are from Guigo II, *The Ladder of Monks and Twelve Meditations,* trans. Edmund Colledge, O.S.A., and James Walsh, S.J., Cistercian Studies 48 (Collegeville, Minn.: Liturgical Press, 1979).

8. John of the Cross, *Dark Night of the Soul,* Book 2.18.1. For another example, see John Cassian, *Conferences,* 12.11.2.

9. See Kallistos Ware, "Introduction," in John Climacus, *The Ladder of Divine Ascent,* trans. Colm Luibheid and Normal Russell (Mahwah, N.J.: Paulist, 1982), 10–11.

10. See Victor P. Hamilton, *The Book of Genesis,* 2 vols., New International Commentary on the Old Testament (Grand Rapids, Mich.: Eerdmans, 1990), 2:239–40: "The Hebrew word here is *sullām,* which occurs only here in the Hebrew Bible. Many commentators have connected *sullām* with the verb *sālal,* 'heap up,' and accordingly suggest for the noun something like 'ramp' or 'stairlike pavement.' More likely is the suggestion that Heb. *sullām* is to be connected (through metathesis) with Akk. *simmilitu,* 'stairway.' [Note: LXX *klímax* and Vulg. *scala* are ambiguous—both can mean "ladder" or "stairway."] . . . This interpretation posits a parallel between Jacob's 'ladder' and the stairways of the ziggurat in Mesopotamia." Hamilton's point here explains why ancient translators used words that can mean either "ladder" or "stairway" (Greek *klimax;* Latin *scala*) (Genesis 28:12 Greek Septuagint and Vulgate).

11. For a photo of a ziggurat stairway at Ur, see John H. Walton, ed., *Zondervan Illustrated Bible Backgrounds Commentary,* vol. 1, *Genesis, Exodus, Leviticus, Numbers, Deuteronomy* (Grand Rapids, Mich.: Zondervan, 2009), 107.

12. For example, the prophet Micah foretells that in the latter days, when the "kingdom" would finally come, the people of Israel would "sit every man under his vine and under his fig tree" (Micah 4:1–8). Likewise, the prophet Zechariah foretells that when the messianic king named "the Branch" finally comes,

"every one of you will invite his neighbor under his vine and under his fig tree" (Zechariah 3:8–10).

13. See Rudolf Schnackenburg, *The Gospel according to St. John*, trans. Kevin Smith, vol. 1 (New York: Herder & Herder, 1968), 317: "The usual explanation appeals to the rabbinical phrase 'to sit under the fig-tree' and the custom of the doctors of the law, of sitting under a tree to study Scripture." See, e.g., *Genesis Rabbah* 62:2: "Rabbi Akiba and his disciples used to *sit and study under a fig-tree*." In *Genesis Rabbah*, trans. H. Freedman, 2 vols. (London: Soncino, 1983), 2:551. See also Jerusalem Talmud, *Berakoth* 2:8: "Once . . . R. Aqiba and his associates, were sitting discussing Torah under a certain fig tree," and *Ecclesiastes Rabbah* 5.11.2: "R. Akiba and his disciples were sitting and studying beneath a fig tree." In Jacob Neusner, ed., *The Jerusalem Talmud: A Translation and Commentary* (Peabody, Mass.: Hendrickson, 2008), loc. cit., and *Ecclesiastes Rabbah* (L. Rabinowitz; London: Soncino, 1983), 151. For these references, see Craig S. Keener, *The Gospel of John: A Commentary*, 2 vols. (Peabody, Mass.: Hendrickson, 2003), 1:486.

14. Schnackenburg, *Gospel according to St. John*, 317: "Nathanael, then, hidden from the eyes of others under a sheltering fig-tree, *would have been studying Scripture*, especially the Messianic prophecies. If so, his reaction to Jesus' revelation, his acknowledging him as the Messiah, is still more understandable" (emphasis added).

15. See Mariano Magrassi, *Praying the Bible: An Introduction to* Lectio Divina, trans. Edward Hagman, O.F.M. Cap. (Collegeville, Minn.: Liturgical Press, 1998).

16. The various manuscripts of Guigo's treatise have multiple titles, such as the "Ladder of Paradise" (Latin *Scala Paradisi*) and "Ladder of Monks" (Latin *Scala Claustralium*). Here I will use the former in order to emphasize that the four steps of *lectio divina* are not just for cloistered monks but can be used by all Christians. For example, see Benedict XVI, Post-Synodal Apostolic Exhortation *Verbum Domini* (The Word of the Lord), nos. 86–87, who refers to these four as "the basic steps" of *lectio divina*.

17. Robertson, *Lectio Divina*, 224, describes Guigo's *Ladder* as "a didactic summary of the whole *lectio divina* tradition."

18. Guigo II, *The Ladder of Paradise*, 2.

19. Guigo II, *The Ladder of Paradise*, 2.

20. Ambrose of Milan, *De Officiis*, 1.20.88. In Ambrose, *De Officiis*, ed. Ivor J. Davidson, vol. 1, *Introduction, Text and Translation* (Oxford: Oxford University Press, 2001), 169.

21. Guigo II, *The Ladder of Paradise*, 2.

22. Guigo II, *The Ladder of Paradise*, 14.

23. Guigo II, *The Ladder of Paradise*, 14.

24. Justin Martyr, *1 Apology*, 1.65–67. Cited in *CCC* no. 1345.

25. See Benedict XVI, *Verbum Domini*, no. 86: "*The privileged place* for the prayerful reading of sacred Scripture *is the liturgy,* and particularly *the Eucharist* . . . In some sense the prayerful reading of the Bible, personal and communal, must always be related to the Eucharistic celebration. Just as the adoration of the Eucharist prepares for, accompanies and follows the liturgy of the Eucharist, so too prayerful reading, personal and communal, prepares for, accompanies and deepens what the Church celebrates when she proclaims the word in a liturgical setting. By so closely relating *lectio* and liturgy, we can better grasp the criteria which should guide this practice in the area of pastoral care and in the spiritual life of the People of God."

21: The Battle of Prayer

1. See John Climacus, *Ladder of Divine Ascent*, 1.8: "Violence and unending pain are the lot of those who aim to ascend to heaven with the body, and this especially at the early stages of the enterprise. . . . It is hard, truly hard."

2. Agathon, *Sayings of the Fathers*, no. 9. In Benedicta Ward, S.L.G., trans., *The Sayings of the Desert Fathers: The Alphabetical Collection* (Kalamazoo, Mich.: Cistercian Publications, 1975), 22.

3. John Cassian, *Conferences*, 18.13.4.

4. Thomas à Kempis, *The Imitation of Christ*, 1.3.3. See also ibid., 25.3: "The one thing that keeps many from advancing spiritually and from fervently amending their lives is the dread of difficulty and the hard work required."

5. *CCC* no. 2725, 2015 (emphasis added).

6. Victor P. Hamilton, *The Book of Genesis*, 2 vols., The New International Commentary on the Old Testament (Grand Rapids, Mich.: Eerdmans, 1990), 2:329.

7. This ambiguity about whether the patriarchs encounter God, an angel, or a human being is not uncommon in Jewish Scripture (cf. Genesis 18).

8. As Old Testament scholars have shown, the word "thigh" (Hebrew *yarek*) is used elsewhere as a word for "loins," as when Abraham's servant places his hand under his "thigh" (Genesis 24:2, 9; cf. 47:29) or when the seventy offspring come from "the thigh of Jacob" (Exodus 1:5, author's translation). In other words, God ends the wrestling match by dealing Jacob a crushing blow to his loins. See S. H. Smith, "'Heel' and 'Thigh': the Concept of Sexuality in the Jacob-Esau Narratives," *Vetus Testamentum* 40 (1990): 466–69; Hamilton, *Book of Genesis*, 2:331–32. Although at first glance this might strike us as comical, the text is making a rather serious point about the intensity of the pain and the permanence of the wounds that are often part of the spiritual journey. In John Cassian, *Conferences*, 12.11.2, Jacob's wrestling with God will become a symbol for the triumph of chastity in the spiritual battle.

9. Augustine, *Sermon* 5.6: "And he blessed Jacob. How? By changing his name." In Mark Sheridan, ed., *Genesis 12–50*, Ancient Christian Commentary on Scripture, Old Testament II (Downers Grove, Ill.: InterVarsity, 2002), 220.

10. F. Brown, S. R. Driver, and C. A. Briggs, *A Hebrew and English Lexicon of the Old Testament* (Oxford: Clarendon, 1977), 975: the Hebrew word *sarah* means to "persist, exert oneself, persevere."

11. See Francis de Sales, *Introduction to the Devout Life*, 2.9: "If it should happen that you find no joy or comfort in meditation . . . , I urge you not to be disturbed. . . . Repeat Jacob's words, "Lord, I will not let you go until you bless me."

12. Frederick William Danker, ed., *A Greek-English Lexicon of the New Testament and Other Early Christian Literature*, 3rd ed. (Chicago: University of Chicago Press, 2000), 755, 272.

13. For God's particular attentiveness to the prayers of widows, see also Sirach 35:13–15.

14. See Joseph A. Fitzmyer, S.J., *The Gospel according to Luke,* 2 vols., Anchor Bible 28–28A (New York: Doubleday, 1983–85), 2:1179.

15. Danker, *Greek-English Lexicon,* 1043: "Strike under the eye," or "give a black eye," "strike in the face." Compare Paul's use of the same word in 1 Corinthians 9:26–27.

16. The Hebrew expression for this mode of argument is *qal va chomer;* the Latin, *a fortiori.*

17. Cyril of Alexandria, *Commentary on Luke,* Homily 119: "The present parable [of the persistent widow] assures us God will bend his ear to those who offer him their prayers, not carelessly nor negligently but with earnestness and constancy." In Arthur A. Just Jr., ed., *Luke,* Ancient Christian Commentary on Scripture, New Testament III (Downers Grove, Ill.: InterVarsity, 2003), 276.

18. See Danker, *Greek-English Lexicon,* 818–19.

19. John Climacus, *Ladder of Divine Ascent,* 26.104. In the same passage, Climacus states that the spiritual battle with evil begins upon rising in the morning: "There is a demon called the forerunner. He lays hold of us as soon as we awaken and defiles our very first thought." In 19.2, Climacus states, "Just as too much drinking comes from habit, so too from habit comes overindulgence in sleep. For this reason one has to struggle against it especially at the start of one's religious life, because a long-standing habit is difficult to correct."

20. Thomas à Kempis, *The Imitation of Christ,* 1.20.2 (emphasis added).

21. Ephrem the Syrian, *Commentary on Genesis,* 30.3: "[Jacob] learned how weak he was and how strong he was." In Sheridan, *Genesis 12–50,* 223.

22. John Cassian, *Conferences,* 9.3.3. See also ibid., 1.13.2: "When we have lost sight of him even briefly, let us turn our mind's regard back to him, directing the eyes of our heart as by a very straight line."

23. John Climacus, *Ladder of Divine Ascent,* 4.92.

24. CCC no. 2729 (emphasis added).

25. John Climacus, *Ladder of Divine Ascent*, 19.7: "No one should undertake any additional task, or, rather, distraction, during the time of prayer."

26. CCC no. 2728.

27. Evagrius of Pontus, *On Prayer*, no. 34. Cited in CCC no. 2737 (emphasis added).

28. Francis de Sales, *Introduction to the Devout Life*, 2.9.

22: The Dark Night

1. John Climacus, *Ladder of Divine Ascent*, 1.12.

2. Thomas à Kempis, *The Imitation of Christ*, 2.9.3.

3. Francis de Sales, *Introduction to the Devout Life*, 4.15. See also Ignatius of Loyola, *Spiritual Exercises*, no. 315: during the purgative way, it is "characteristic" of the Holy Spirit to give "consolations" and "inspirations" by "making all easy . . . so that the soul goes forward in doing good."

4. See, e.g., John Cassian, *Conferences*, 4.2–6; John Climacus, *Ladder of Divine Ascent*, 4.58; Francis de Sales, *Introduction to the Devout Life*, 4.15: "When God orders spiritual joy to be taken away from them . . . they think they are neither in heaven nor on earth and that they shall remain buried *in everlasting night* . . . suddenly left in a state of aridity, deprived of all consolation, and plunged into interior darkness"; John Paul II, Apostolic Letter *Novo Millennio Ineunte* no. 33: "The great mystical tradition of the Church of both East and West . . . shows how prayer can progress. . . . It is a journey totally sustained by grace, which nonetheless demands an intense spiritual commitment and is no stranger to painful purifications (*the 'dark night'*)."

5. John Climacus, *Ladder of Divine Ascent*, 4.58. Although the subject in this sentence that "he" refers to is "the devil," Cassian immediately makes clear that it is actually *God* who allows the "providential withdrawal" of "what seem to be" spiritual goods in order to increase the soul's humility.

6. Thomas à Kempis, *The Imitation of Christ*, 2.9.4.

7. John of the Cross, *Dark Night of the Soul*, Book 1.8.1, 3 (emphasis added).

8. In *Dark Night of the Soul*, John of the Cross actually speaks of *two* "dark nights," both of which have both active and passive dimensions. The first night, which John calls "the night of the senses," happens to many *beginners* as they transition from the first stage of spiritual growth (which John calls "the purgative way") to the second (which he calls "the illuminative way"). For a full discussion of the dark night of the senses in its active and passive forms, see John of the Cross, *The Ascent of Mount Carmel*, Book 1.1–15 and *Dark Night of the Soul*, Book 1.1–14. The second night, which John calls "the night of the spirit," happens to those who are more *advanced* in the spiritual life, in the transition between the second stage (the illuminative way) and the third (which he calls "the unitive way"). For a full discussion of the dark night of the spirit in its active and passive forms, see John of the Cross, *The Ascent of Mount Carmel*, Books 2.1–3.45 and *Dark Night of the Soul*, Book 2.1–25. In this chapter, I am focusing primarily on the involuntary deprivation of consolation during prayer known as the passive night of the senses.

9. See John of the Cross, *Dark Night of the Soul*, Book 1.9.1–9.

10. In support of this stands the fact that John himself interprets this psalm as King David's firsthand description of "when he was in this night"—meaning the night of the senses (John of the Cross, *Dark Night of the Soul*, Book 1.13.6).

11. See Frank-Lothar Hossfeld and Erich Zenger, *Psalms 2: A Commentary on Psalms 51–100*, trans. Linda M. Maloney, Hermeneia (Minneapolis: Fortress, 2005), 277, who rightly point out that "the night" being described is "the time when one speaks to one's own heart, the time of brooding, of theological seeking" and that the psalmist "turns inward" in a "retreat into interiority."

12. See John of the Cross, *Dark Night of the Soul*, Book 1.11.1–2.

13. RSV, slightly adapted.

14. Frank-Lothar Hossfeld and Eric Zenger, *Psalms 3: A Commentary on Psalms 101–150*, trans. Linda M. Maloney, Hermeneia (Minneapolis: Fortress, 2011), 574.

15. Hossfeld and Zenger, *Psalms 3*, 575: the psalmist asks "for an end to the hiddenness of God's countenance, for an experience of divine concern."

16. It is worth noting here that John of the Cross connects Jesus' famous cry of dereliction on the cross: "My God, my God, why have you forsaken me?" (Matthew 27:46)—in which he is quoting Psalm 22:1—with the second of the two nights: the "dark night of the spirit" (John of the Cross, *The Ascent of Mount Carmel*, Book 2.7.11). Since we are focused here on the dark night of the senses experienced by beginners in the purgative way, an explanation of Psalm 22 and Jesus' cry of dereliction lies beyond the scope of this study.

17. In antiquity, the word "friend" (Greek *philos*) is ordinarily used to describe someone who is "beloved" or "dear"—not merely an acquaintance. See Frederick William Danker, ed., *A Greek-English Lexicon of the New Testament and Other Early Christian Literature*, 3rd ed. (Chicago: University of Chicago Press, 2000), 1059.

18. Joseph A. Fitzmyer, S.J., *The Gospel according to Luke*, 2 vols., Anchor Bible 28–28A (New York: Doubleday, 1983–85), 2:910: "Luke's Greek word for 'persistence' actually means 'shamelessness.'" The term comes from "self-respect" or "respect" (Greek *aidōs*). The envisioned setting is a single-room home with family members all sleeping in the same space, such that rising to show hospitality to an unexpected guest would disturb the entire family (ibid., 2:912).

19. Fitzmyer, *Gospel according to Luke*, 2:914.

20. See Cyril of Alexandria, *Commentary on Luke*, Homily 79: "Sometimes we pray without discernment or any careful examination of what truly is to our advantage, and if granted by God would prove a blessing or would be to our injury if we received it. . . . When we ask of God anything of this kind, we will by no means receive it."

21. Fitzmyer, *Gospel according to Luke*, 2:914.

22. John of the Cross, *Dark Night of the Soul*, Book 1.8.1, 4.

23. Francis de Sales, *Introduction to the Devout Life*, 4.13.1.

24. John of the Cross, *Dark Night of the Soul*, Book 1.10.2 (emphasis added).

25. John of the Cross, *Dark Night of the Soul,* Book 1.10.4. John later clarifies that a person should stop meditating only when it is "no longer possible," since times of dryness can alternate with times of consolation. See ibid., Book 1.10.6; 1.14.5.

26. See John of the Cross, *Dark Night of the Soul,* Book 1.13.5: "*All the virtues* . . . are practised by the soul in these times of aridity." See also Book 1.11.4: "This night quenches within it all pleasures, whether from above or from below, and makes all meditation darkness to it, and grants it innumerable other blessings in the acquirement of the virtues."

27. Francis de Sales, *Introduction to the Devout Life,* 4.15: "We must never lose courage during these interior troubles. . . . During the night we must wait for the light."

28. John of the Cross, *Dark Night of the Soul,* Book 1.12.2.

29. John of the Cross, *Dark Night of the Soul,* Book 1.13.7.

30. John of the Cross, *Dark Night of the Soul,* Book 1.13.11.

23: The Living Water

1. John Chrysostom, *Homilies on Romans,* 14 (on Romans 8:27). In Gerald Bray, ed., *Romans,* Ancient Christian Commentary on Scripture, New Testament VI (Downers Grove, Ill.: InterVarsity, 1998), 230–31.

2. Thomas à Kempis, *The Imitation of Christ,* 2.9.4.

3. Teresa of Avila, *The Way of Perfection,* 19.6.

4. See, e.g., Gregory of Nyssa, *Homilies on the Song of Songs,* 9: "The Lord says to the Samaritan woman, 'If you knew the gift of God. . . .' She contains the inflow within *the well of her soul* and so becomes the storehouse of that living water." In Gregory of Nyssa, *Homilies on the Song of Songs,* trans. Richard A. Norris, Jr., Writings from the Greco-Roman World 13 (Atlanta: Society of Biblical Literature, 2012), 307, 309. See also Guigo II, *The Ladder of Monks,* 13: "[Jesus] demanded *prayer* from her: 'If you only knew the gift of God . . . you would perhaps ask Him for living waters.' . . . Filled with desire for it, she had recourse to prayer, saying: 'Lord, give this water'"; Teresa of Avila, *Life,* 30.19: "Oh,

how often do I remember the living water of which the Lord spoke to the woman of Samaria! I am so fond of that Gospel. I have loved it ever since I was quite a child . . . and I used often to beseech the Lord to give me that water. I had a picture of the Lord at the well, which hung where I could always see it, and bore the inscription: *'Domine, da mihi aquam'* [Latin, 'Lord, give me this water']." In Teresa of Avila, *The Life of Teresa of Jesus: The Autobiography of Teresa of Ávila*, trans. and ed. E. Allison Peers (New York: Image, 2004), 257–58.

5. Baruch A. Levine, *Numbers 1–20*, Anchor Bible 4 (New York: Doubleday, 1993), 468: "*Mayîm hayyîm* means, in effect, fresh water from a source, not from a cistern or the like (cf. Gen 26:19; Jer 17:13)."

6. RSV, slightly adapted.

7. RSV, slightly adapted. See Johannes Beutler, S.J., *A Commentary on the Gospel of John*, trans. Michael Tait (Grand Rapids, Mich.: Eerdmans, 2017), 116.

8. Artur Weiser, *The Psalms*, trans. Herbert Hartwell, The Old Testament Library (Philadelphia: Westminster, 1962), 348: "What he longs for is only and solely that he may be permitted to appear before God's 'face' and, coming into close contact with him, may have the most intimate communion with him."

9. See Jack R. Lundbom, *Jeremiah 1–20*, Anchor Bible 21A (New Haven: Yale University Press, 1999), 268.

10. See, e.g., John J. Collins, *The Scepter and the Star: Messianism in Light of the Dead Sea Scrolls*, 2nd ed. (Grand Rapids, Mich.: Eerdmans, 2010), 39.

11. For a fuller discussion, see Brant Pitre, *Jesus the Bridegroom: The Greatest Love Story Ever Told* (New York: Image, 2014), 55–81.

12. As Marianne Meye Thompson, *John: A Commentary*, New Testament Library (Louisville, Ky.: Westminster John Knox, 2015), 175–76, rightly points out, the Greek is ambiguous regarding exactly whose "heart" Jesus is referring to here: his own or the believer's.

13. Beutler, *Gospel of John*, 117.

14. RSV, slightly adapted.

15. See Beutler, *Gospel of John,* 492.

16. See Beutler, *Gospel of John,* 115: "Against the background of other texts of the Fourth Gospel, Jesus's request can be seen as the expression of his thirst for man's salvation. Relevant here are the words of Jesus immediately before his death on the cross: 'I thirst' (John 19:28). They too are not an expression of Jesus's physical thirst only."

17. CCC no. 1995 (emphasis added); cf. ibid., no. 2672: "The Holy Spirit . . . is the interior Master of Christian Prayer."

18. CCC no. 2560, quoting John 4:10 (emphasis added).

19. Thérèse of Lisieux, *Story of a Soul,* 9 1v (emphasis altered).

ABOUT THE AUTHOR

⁓

DR. BRANT PITRE is Distinguished Research Professor of Scripture at the Augustine Institute. He earned his PhD in theology from the University of Notre Dame, where he specialized in the study of the New Testament and ancient Judaism. He is the author of the bestselling books *The Case for Jesus, Jesus and the Jewish Roots of the Eucharist, Jesus and the Jewish Roots of Mary,* and *Jesus the Bridegroom.* Dr. Pitre has also produced dozens of video and audio Bible studies in which he explores the scriptural roots of Christianity. He lives in Louisiana with his wife, Elizabeth, and their five children.

More information about Dr. Brant Pitre's work can be found at www.BrantPitre.com.

ABOUT THE TYPE

This book was set in Legacy, a typeface family designed by Ronald Arnholm (b. 1939) and issued in digital form by ITC in 1992. Both its serifed and unserifed versions are based on an original type created by the French punchcutter Nicholas Jenson in the late fifteenth century. While Legacy tends to differ from Jenson's original in its proportions, it maintains much of the latter's characteristic modulations in stroke.